GLOBAL
SOUTH
ASIA

BHAKTI AND POWER

DEBATING INDIA'S RELIGION OF THE HEART

Edited by

John Stratton Hawley, Christian Lee Novetzke, and Swapna Sharma

A Samuel and Althea Stroum Book

UNIVERSITY OF WASHINGTON PRESS

Seattle

Bhakti and Power was made possible in part by a generous grant from the Samuel and Althea Stroum Endowed Book Fund.

Additional support was provided by Yale University's Department of Religious Studies, Lex Hixon Fund, South Asian Studies Council, Edward J. and Dorothy Clarke Kempf Memorial Fund, and Whitney and Betty MacMillan Center for International and Area Studies.

The Faculty Research Fund of Barnard College also assisted the publication of this book.

Printed and bound in the United States of America

Composed in Minion, typeface designed by Robert Slimbach

23 22 21 20 19 5 4 3 2 1

UNIVERSITY OF WASHINGTON PRESS
www.washington.edu/uwpress

LIBRARY OF CONGRESS CATALOGING-IN-PUBLICATION DATA
LC record available at https://lccn.loc.gov/2018046958
ISBN (paperback): 978-0-295-74550-3
ISBN (hardcover): 978-0-295-74551-0
ISBN (ebook): 978-0-295-74552-7

Cover illustration: Abdur Rahman Chughtai (1894–1975), *Heer.* Courtesy of Chughtai Museum Lahore, represented by Arif Rahman Chughtai

The paper used in this publication is acid free and meets the minimum requirements of American National Standard for Information Sciences—Permanence of Paper for Printed Library Materials, ANSI Z39.48–1984.∞

CONTENTS

ACKNOWLEDGMENTS

Many people and institutions made it possible for this volume to take shape, and we are grateful to each of them. We are deeply indebted to Kasturi Gupta and the South Asia Council at Yale University for suggesting to Swapna Sharma that she host the conference in May 2016 where contributors to this volume first gathered to share their work. The Edward J. and Dorothy Clarke Kempf Memorial Fund generously supported the conference. In addition we are grateful to the Macmillan Center at Yale for providing a publication subvention and to Barnard College for additional publication funds.

We thank the British Library for permission to reproduce the Assamese paintings Phyllis Granoff analyzes in chapter 9 and Phyllis Granoff for donating a portion of her faculty research funds so that these images could be shared with readers of this book. We owe a similar debt of gratitude to the Metropolitan Museum of Art, the Victoria and Albert Museum, a private New York collector, and Oliver Forge and Brendan Lynch, Ltd., for providing images that appear in chapter 11 and allowing them to be reproduced.

Our heartfelt thanks go to Lorri Hagman and her colleagues Michael Baccam, Niccole Coggins, and Margaret Sullivan at the University of Washington Press for shepherding this volume through many changes and giving it close and careful attention at every stage. We are also grateful to the editors of the press's Global South Asia series—Padma Kaimal, K. Sivaramakrishnan, and Anand A. Yang—for their confidence in the book's importance, and to the two anonymous reviewers who provided us excellent guidance for revision. Our thanks to Sarah C. Smith, who copyedited our book and to Chris Dodge, our indexer.

Finally, we three editors wish to acknowledge the attentiveness and team-spiritedness of each of our contributing authors. On occasion this required a willingness to dispense with whole swaths of persuasive prose so that the book could fit between its two covers—a willingness cheerfully offered. It has been a great pleasure to work with scholars such as these.

NOTE ON TRANSLITERATION

India is a land of many languages, and the systems used to transliterate the words that fill them are diverse. We standardized terms that occur frequently across the chapters comprising this book, but since local context is so important, we have allowed a considerable amount of diversity to remain. The index is the best place to turn should confusion arise: if more than one scheme of transliteration has been used to render a single term, the several options can usually be seen side by side there. Typically these variations register the difference between standard anglicized forms and spellings that are in line with more precise systems of transliteration, which in turn vary from language to language. Here are some examples:

Brahman, Brahmin, brahman (where the capital letters merely convey traditional English usage, not the sense that this caste group is more important or deserving than any other; where ultimate reality is meant, only the spelling Brahman is used)
Chaitanya, *caitanya* (as in the title *Kṛṣṇacaitanyacaritāmṛtamahākāvya*)
dharma, *dharm*
kirtan, *kīrtan*
Shiva, Śiva, Shiv (as part of a name with several components)
Virashaiva, *vīraśaiva*

Titles may also be quoted in shorter or longer forms, depending on the preference of individual contributors, for example, *Caitanyacaritāmṛta* and *Kṛṣṇacaitanyacaritāmṛtamahākāvya*. We hope that such variants will not prove too disconcerting and that readers will be able to move easily and confidently from one chapter to another.

BHAKTI AND POWER

INTRODUCTION

The Power of Bhakti

WHAT is bhakti? Though born in South Asia, this concept is fast becoming a term of general usage in the study of religion as practiced around the world, and it has important implications for historical, humanistic, and social scientific studies more broadly. The *Bhagavad Gītā* has made *bhakti* a household word for vast numbers of people. The *Gītā* is two thousand years old—many Hindus say older—but the power it exerts on the global imagination is relatively new. The *Gītā*, of course, is a book, but bhakti doesn't just lie on the page. It is the animating force behind *kīrtan*-chanting performances in eastern Europe, the Just Love Festival in Germany, and raucous Holi celebrations on many college campuses in the United States. A monumental Bhakti Fest convenes each September at Joshua Tree National Monument in southern California (fig. I.2). From yoga studios to soothing musical chants, bhakti seems to be everywhere.

But what exactly is it? Suppose we poll the three editors of this volume. Jack Hawley had this to say in a recent book:

> Bhakti, as usually translated, is devotion, but if that word connotes something entirely private and quiet, we are in need of other words. Bhakti is heart religion, sometimes cool and quiescent but sometimes hot—the religion of participation, community, enthusiasm, song, and often of personal challenge, the sort of thing that coursed through the Protestant Great Awakenings in the history of the United States. It evokes the idea of a widely shared religiosity for which institutional superstructures weren't all that relevant, and which, once activated, could be historically contagious—a glorious disease of the collective heart. It implies direct divine encounter,

I.1 Swamini Vishwamohini offering to daub sanctified sandalwood paste on the foreheads of European devotees at the inauguration of Bhakti Marga's new temple-ashram in Vrindavan, North India, December 2016. Photo by Jack Hawley

> experienced in the lives of individual people. These people, moved by that encounter, turn to poetry, which is the natural vehicle of bhakti, and poetry expresses itself just as naturally in song. There is a whole galaxy of bhakti poets who have been moved to song in the course of Indian history, and their songs are still sung today, everywhere across the subcontinent and in all its major languages.[1]

Swapna Sharma pursues this line of thinking into a more specific domain. Referring to the Braj region of northern India, where she was born, she directs our attention to a cross-regional bhakti heritage that situates Braj in a much larger domain. She praises the contribution made by a family that produced one of Braj's leading bhakti poets, saying that commonalities of bhakti expression widely shared throughout India made them

> able to combine the adopted Braj culture with sensibilities and practices that reflected their own southern roots. They showed

I.2

Bhakti Fest, Joshua Tree, California. Photo by Drew Thomases

> us that you can keep adopting and editing and modifying things at all levels in your life regardless of religion, culture, and language without losing your dignity and roots. That keeps any culture, religion, and community singing and dancing for centuries, just as the Bhatt family has done.[2]

Christian Lee Novetzke adds to this by showing how bhakti creates its own publics:

> Unifying the myriad forms that bhakti has historically taken and continues to take is the idea of a public, which I think of as a social unit created through shared cultural phenomena, and reinforced by demonstrations in public of these shared cultural phenomena. . . . In the context of bhakti, this concern with responsibility and constituency can be transposed to an understanding of what forms the social environment of bhakti. Images of bhakti are associated with acts of sharing through religious performances (*kīrtan*, *bhajan*, *rāslīlā*) and communities of pilgrimage. . . . The sense in which

> bhakti enters the history of India is not through the private realm but through the . . . social world. . . . Bhakti, as a subject for cultural history, must be taken in its social forms and not theorized solely within the sphere of an individual's consciousness. . . . [Therefore] any study of bhakti must always be a social or, I would say, a public subject.[3]

In this volume, bhakti holds all of the meanings just expressed—these and many more. Bhakti derives a good bit of its power from the fact that it can signify so many things in such diverse settings across a vast expanse of space and time. Each chapter speaks to its own understanding of what bhakti means, and doubtless the power of bhakti varies from context to context, but can we arrive at some shared sense of what that power typically entails?

It has long been claimed that bhakti has had a salutary effect on Indian life and that bhakti's devotional impulse creates a widely shared affective realm to which the downtrodden, subaltern, disenfranchised, excluded, and rejected have just as much access as do the rich, the educated, and those who exert control over others in the populations to which they belong. Thus we hear, in the words of the great Sanskritist V. Raghavan, that bhakti is "a democratic doctrine which consolidates all people without distinction of caste, community, nationality, or sex." Raghavan says, as many others have, that bhakti expressed itself in Indian history as a "bhakti movement" that originated in the fifth and sixth centuries in south India and in the course of spreading elsewhere changed the face of South Asian history. He gives due weight to several special features of "this song-literature of the saints": a shared emphasis on the name of the Lord and on the guru; a clarity about the true, simple form of worship; a "reformist zeal and denunciation of sham and deception as also of empty formalism"; and a "sense of the unity of all paths" and concomitantly a certain "*advaitic* tone and the preference for monism." At the end of the day, however, Raghavan is most pointedly attentive to bhakti's socially inclusive nature. Yes, the tone of bhakti expression is catholic in that it involves people from all social stations and all walks of life, but in Raghavan's belief its deepest claim to social significance goes beyond such catholicity. "The large galaxy of saints from all over the country," he says, "is made up largely of those who arose from the non-literary classes." This had great significance in "preparing the ground for centuries for the evolution of an increasing sense of equality, and in the bringing up of the masses and educating them in the essential culture of the land."[4]

Here we see the idea that bhakti empowers the downtrodden and ostracized, that it has the ability to provide a voice to those who have no voice—members of nonelite groups. The home-grown "democratic doctrine" that Raghavan finds at the heart of bhakti is an enduringly important way to identify the site where bhakti meets power, but it is only one way; there are others. That modern saint of power, Michel Foucault, forcefully argued that power is both a repressive and a productive force in society, a system of relations that operates upon the body-mind complex of any individual and collectively on social order as a whole. It is easy to see that Raghavan has said nothing about the repressive aspect of Foucault's characterization. For Raghavan, the discipline that bhakti offers is purely productive, not repressive. In his eyes, and in the opinion of many others before and since, bhakti serves to mediate, moderate, and generally address power through the mind and heart of an individual who is linked to a community or an imagined collective of like-minded devotees. In this view, the power of bhakti is that it enables people—often quite ordinary people—to imagine an alternative world and to participate in that very world in the course of imagining it, even if it remains unactualized in the rest of daily life. And we are not speaking of a single moment, a single inspiration, a single kindling of the imagination. Rather, as Raghavan implies, bhakti is actually a general movement or momentum in South Asian history. One of the most important facets of its power is that it engenders continuing traditions of practice. In bhakti, imagination lasts.

At some level, no doubt, all this is true, but as several contributions to *Bhakti and Power* make clear, the relationship between bhakti and power is far more complex than such a description makes it seem. Whole swaths of the South Asian population, including many of those to whom Raghavan specifically alluded, have historically been excluded from realms in which bhakti is celebrated. Such people may therefore deny that they have any deep relationship to such a sphere or disclaim any such relationship at all. Their discontents are registered primarily along two gradients—caste and gender—and the heavy hand of power descends on each.

Gender and caste are subjects that run through most of the essays in this volume, and they are deeply intertwined. Whenever one is talking about caste, gender is inevitably relevant, since caste as a practice is deeply invested in endogamy, patriarchy, and the maintenance of property in any given community. Yet while many people have talked about what happens to caste in a bhakti context, many fewer have trained their eyes on gender. This is a striking fact, considering that love relationships tend to be such prominent bhakti themes, and anyone who has ever fallen in love knows that love is a form of power. Perhaps bhakti's gender aspect has been so thoroughly internalized that it seems less important to discuss than caste. But there is indeed an important question that arises in gendered bhakti: what difference does it make when a divine dimension is imputed to love?

Heidi Pauwels and Manpreet Kaur particularly address this question in chapters 3 and 8, but we do not have to wait for their chapters to find ourselves in the midst of this bhakti-gender-power conundrum. Our volume begins there. It opens with an essay in which Karen Pechilis engages the voice of Kāraikkāl Ammaiyār (ca. sixth century CE), a female devotee and self-designated servant of Shiva whose love for him was expressed in an unconventional way. She made herself his "ghoul" and went to the cremation ground to conjure him up. Was it the divine in Shiva that compelled this sort of response in his enraptured devotee?

It is a striking feature of the literature of bhakti that questions about power relationships between humans and gods are often asked in a female voice, and it is equally striking that every major bhakti community has female protagonists. Indeed, the female presence can be felt at almost every point in the long history of bhakti—from the first uses of the term *bhakti* in the Buddhist *Therīgāthā* (ca. sixth century BCE), written in Pali, to the famous bhakti voices of Āṇṭāḷ, Janābāi, and Mīrābāī.[5] Yet in the annals of bhakti poetry gender hardly seems to get a balanced treatment. Apart from the *Therīgāthā*, all the great anthologies of bhakti verse were written by men, and male poets far outnumber female ones as they proceed. True, the female bhakti poets carry a degree of influence that helps to compensate for their numerical weakness. Who among the Tamil poets can rival the compelling persona of Āṇṭāḷ? Who among Hindi poets is better known than Mīrābāī? Still, we must ask just whose power is this. Is it women's own, or in some cases are we hearing the voices of men?

Indeed, there are hidden difficulties along these lines. For example, Karen Pechilis has observed that we cannot be 100 percent sure Kāraikkāl Ammaiyār's poetic utterances were produced by a woman: probably so, but a certain element of doubt remains. This doubt arises not only because the vast majority of literate people in India's long history have been men but because it is a long-held, well-known practice for men to adopt the female voice in some of their poetic compositions. Tamil, the language Kāraikkāl Ammaiyār spoke, provides some good examples of poetry attributed to female authors, dating all the way back to the language's classical pre-bhakti roots.[6] Of course, women may also have composed as men, crossing the gender line in the other direction, but if so, tradition does little to mark that fact. Harshita Mruthinti Kamath, a scholar of premodern Telugu literature, had to do some careful digging before she could confidently argue that many if not all of the poems attributed to the male poet Kṣetrayya may actually have been composed by women—courtesans.[7] There may have been other, similar instances in the long course of bhakti history, but on the whole it is much easier to suppose that the gender-bending went the other way. Given men's much greater access to public roles of performance, it is likely that certain poems attributed to Āṇṭāḷ, Janābāi, Mīrābāī, and Kāraikkāl Ammaiyār may have been composed by men—bhakti female impersonations. Do power differentials such as this make a difference where bhakti is concerned? The answer is certainly yes, even when the nature of the power in question is not always easy to name.

Things play out differently in relation to caste. Consider the famous moment in 1956 when B. R. Ambedkar, India's best-known champion of Dalit rights, disavowed Hinduism and led his Dalit followers into the embrace of Buddhism.[8] In doing so, he not only rejected the exclusive canons of the Vedic religious practices most closely associated with Brahmanical intellectual hegemony; he also rejected bhakti as a force that had been ineffective in combating such top-down visions of religion.[9] Ambedkar was disputing the bhakti movement—that legendary picture of the past that understood early Tamil- and Kannada-language bhakti to have laid the basis for Marathi, Gujarati, Hindi, and other bhakti literatures yet to come. He didn't question that such a movement existed; he merely thought it had been a washout. What had bhakti done for his fellow Dalits, even when it purported to speak through Dalit life-stories and in the voices of Dalits themselves? For Ambedkar it was not just that bhakti lacked the power to alleviate the social and economic suffering of his fellow Dalits; it was that bhakti's true power seemed too often to lie in its ability to dissuade people from taking political action because of the theological emollients it provided. It was an opium of the people in a fully Marxist sense.

Ambedkar had a good purchase on his ideas. He walked in the corridors of political and intellectual power. Though born into poverty and the object of plenty of upper-caste abuse in his childhood, he ended up studying at the London School of Economics and at Columbia University and gaining admission to the bar at the heart of imperial power, London. He went on to become the principal drafter of the Indian constitution, which was enacted in January 1950. Hence it was a matter of deep significance for the nation as a whole that six years later he closed his own personal book on bhakti, making it clear that bhakti had failed to do the historical job that Raghavan would still claim for it in 1964. Six million people followed Ambedkar into Buddhism—with a fervor that might be called a bhakti of its own.

This single anecdote from the history of modern India reveals the depth of disagreement that can and does arise when one asserts that bhakti has a certain power to impart. In every way Ambedkar's dramatic departure from the Hindu fold reveals that bhakti's relationship to various forms of power needs urgently to be investigated. That is what we hope to do in this book—with regard to gender, caste, and all the rest.

Initially, all our contributors were invited to address the question "Is Bhakti a language of power or protest?" They were to bring forth particular instances that would show how bhakti has been active in the life of the religious imagination. That frame quickly proved too limiting. Not only does bhakti spread itself unevenly along the scale that extends from power to protest, but it makes one ask how adequate such an external scale of measure can be. Bhakti often turns out to be a way of asking what power really is—or protest, for that matter. There are instances when a sense of powerlessness is claimed to lie near the core of bhakti, yet the practice of the bhakti that surrounds it may turn out to be anything but shy and retiring. And the pattern can also be reversed. Bhakti may proclaim the Lord's power, but does it really leaven ordinary life? Power means many things, and bhakti seems to command only a certain band of them. Thus we must think about whether some forms of power are intrinsic to bhakti and its historical expressions, while others are not. And we must not shrink from asking about ways in which certain forms of power have made use of bhakti—or simply left it behind.[10]

The stakes here are high. These are the stakes with which both Ambedkar and Raghavan were dealing, and they have hardly diminished in the present day. Hindu nationalists aligned with the Bharatiya Janata Party (BJP) sometimes call their opponents "sickularists," and when those opponents retort by calling their BJP adversaries *bhaktas*, they don't mean it as a compliment. Such people are unenlightened Hindu bigots, they imply, holdovers from an age that ought now to be gone.

Consider too, a different sort of scene. In January 2017 a conference was convened at FLAME University on the outskirts of the west Indian city of Pune to which one of our editors, Jack Hawley, was invited. The conference was called Shabd aur Sangeet [Word and Song]: Unravelling Song-Texts in the Indian Situation, and it addressed itself often to sung bhakti texts. From a power point of view, the site was right. The city of Pune has played a significant role in the annals of bhakti and especially in regard to relations between bhakti and power, since in the course of the seventeenth century it was the seat of the regime established by the iconic Maharasthrian rebel leader and then king Shivaji Bhonsle. The story of Shivaji is a famous one, and an important part of that story concerns Shivaji's special relationship to his preceptor Rāmdās, who is often regarded by Marathi speakers as being a definitive example of what a bhakti saint should be. The claim is made that in the act of being passed from Rāmdās to Shivaji, bhakti made history. It established the independent power of a Maratha state.

Such matters played no explicit role in the FLAME conference, but the issue of bhakti's relationship to power nonetheless crept in. There was a good bit of praise for the expressive force of bhakti in Indian history—its power to motivate and envelop. One heard, for example, how bhakti had been a means of female empowerment in the life of the ninth-century Tamil poet-saint Āṇṭāḷ, yet discordant notes were also sounded. Many participants worried about the sanitizing role that bhakti has played in the domain of Indian music: the way it has been used to mute and sweeten expressions of protest against patterns of social injustice. It was not that the injustices remained unvoiced—to the contrary, they might pointedly rise to the surface—but their force, once turned to music, was not so raw.

This theme emerged most dramatically in a set of papers that were grouped so as to form a panel entitled Protest: Issues of Caste and Community Identity in Song-Texts. Here one learned about songs by Maharashtrian Dalits addressed not to the ordinary bhakti saints but to "saint" Ambedkar—*bhīm gīt*, as these songs are called. The panel also screened a clip from a recent movie made by Punjabi Dalits in which the women take up arms rather than put up any more with stories of how Jat boys make it a habit to sleep with lower-caste women like themselves. The lead fighter wears a black turban and carries a gun, and it's the throbbing pulse of bhangra all the way. All this, of course, is contemporary, well after the enacting of Ambedkar's constitution, but it makes you wonder about similar songs that might not have survived from the past to the present, since the ability to record a song for posterity would have been greatly aided by writing it down, and that required the help of the literate classes. Songs of protest do emerge from the past, but they tend to be religiously inflected. Perhaps there were many more in which appeal was not made to the Lord—songs like those we can see to have made the transition from nonreligious expression to religious in the present day. All you have to do if you're a musician is change a few words, and suddenly you're singing bhakti.

Then there are figures like Mantesvāmī, the Kannada Dalit saint said to have lived in the fourteenth century whose story, songs, and legend are kept alive by Nilgara performers of the Deccan. Some consider Mantesvāmī to have been a reincarnation of the Vīraśaiva bhakti saint Allama Prabhu, but that does not rob Mantesvāmī of the radicalness of his social criticism. Here was a man said to have appeared in the house of a menstruating woman and asked to worship Shiva there. When she revealed her bodily state and recommended that he go elsewhere so as to preserve the generally accepted canons of religious purity, he refused. The entire world, he said, is created of blood, so what better place to worship Shiva than where menstrual garments were being washed? This was a religious song that nonetheless defied religion—a bhakti song for sure.[11]

The questions raised at the Pune conference echo in Indian society at large. Two weeks after it concluded, one of Mumbai's daily papers carried a feature called "Songs of Protest." There the well-known Carnatak vocalist Vasumathi Badrinathan reviewed the songs of anguish produced by many bhakti saints over many centuries and reflected implicitly on her own role in singing them. What pain had she alleviated by doing so? Like a number of the writers who contributed to the present volume, she responded to this implicit question by widening the lens. "A protest," she observed, "is not always anti-establishment. It is also a voice for an alternative ideology, a parallel course of action, a plea that could have shades of defiance, of courage, of quiet persistence, a course of self-expression especially when it is threatened. Music allows you to do all this, melodiously." And so did a photograph that accompanied her interview in print. It showed the actor and singer Danapani Desikar playing the seventh-century Tamil Dalit saint Nandanar on the cinema screen. Desikar himself was hardly Dalit—except, perhaps, from a bhakti point of view.[12]

Thus Bhakti's power is something complex. But however complex it may be, there is no avoiding the age-old question of power and protest—seemingly such a simple one. The question is this: when religion is the vehicle, and when the message is protest, why does so little seem to change?

THEMES AND CHAPTERS

We have assembled the chapters that follow into three parts—"Situations," "Mediations," and "Solidarities"—although the cross-currents are far more complex than such labels suggest. We begin with "Situations" in an effort to proceed from the ground up: how has bhakti existed in relation to power in a number of historically and geographically specific settings? Then we proceed to "Mediations," where we highlight the cross-cutting roles that various forms of bhakti expression have played, as well as considering the central question of whether in some necessary sense bhakti is about relationship—mediation itself. Finally, we proceed to "Solidarities," bringing to light different sorts of instances in which bhakti has served as social, religious, and political glue—or was presumed to do this job. We offer these thematic distinctions as heuristic aids to the reader, though the chapters themselves do not have to be read in a specific order. Ultimately each essay stands alone in the way it addresses our shared question.

Most of the chapters engage with a textual or written bhakti archive, as is the norm in the study of bhakti, but some look to other archives as well. One can speak, perhaps, of a many-sided "bhakti archive"—an archive to which these chapters contribute. Archives are not accidents of history. They are formed by intentional, powerful forces, and often these forces have excluded others on the basis of class, caste, gender, and language. In this way, historically speaking, bhakti has been edited at the source by the desires of the archivist or the archive's sponsor. Doubtless this is true of this book as well, but we have tried to be wide ranging. Graves, Lee, Haberman, Kini, and Pinch make use of ethnography; Graves, of performance arts; Kini and Pinch, architecture; Granoff and Hawley, visual culture; and Davis, even the record provided by syllabi developed in American classrooms. We three editors—textualists who have also pursued non-text-based studies—feel that the archival sources assembled here provide a helpful snapshot of the field of bhakti studies as it exists today. Yet we hope that the archive for bhakti continues to deepen, not just in terms of caste, gender, language, and region, but also in the kinds of materials it represents. Bhakti is at work across a considerable spectrum of human expression.

Situations

In chapter 1 Karen Pechilis introduces a figure who from her own historical moment in the sixth century to the present day has served as a textbook example of bhakti protest against normal ways of doing business in the world. This is Kāraikkāl Ammaiyār, a Tamil woman (prior caveats aside) who is remembered as a poet-saint—and a challenging one at that. Pechilis asks whether the bhakti envelope in which her canonical biographer Cēkkiḻār attempted to place her may actually have been somewhat suffocating—different from Kāraikkāl Ammaiyār's own understanding of religious reality, not to mention her own life. Here is someone who describes herself as a ghoul (*pēy*) at the cremation ground where Shiva dances—someone who, by contrast to Cēkkiḻār's much later account, makes no effort to measure herself by the conventions of ordinary life. Her own bhakti takes her far from all that. Its affective power is so great that the conventions of ordinary life are no longer even a point of reference for the person she becomes in Shiva's presence.

In chapter 2, Gil Ben-Herut traces Shiva-bhakti into its most celebrated moment in some of the regions that border Tamilnadu to the west—regions where Kannada is spoken. It has usually been believed that a bhakti revolution occurred in Kannada Shaiva history in the twelfth century. It was then that a group of poet-saints who would later be called Virashaivas (Vīraśaivas, heroic Shaivas) sang—or spoke—their unsettling *vacana* rhetoric. Well before the publication of A. K. Ramanujan's widely read book *Speaking of Śiva*, which celebrates the Virashaivas, this group of poet-saints was adulated by many Kannada speakers as the greatest democratic revolutionaries the subcontinent had ever known. They questioned caste, they included women in their inner precincts, and they disputed the authority of Brahmans—or so the story goes.

Ben-Herut questions this orthodox historiography. Focusing on the first collection of saints' lives to appear within the Virashaiva orbit, the *Śivaśaraṇara Ragaḷegaḷu* of the thirteenth-century poet Harihara, he demonstrates that each of the above contested arenas—caste, gender, and Brahmanism—was treated with a complexity that defies modern expectations about what democratic and egalitarian values ought to mean. Ben-Herut draws attention to several intriguing stories in Harihara's text—about a poor potter who becomes a paragon of bhakti, about a female devotee who pays dearly for walking away from marriage, and about a few privileged Brahmins—and shows how these stories are less testaments to the value of outright protest than new ways of negotiating old forms of social and religious power.

Heidi Pauwels also addresses questions of caste and gender, and in doing so she pays close attention to issues of method that must be kept in mind when one uses premodern literary texts to make broad claims about what bhakti does or does not do. Pauwels takes special issue with any simple dichotomizing of the progressive *nirguṇa* and conservative *saguṇa* registers of bhakti that have so often been assumed in the historical study of North Indian bhakti—on the one hand, *bhaktas* who would deny that divine reality can be approached through the vocabulary of the senses and within the confines of accepted social categories; on the other, *bhaktas* who affirm those very things. She also weighs genres carefully against each other—hagiography against literary anthology, *bhaktas'* understandings of their pasts as against what they perceive about their present. To make these distinctions clear, Pauwels considers the case of the sixteenth-century Brahman bhakti poet Harirāmvyās, who lived in the newly established town of Vrindavan and thus inhabited Krishna's world. While being a decidedly *saguṇa bhakta*, at the same time Vyās saw himself as also being heir to *nirguṇa bhaktas* such as Kabīr and Raidās, who made a point of valorizing spiritual kinship above worldly social considerations, and he condemned any of his high-caste contemporaries who might refuse to eat with their low-caste bhakti peers. Harirāmvyās was certainly progressive in this way, yet he stopped well short of championing social reform outside of a devotional context. He had his eye on a specifically bhakti sort of canon instead.

Chapter 4 carries us into contemporary times. Eben Graves introduces us to a moment in 2012 when a group of Bengali musicians sought to assemble what he calls, following Partha Chatterjee, a "contingent political society" that would serve the purpose of securing state subvention for the art they practice. *Kīrtan* and bhakti are the banners under which they gather (in Bengali, *kīrtan* connotes a specifically Vaishnava lyrical form), and it is interesting to see, once again, how the regional use of the vernacular—now Bengali—seems to carry a power of its own, a power invested in music. Yet this is an appeal being made to the instruments of state—power of a different order. Echoes of some of the tensions explored in earlier essays can certainly be heard, but in this very different, more internally focused context. These are bhakti professionals.

In the last chapter in "Situations," Joel Lee shows that the effort to fling wide the cloak of Hindu bhakti so that it would cover a wide range of Dalit groups living in North India was just that—an effort, not a fact. It occurred at the specific and politically motivated behest of the Arya Samaj, eager to consolidate a Hindu majority by persuading Dalits to identify as Hindu. Many Dalits found this strange, intrusive, and frankly motivated by the desire to co-opt, and the lengthy passages Lee quotes from the Arya Samaj's *Śrī Bālmīki Prakāś* shows why they may have felt this way. Thus Lee makes us aware once again of a world where Dalits stand apart from the moods and concerns of bhakti. They perceive it as an instrument of power that they largely prefer to resist, however much figures drawn from their own social and occupational group might be lionized as bhakti saints. The leatherworker Ravidās is such a figure, and so is the person called Vālmīki, whether he is understood as a hunter, as a robber, or specifically as a *chāṇḍāl* "untouchable." Lee makes these Vālmīkis the title of his chapter. To present the full force of the Dalit resistance he describes, and concomitantly the force of the bhakti "cloak" it tries to shed, Lee takes us to the realm of sensory experience—the sense of smell and the revulsion it provides as Dalits go about the sanitation work to which the wider Indian society has assigned them. Karen Pechilis had exalted "affect" as an important aspect the theater of bhakti. Lee casts the realm of affect in very different terms.

Mediations

The chapters grouped under "Mediations" also offer us glimpses into specific places and moments where bhakti has been and is performed—"situations" as we have called them—but while doing so, they bring to the fore questions of relationality. Such questions have received much attention on the part of scholars and devotees attempting to understand what bhakti is. Following in this lineage, David Haberman and Jack Hawley, whose essays conclude this part of the book, claim in different ways that bhakti quite simply *is* relationship—or if not relationship, then more broadly, perhaps, mediation.

Working through the paradigm created by Sheldon Pollock in his influential work *The Language of the Gods in the World of Men*, Christian Lee Novetzke argues in chapter 6 against the idea that religion was of secondary importance for vernacularization and shows instead that there was indeed something revolutionary in the earliest expressions of Marathi bhakti—namely, an appreciation and valorization of life as lived in a quotidian world. The force of the use of a vernacular language for religious expression, by contrast to classic Sanskrit, was indeed revolutionary, at least in the Marathi context. An important aspect of Novetzke's essay concerns various ways in which the Yadava rulers of the eleventh to thirteenth century were a part of this picture. With their inscriptions they seemed to want to tap into a power of bhakti that they themselves did not wield but with which they wished to be associated. The earliest layers of Marathi bhakti literature appear to have been concerned not with courtly life but with the everyday. They comment on social inequality in the context of gender and caste in the course of proclaiming access to salvation for the ordinary person.

John Cort shifts the focus from western India to the Braj country, which lies along the River Yamuna in northern India. He takes us to Agra in the sixteenth century and also offers a hint of what would happen in Jaipur at the beginning of the eighteenth century. Unexpectedly, given the usual dimensions of bhakti studies, he plunges us into the world of the Jains, whose relation to the domain we familiarly call Hindu is a complex one—so complex, with respect to bhakti, that he pleads with us to talk not of bhakti but of bhaktis. Envisioning a broad shift in Jain intellectual life in the sixteenth and seventeenth centuries in North India—a broadening of learning such that many more rank and file Jains took on literary work—Cort shows how the shaping of expressive and doctrinal bhakti compositions, especially in Brajbhāṣā, the language of Braj, was really just part of a much more complex productivity, one in which the relationship between Sanskrit and the vernaculars played a critical role. Did bhakti as a genre mediate between these two, then? Yes, but in that it was not alone. In Cort's portrait of seminars, sermons, poetry performances, and study circles in Mughal Agra, he brings to light a literary culture that has rarely been included in historical assessments of bhakti, enabling us to form an implicit contrast with the Vaishnava realm portrayed by Pauwels, its center not far up the Yamuna in Vrindavan. Both emerge as more complex than we have been led to expect, but in quite different ways.

Manpreet Kaur carries some of these themes forward by moving us into the next century and taking us north toward the Punjab. Her focus is on poetry that gives expression to the love story of Hīr and Ranjhā, which is eloquently present in the lyric poetry (*kāfī*) of Bulleh Shāh and an epic *qissā* of Warīs Shāh. Both Bulleh Shāh and Warīs Shāh are eighteenth-century poets—and they are Sufis. Here there is much to mediate. Making occasional mention of the well-known bhakti poet-saint Mīrābāī, Kaur shows that one of the most important themes in the story of her life and in her poetry—her deep love for Krishna as an absconding yogi and her commitment to joining him in that life—also appears in the classic romance of Hīr and Ranjhā. There too we see both hero and heroine assuming the roles of yogis, and their encounter with yoga (more specifically the form of yoga practiced by followers of Gorakhnāth) lifts their love to a new level. Kaur asks what work of mediation is going on here. And what difference does it make that the principal religious overtones of the Hīr-Ranjhā legend are Sufi and Muslim rather than bhakti and Hindu? Resonances to the literature of the Sikhs are also present. This is a complex set of mediations, and it seems that this time bhakti is less a mediator than an object of mediation. Poetry inspired by the story of Hīr and Ranjhā serves a mediating function that relates bhakti to kindred realms—ordinary human ("secular") love on the one hand, Muslim understandings of yoga and love on the other.

In chapter 9 we move ahead to the nineteenth century, and our guide is Phyllis Granoff. In the course of introducing us to rapidly developing religious and literary contours among what I. P. Gupta has called "a professional class," John Cort had been careful to distinguish that class's position from the world inhabited by kings and their primarily Brahman advisors, scholars, and ritual specialists. This is precisely the world that Granoff brings to life. She takes us to the court of the Assamese king Purandara Sinha, where the meanings of bhakti mediation once again change. Granoff opens before our eyes the pages of a beautiful Assamese rendering of the first chapter of the *Brahmavaivarta Purāṇa*, a celebration of Krishna originally written in Sanskrit but now expressed in vernacular Assamese. Here one feels the indirect impact of the great Assamese bhakti poet-saint Śaṃkaradeva, but Granoff's special interest is showing how the writer and illustrator of this illustrated manuscript caused the *Brahmavaivarta Purāṇa* to take on special meaning in relation to their patron, Purandara Sinha. Through them bhakti becomes a language of mediation between religious and political realms, between languages that have distinct registers, and between words and images. Granoff investigates the challenges an artist must face when required to give visual form to a text that sometimes adulates the Lord in devotedly formless terms. One could make a case that this is the hardest and most fundamental challenge bhakti has to face when it serves as a language of mediation.

David Haberman pursues the "formless yet formed" theme in his chapter on bhakti as relationship per se. He begins by considering the way this conundrum was classically framed in the *Bhagavad Gītā* and suggests how it was crucial to some of the Gauḍīya theorists who lived in sixteenth-century Vrindavan. He then moves quickly and dramatically to Mount Govardhan on the other side of Braj. There he explores what it means to make a mountain—or a stone of that mountain—into a person in the act of worship. In his analysis Haberman offers a radical and radically embodied correction to any view of bhakti that would stress its analogies to the Protestant Christian bhakti, so renowned for its principled and deeply felt disembodiedness. Like Granoff's Assamese Vaishnava bhakti, the bhakti world Haberman explores lends itself forthrightly to art.

In chapter 11 Jack Hawley continues the mediational theme and as well the engagement with art but takes a somewhat different tack. Rather than focusing on one realm or moment in which bhakti was understood to play the role of mediator, he proposes that this element has been crucial to the ways Hindus have thought about bhakti across many centuries and regions. By his count, no fewer than fifteen such mediations are involved. After discussing the first fourteen he concludes with the arena that has provoked us time and again, the apparent polarity between power and protest, drawing attention to the elusive, seemingly ever-shifting way bhakti inhabits each in relation to the other. Bhakti is the mediator, as he says in his title, but just how?

Solidarities

In the final section we turn the tables. Without leaving aside the situated nature of individual expressions of bhakti over time and place and without abandoning the insight that most if not all fields of bhakti expression characteristically involve an element of mediation, we now advance to new terrain: How does bhakti create solidarity or solidarities? And how do social and economic solidarities sometimes seize on bhakti to project an aura of religious truth? Finally, are there instances in which it really doesn't make sense to speak as if one could start either with bhakti or with power and proceed from one to the other? Are there times when the two are already one?

We begin with two explorations of significant events in the life of the religious community that formed around the charismatic personality of Chaitanya in the early sixteenth century, the movement or sect familiarly called the Gauḍīya or Bengali Sampradāya. In chapter 12 Kiyokazu Okita focuses especially on two events that brought the fledgling bhakti community of Chaitanyites into conflict with governmental structures created and largely staffed by powerful Muslims. Investigating two of the most important collective biographies to emerge from the Chaitanyite community in the first hundred years of its life, Okita shows how these contestational encounters were interpreted as displaying the vigor of the sort of bhakti life Chaitanya had established. These sources are sometimes quite different in their understanding of the bhakti solidarities they display. Okita believes we can account for such differences in terms of the rather different political circumstances that shaped the environments in which these hagiographical accounts were written. One was composed in the middle of the seventeenth century, the other at its conclusion; one emerged from Bengal, the other from Braj. The earlier Bengali milieu was far more riddled with conflict than the later Braj one. Little wonder, then, that bhakti inclines toward violent protest in the first and favors more subtle and muted negotiations with power in the second.

For purposes of this chapter, at least, Okita thinks of power as inhabiting first and foremost the instruments of state. Working with some of the same sources and incidents, however, Shrivatsa Goswami moves in a different direction in chapter 13. Speaking from his own experience—he is one of the most important leaders within the Chaitanya Sampradāya today—he focuses not so much on how bhakti interacted with external sources of power but on how the personal impress of Chaitanya caused his brand of bhakti to generate a power of its own. Goswami keeps in mind the political fields of contestation and mutual support that affected the life of this new bhakti movement, but his primary concern is to explain how its most important intellectual structures tried to name the intrinsic powers of bhakti. And he gives us a vivid sense of how that act of theological naming has had powerful, long-lasting effects. Perhaps because Goswami bases his discussion largely on canonical works that were produced in Vrindavan—that is, in Braj and in proximity to Mughal and Rajput corridors of power—he takes the view that the new bhakti solidarity Chaitanya produced, through his followers, had an irenic and pluralistic orientation. He insists in concluding that its teachings with respect to social justice were nondiscriminatory and all-embracing.

Divya Cherian's chapter 14 takes another look at such perspectives. Through new and remarkable explorations of the archives of the erstwhile Marwar state in southwest and central Rajasthan, she provides an account of what could happen when intellectual and social formations such as the Chaitanya Sampradāya and its cousin the Vallabh Sampradāya became the wedges around which an "expanding Vaishnava public" came to be fashioned. All this happened in the latter years of the eighteenth century. In Marwar, certainly, the Vallabh Sampradāya was far more important than its Chaitanyite cousin: the maharaja of Jodhpur sought initiation into that community in 1766, unleashing or at least participating in a cascade of changes. The social and legal dramas that emerge from Cherian's painstaking studies are remarkable, taking us well beyond the realm of theology and hagiography into the sort of records with which scholars of religion too rarely deal. Here we can clearly see how different segments of society—merchants, leatherworkers, Brahmans, Muslims, and many others—appealed to the state in the face of changes ushered in by the expanding influence of this new sectarian Vaishnava public. Here we see a new kind of power of bhakti for sure, but we also see how people who found themselves suddenly excluded from the new

Vaishnava orbit it hoped to define came up with ways to fight back. Their protests, insofar as Cherian is able to envision them through state records, had far more to do with claims of traditional practice than with assertions of bhakti enfranchisement.

In chapter 15 Tyler Williams, working in the same geographical area but focusing on a somewhat earlier period of time, provides a view of bhakti institutions that is complementary to Cherian's. Focusing on the Dādū Panth and the Nirañjanī Sampradāya, he shows how they developed in realms that were largely independent of the state but sometimes comparable to it—bhakti powers of their own, you might say. The domains over which they considered themselves to rule challenged the familiar distinction between spiritual (bhakti) and temporal (power), fusing them instead. Such bhakti solidarities bear many interesting marks. Most fascinatingly—in their institutional structuring, their narrative self-representation, and their hymnody—they come across as deeply marked by the economic lives of the communities out of which they emerged: merchants of many stripes. Renunciation can have its place in such enactments of what bhakti is about, but the world's give-and-take is never left behind. It is hard not to think of Weber's study of European Protestant inner-worldliness when we follow Williams into communities where the individual is encouraged, through bhakti, to sever emotional attachments to the ordinary world without disrupting attachments that are bodily and socially given. By performing that act of alchemy, these *bhaktas* transvalue the world itself, and the guru emerges as the most successful merchant within it. Reports of the guru's activities sometimes read like a merchant's ledger book, Williams remarks, and seen against the background of what he argues, well they might.

In the penultimate chapter of the book, Aditi Natasha Kini and William Pinch move forward into the nineteenth century while at the same time evoking the powerful memory of a poet who stands at the cusp of what we might call the bhakti era in North India. Kini and Pinch translate and explore a text called *Āīna-i-Tirhut*, or "Reflections on Tirhut," a name that refers to the region more commonly known these days as Mithila, in north Bihar. This nineteenth-century treatise by Bihārī Lāl Fitrat frequently invokes the great poet-saint Vidyāpati, the fifteenth-century doyen of Maithili bhakti, along with the patron to whom Vidyāpati often addressed himself, Raja Shiv Singh of the Oinwar dynasty, who employed Vidyāpati. One is reminded of the sixteenth-century saint Śaṃkaradeva in nineteenth-century Assam, as described by Phyllis Granoff. Kini and Pinch move us into a new terrain in which the physicality of bhakti is experienced: the waterscape of north Bihar with its distinctive tanks and ponds. In Fitrat's *Āīna-i-Tirhut* Vidyāpati is remembered not just for his poetry but for his ministerial role at court. His memory is especially tied to the creation of the agrarian infrastructure on this fertile part of the Gangetic Plain. Here—in memory at least—we have the power of bhakti registered in the land itself, a true solidarity if ever there was one.

And with that we come to the final chapter, in which Richard Davis describes what it means to teach bhakti in an American classroom. He offers us a recapitulation of many themes that animated the chapters that came before his, showing how they take on a life of their own when subjected to the conditions that govern a semester-long course on bhakti. Davis's students are undergraduates living far from India. Typically they are unable to read any Indian language, so the bhakti they experience relies in large part on the power of translation. Davis shows us how the protest theme so often voiced in the literature of *nirguṇa bhakti* is inevitably more persuasive in a classroom like his than its more gentle *saguṇa* cousin, which American undergraduates may even find insipid. Yet he also reports that there is a bookstore just down the block from where he teaches that has been named after one of the most prominent of those *saguṇa* bhakti saints: Mīrābāī.

What is the relationship between power and bhakti? The chapters in this book establish no definitive answer. But implicitly, at least, they make a common affirmation. They testify to the fact that the idea of bhakti has for centuries had the power to generate texts, poems, performances, politics, and, yes, chapters in books that seek to understand what Jack Hawley has called India's "religion of the heart." Yet two great questions remain, whether at the corporate or the individual level, and it seems they always will. First, does such a vision of the true domain of religion pertain to everyone—does everyone have such a heart? And second, if so, how can we keep that heart from breaking? To what extent has bhakti served to countermand hatred, injustice, and human need? As bhakti's increasingly felt presence on the global scene attests, these are questions that echo far beyond South Asia.

NOTES

1 Hawley, *A Storm of Songs*, 2.
2 Sharma, "Gadadhar Bhatt and His Family."
3 Novetzke, *Religion and Public Memory*, 13, 18–19, 21–22.
4 Raghavan, *Great Integrators*, 31–32, 47, 16.
5 For the *Therīgāthā*, see Pechilis, *Interpreting Devotion*, 9ff.; Hallisey, *Therigatha*. For Āṇṭāḷ, see Venkatesan, *Secret Garland*. For Janābāi, see Novetzke, *Religion and Public Memory*, 68–79, 96–98. For Mīrābāī, see Hawley and Juergensmeyer, *Songs of the Saints*, 119–40.
6 Pechilis, *Interpreting Devotion*, 10–13.
7 Kamath, "Kṣētrayya."

8 *Dalit* is a Marathi/Hindi word that means "downtrodden" and is the term we have elected to use in lieu of other terms such as *untouchable* or *Harijan*. In this, we follow standard current practice, a practice established by Dalits themselves.

9 Keune, "God Eats with Mahars"; Vajpeyi, *Righteous Republic*, 202–42.

10 We are deeply grateful to one of our contributors, Joel Lee, for pressing this point, and readers will see how it echoes through his essay.

11 Papers discussed in the paragraphs just concluded are: Chitra Sreedharan, "Finding Shakti through Bhakti: Andal—the Empowered One!"; Sarvapriya Raj, "Not Just Protest! An Exploration into the Politics of Representation in Popular Musical Culture of Punjab"; Tushar Mesharam, "Contemporary Dalit Musicality and Identity in Marathi Bhim Geet"; and Mohit Kaycee, "The Oral Epic of Manteswamy and Neelgara Tradition" (FLAME University, Pune, January 22, 2017). Print versions of the essays by Sreedharan and Mesharam appear in Mudgal et al., *Shabd aur Sangeet*.

12 *Asian Age*, February 6, 2017, 16.

SITUATIONS

CHAPTER ONE

AFFECT AND IDENTITY IN EARLY BHAKTI

Kāraikkāl Ammaiyār as Poet, Servant, and Pēy

KAREN PECHILIS

Is bhakti a comfortable space? Bhakti's mode of devotional participation has been interpreted and deployed to provide scaffolding for the certitude and self-righteousness of a social identity, especially in the context of launching protest or consolidating power. In such cases, bhakti is made to enframe and subordinate other social identities, especially inherited ones. Yet before a desire to replace received identity can become mobilized for individual, community, or political ends, the very act of questioning identity must be generated and recognized as a viable and accessible mode of thought. Such a project demands an exploratory subjectivity. The sixth-century Tamil Śiva bhakti poet-saint Kāraikkāl Ammaiyār was an early proponent of such exploratory questioning, a willful subject who in her poetry crafted a devotional subjectivity through the affective identities of servant and *pēy* to Śiva.[1]

In the poetry of Kāraikkāl Ammaiyār, bhakti is a space more of exploration than of comfort and consolidation. Kāraikkāl Ammaiyār does not at all overtly furnish herself with a social identity in her poetry. In a cultural tradition where precise social identity was and is the norm, we hear nothing of her caste community, her socioeconomic status, or even her gender. The name Kāraikkāl Ammaiyār—the woman saint from Kāraikkāl—which clearly marks her gender, comes from her biographer, who also provides details about her caste community and socioeconomic status as he portrays a domestic drama of marriage at the center of her devotional story.[2] Instead of relying on inherited identity, Kāraikkāl *pēy* constructs two other quite different identities. One is that of a servant, which is embedded in a poetic discourse that oscillates between certainty and doubt. The other is that of a *pēy* (ghoul; one who delights in the morbid), which is embedded in a poetic description of the horrifying elements of the cremation ground.[3] In fact she uses the latter for her "signature verses" in three of her four poems; her self-reference there is Kāraikkāl *pēy*, or the "ghoul from the shore," or perhaps "the ghoul from [the proper name of] the town Kāraikkāl." And so I shall call her Kāraikkāl *pēy* from here on out.

In her poetry, she is both observing and fashioning herself. Her poems have been identified as autobiographical since the twelfth century and there is no dispute—to date—on the number and content of poems attributed to her.[4] A study of her own poetry is an enterprise quite distinct from analyzing what people have said *about* her. Her most important biographer, the court minister Cēkkiḻār, attempts to include at least one representative of named, diverse social identities in his comprehensive twelfth-century biographies of the Tamil Śiva bhakti saints–including one female poet-saint, Kāraikkāl Ammaiyār, and two other female saints who are not authors. That way of placing her has been very influential, but in her own poetry we encounter quite a different range of concerns.

The critic John Berger has remarked that "autobiography begins with a sense of being alone. It is an orphan form," and yet in his next sentence he decenters this solitude by saying that he is most interested in "common moments" with kin, which "if I relate them well enough—will join countless others lived by people I do not personally know."[5] His comment suggests that autobiography engages the in-between-ness of self and self-observation, self and world, self and kin, and self and other beings. These in-between spaces are the modalities of affect, according to Gregory J. Seigworth and Melissa Gregg in their beautifully titled article, "An Inventory of Shimmers."

> At once intimate and impersonal, affect *accumulates* across both relatedness and interruptions in relatedness, becoming a palimpsest of force-encounters traversing the ebbs and swells of intensities that pass between "bodies" (bodies defined not by an outer skin-envelope or other surface boundary but by their potential to reciprocate or co-participate in the passages of affect). Bindings and unbindings, becomings and un-becomings, jarring disorientations and rhythmic attunements. Affect marks a body's *belonging* to a world of encounters or a world's belonging to a body of encounters but also, in *non-belonging*, through all those far sadder (de)compositions of mutual in-compossibilities. Always there are ambiguous or "mixed" encounters that impinge and extrude for worse and for better, but (most usually) in-between.[6]

Relationality is to the fore, which is also a hallmark of bhakti. Applying affect theory to the poetry of Kāraikkāl *pēy* illuminates her pronounced and provocative emphasis on visual and visceral imagery to imagine her relationship to Śiva as both servant and *pēy* through unscripted encounters.

Her encounters in her longest poem, the one-hundred-verse *Aṟputat Tiruvantāti*, or "Sacred Linked Verses of Wonder," are with an intensely visualized Śiva, whom she describes in detail in many cases by selectively drawing from mythology. It is strictly in relation to him that Kāraikkāl *pēy* on a few occasions describes herself in the first-person singular, and these verses are found only in her longest poem. On these occasions she declares her identity as that of servant to Śiva.[7]

> I aspired to only one thing.
> I settled on that one thing and left the rest.
> I kept inside my heart only that one thing;
>   the lord who bears the Gaṅgā
>   the lord whose locks are adorned with the sun and the moon
>   the lord whose palm holds the flaming fire;
> and I have become a servant to him. ("Wonder" v. 11)
>
> Oh foolish heart,
> worship the feet of the servants
> who recite hymns devoted
> to the only lord who wears the moon as a garland,
> eschewing any association
> with those who do not take him to heart. ("Wonder," v. 40)
>
> Our love is for him alone
> whom we will serve for seven births;
> besides the lord
>   who is adorned with the crescent moon
>   in his thick matted locks
> we will never become servants of any other. ("Wonder," v. 3)[8]

Verse 11 illustrates the affective core that constitutes the identity of servant. To make her aspiration a reality requires the single-minded emotional commitment that is encapsulated in the relational term *servant* and dramatized in her detailed description of Śiva's body. With an assist from mythology, Śiva is portrayed as the master of the intertwined elements of water, sun, moon and fire, and, via her heart, the "element" of humankind.

In Kāraikkāl *pēy*'s rendering, a servant is a category of humanity distinguished by its attention to a singular divine reference, not by a focus on an individualized human actor. Kāraikkāl *pēy* is a member of a *human* community that values shared humanity over individual virtuosity. In verse 40 she recognizes others who are servants by the same criterion of a heart dedicated to the singularity of Śiva, and in verse 3 she locates herself within that community of servants to Śiva, sharpening his specificity as the *only* "lord who wears the moon as a garland." As these verses limn the devotional subjectivity of the servants, they also draw a contrast: she says that there are other human beings who do not have Śiva in their hearts (v. 40) and who, by implication (v. 3), could offer servitude to another deity.[9]

This suggests that for her, identity is made, not inherited. What aids the social palatability of this assertion is that for devotees of Śiva, such self-made identity is subordinated labor to Śiva's own established identity—an identity of power that benefits others. When Kāraikkāl *pēy* describes him as the "lord who bears the Gaṅgā" or as the "lord who is adorned with the crescent moon," she cites his portrait from Sanskrit mythology, which was being circulated in Tamil literature by late classical works such as the *Cilappatikāram* and the *Kalittokai*. Throughout her longest poem, her preference is for the Gaṅgādhara-mūrti (lord who bears the Gaṅgā) and the Viṣāpa-haraṇa-mūrti (the lord as the swallower of poison), protective forms of Śiva whose deeds are memorialized by emblems on his body. She also describes forms that became categorized as Śiva's Eight Heroic Deeds, especially the Tripurāntaka-mūrti, or destroyer of the *adharmic* (against the cosmic order of dharma) triple cities.

On one level, then, Kāraikkāl *pēy*'s exploration of a self-determined human identity is validated by her appeal to a standardized identity of divinity. This grounding is one mechanism by which bhakti fosters a protected self-exploration, by investing with a devotional motive a person—in this case a woman—who might otherwise be socially viewed as an unacceptably willful subject. A contrastive note here is that the three later and more famous male saints in Tamil Śiva bhakti all specified in their own poetry that it was not their own action but Śiva's that initiated their transformation to servanthood. Campantar says he was a mere child who was "possessed" by Śiva via his gift of "divine food in a golden cup"; Appar states that his stomach and bowel ailments were Śiva's "punishment" for his "ignorance," which pushed him to become the lord's "servant"; and Cuntarar reports that he was captured and enslaved by Śiva.[10] But Kāraikkāl *pēy* defines herself as inhabiting a self-generated devotional subjectivity. Here I am making an argument that is different from A. K. Ramanujan's famous suggestion that in the Tamil stories of saints, men are depicted as needing to convert but women are already steadfast of heart, beings who naturally give themselves to total dedication or surrender—*prapatti bhakti*.[11] I am arguing that Kāraikkāl *pēy* was speaking a deeply affective self-determined identity through her habitation of a self-defined devotional subjectivity. She is a willful subject, not an accommodating one:

Birth in this body
enabled me to express
my overflowing love
through speech,
and I reached
your sacred henna-red feet.

And now I ask,
oh, lord of the gods
  whose neck shimmers black,
when will the afflictions
that birth in this world also enables ever end? ("Wonder" v. 1)

On another level, her exploratory positionality is less constrained by inherited images of who Śiva is than one might think. Rather, she extends and disrupts these images in three distinctive ways. In all three, she reshapes the mythology of Śiva. In my first example, she unifies imagery from three distinctive mythological stories of Śiva under a common bhakti theme—the foot:

His revered foot
crushed the powerful many-shouldered giant
who arrogantly lifted the mountain;
foiled holy Brahmā and Viṣṇu
who wept and then joyfully praised him
when they could not find his limits;
and kicked Yama, the god of death, into submission. ("Wonder" v. 80)

In this poem she joins three mythological images—Śiva who transforms the demon-king Rāvaṇa of Lanka, Śiva who manifests himself as the fiery lingam, and Śiva who destroys the lord of death—by the single theme of the lord's foot. "Reaching the lord's foot" became a signature bhakti trope, and here we see an early version of it deployed specifically to enframe the mythology with the *bhakta*'s own devotional subjectivity.

Second, she questions the logic and implications of the mythology itself:

Lord of the third eye
whose throat is darkened—

where did you hide yourself
when Viṣṇu
who is dark like a rain cloud
and even shares your motile body
could not find you in days of yore? ("Wonder" v. 54)

Would the palm of your hand
become red from the flames dancing in it?

Or would the flames
absorb their color from your beautiful palm?
Oh lord
who bears bright flames in your palm
as you dance with anklets ringing
on the fire
at the abode of the ghouls,
make your reply to this. ("Wonder" v. 98)

In these verses, she notes the contradiction that Viṣṇu shares Śiva's body (Harihara), yet he could not find the limit of Śiva's fiery lingam (v. 54). Also, in verse 98, which reads virtually as an iconography of the dancing Śiva, she contemplates the origins of Śiva's red color. In both cases she is concerned with finding Śiva's intrinsic nature through contemplation of his forms; this is amplified in verse 61, in which she—as a servant, dealing with the questions of others as well as her own—directly demands to know Śiva's essence:

I became your servant
though I had not seen
your sacred form;
even today, I have not seen it.
So what will I answer
to those who repeatedly ask,
"Which is the form of your lord?"

What exactly is your true form? ("Wonder" v. 61)

Third, the case can be made that she addresses the question of his essence by seeking out a direct and unscripted encounter with Śiva himself. This encounter takes place at the cremation ground, as described in her two short hymns of eleven verses each. There is a strong bifurcation in her corpus between her two longer poems, which engage themes and images I have already discussed, and these two hymns on Tiruvālaṅkāṭu, which purport to provide an eyewitness description of the scene surrounding Śiva's dance at the cremation ground. In her deployment of such imagery, Kāraikkāl *pēy* is partly in dialogue with Sanskrit mythology, which depicts Śiva as favoring the cremation ground in the company of misshapen beings who constitute his retinue.[12]

> In this miserable burning ground
> young ghouls scavenge the desolate theatre,
> disappointedly find nothing to eat
> and settle for sleep;
>
> While at twilight,
>   flawlessly in time to the rhythm
>   of heavenly drums
>   effortlessly bearing fire in his palm
> the beautiful one dances. ("Decade 2" v. 7)
>
> On ground moistened by melted fat,
> ghouls of hollowed eyes and long teeth
> violently perform the *tuṇaṅkai* dance
> around the burning ground;
> when they see the pyres have extinguished
> they crowd to gorge gleefully on the corpses
> to their hearts' content.
>
> Here in this frightful burning ground,
> bearing fire in his palm,
> the beautiful lord dances. ("Decade 2" v. 2)

She also draws from Tamil Caṅkam or "classical" poetry, which depicts *pēy* or ghouls feasting on the corpses of those who are fallen in battle in its complex rendering of what counts as heroic. That is battlefield as place. Battlefield as spiritual practice is the theme of the classical Sanskrit *Bhagavad Gītā*'s distinctive concern with bhakti as self-knowledge and disciplined action. But if, as the Gita teaches, confrontation with death is both the catalyst and method for a true understanding of bhakti, how would someone who is *not* a warrior go about getting that experience?

For many traditions that originated in India, the cremation ground (*shmashāna*) is the place where one ordinarily confronts death. It is thus an accessible place, but it requires a distinctive perspective to view the cremation ground as a generative place for spiritual practice, rather than a place to ritually dispose of a body. The contrast is made in Kāraikkāl *pēy*'s poetry itself: she describes mourners as "agitated and unable to comprehend, / they bear the dead in biers / to the cremation ground / and perform the rites then light the pyres" ("Decade 1" v. 10), yet describes herself as "Kāraikkāl *pēy* of the blazing mouth and teeth [who] thrives at this burning ground" ("Decade 2" v. 11); her self-identification as *pēy* marks her lingering presence there. The contrast in perspectives is vivid: The burial party is at the cremation ground involuntarily and temporarily to dispose of a body, while grieving and mentally agitated; the spiritual practitioner goes to the cremation ground on a voluntary basis, lingers there, and desires to understand deeply.

By Kāraikkāl *pēy*'s time, the cremation ground had been identified as a field of spiritual practice by several groups, including Buddhists. For Śaivas, *purāṇic* mythology located Śiva as inhabiting the cremation ground, but it was tantra that provided a rationale for Śaivas to go to the cremation ground for spiritual practice.[13] According to Alexis Sanderson, in the period between the Mauryas and the Guptas, worship of Śiva was "common and widespread in the population, and this was the case throughout the subcontinent."[14] Such traditions of lay devotion were characterized by the attainment of "success and security in this life and, after death, the finite reward of ascension to the deity's paradise (*śivalokaḥ*, *rudralokaḥ*), followed, once the merit that earned that reward has been exhausted, by the most desirable of incarnations in the human world."[15] In the context of this lay devotional substratum, specific initiatory traditions of Śaivism developed from the second century to the fifth century CE, which later tradition grouped as Atimārgas: the Pāñcārthika Pāśupatas, the Lākulas or Kālamukhas, and the Kāpālikas or Mahāvratins as adherents of the Soma-siddhānta. All of these initiatory traditions considered themselves to be distinguished from the devotional laity by "offering the individual alone the attainment of the non-finite goal of liberation (*mokṣaḥ*)."[16] Beginning in the middle of the fifth century and extending into the sixth, further initiatory traditions developed, including the Mantramārga or "Tantric Śaivism," which developed on the basis of the Kālamukhas and the Kāpālikas, and the Śakta Kulamārga, which developed specifically from the Kāpālikas. These later traditions "promised not only liberation, but for those initiates consecrated to office, the ability to accomplish supernatural effects (*siddhiḥ*)."[17]

Within this broad history, Kāraikkāl *pēy* is located at the juncture between the Atimārga proto-tantra sects and the emergence of the Mantramārga or tantric Śaivism; between the development of the nonfinite goal of spiritual liberation and the developing emphasis on special powers or *siddhis*. Notably, two of the four literary texts that provide "the earliest clear and datable evidence of full-blown Tantric religion"[18] were authored in south India: Mahendravarman I's *Mattavilāsa* (a satirical play by authored by a Pallava dynasty king, r. 600–630) and Daṇḍin's *Daśakumāracarita* (written under the auspices of the Pallava king Narasiṃhavarman II, r. 690–728).

The Atimārga concept of liberation as nonfinite contrasts with the goal of lay devotion: For the Atimārga, *mokṣa* is a lasting state, not exhaustible merit. To achieve that state, the Kāpālikas practiced rituals associated with death; such rituals are also described in the *Devī Purāṇa*, a Śakta text dated to the sixth century by Lina Gupta. After noting the text's emphasis on initiation, she summarizes its description of such practice:

> Only by following strictly prescribed procedures including control of the senses, cleansing the self of negative inclinations, meditation, penance, and following the ways of justice and truth can a person transcend the *paśu* ["afflicted"] state to become a *vīra* ["freedom from desire"]. . . . One of the most grueling of the Vāmācāra Śākta practices performed by the *vīra sādhaka* is the *nilasadhana* [*nīla-sādhana*]. On a special night, the *sādhaka* must sit on a corpse in a deserted location such as a cremation ground, riverbank, or pond and offer an oblation of consecrated flesh . . . to the fire deity. Through successful completion of the rite, [the practitioner] is united with the deity.[19]

Such rituals are a logical component of a worldview in which the boundary between finite and nonfinite has been disassembled. In contrast to the devotional practice of the laity, the Atimārga and tantric sects did not view liberation as repeating a cycle that resonates with that of birth and death; instead, the finite and the nonfinite were understood to intersect in embodied humankind and to effect liberation from the cycle of rebirth. The way to manifest this intersection was for the initiated to engage cultural signs of non-existence, especially in emulation of Śiva as Bhairava, at the place that both concretized and symbolized the cycle of rebirth and death—the cremation ground.

Tantra established a rationale and a practice for rendering the cremation ground as an effective theater for voluntary spiritual practice that would make it possible to engage with Śiva. Kāraikkāl *pēy*'s experiential vision of the cremation ground suggests that she also viewed the intersection of life and death as generative of spiritual insight, but that she preferred unscripted encounter to Tantra's carefully scripted approach that begins with initiation. Unlike the *nīlasādhana*'s deliberative, ritualistic performance, she offers a poetic description of the chaotic wildness of the cremation ground theater. Instead of emphasizing the controlled central actor as the tāntrika herself or himself, she celebrates the elegant dancer Śiva. Whereas the tāntrika achieves a ritual resolution, Kāraikkāl *pēy*'s poetry displays a tense in-between-ness:

> There, in the thickest darkness
> of the dead of night
> desiccated white fruits of the *vākai* rattle,
> birds of prey screech
> and an alarmed owl flutters on a branch.
>
> In this cremation ground,
> shadowed by dense chaparral,
> dancing elegantly on the flames,
> our father resides at Tiru Ālaṅkāṭu. ("Decade 1" v. 3)

It is the affective dimension that comes to the fore in Kāraikkāl *pēy*'s short hymns, especially the registers of fear, horror, and repulsion. This effect is achieved by her poetic style of making the first part of a given verse describe the scene at the cremation ground, while the second part of the verse locates Śiva as a dancer in the midst of that scene. The two parts are not usually equal; in most verses there is much more description of the context than of the deity, suggesting the visceral prioritization of involuntary horror. But for one who lingers, the unprecedented experience of the simultaneity of the finite and the nonfinite can be transformative. Historically, such an experience even transformed the meaning of the image of the dancing Śiva, but that is a story for another day.[20] Kāraikkāl *pēy*'s poetry suggests that remaining in the cremation ground sublimates human subjectivity into a devotional subjectivity. She does not imagine this process as contingent on initiation or as resulting in the ability to accomplish supernatural effects (*siddhiḥ*) but instead as a moment of profound awareness of humankind's conflicted essence of body and soul held in tension: an edulcorated vision of the perpetual dance of the finite and the nonfinite. Her intensely visual language provokes an affective, visceral situatedness in one who hears or reads her poetry. Deriving meaning from an affective experience of unscripted encounter is the way of the bhakti poet; enacting meaning through scripted transformative experience is the way of the tantric ritualist, as in Thomas Coburn's description of tantra as "a private and ritualized experience of oneness."[21]

The way Kāraikkāl *pēy* lived, as understood from her own poetry, was immersed in the cultivation of a devotional subjectivity that had at its center affective experiences of Śiva. Its aspects of poet, servant, and *pēy* are each potentially accessible to all of humanity. She does not describe her day-to-day activities, which permitted her biographer Cēkkiḻār to imagine a conflict between her bhakti and ordinary gendered social expectations, yet her poetry provides no evidence that she shared such a bifurcated view of her own life. Rather, her poetry provides a framework for humanity in its prioritization of continuous self-(re-)definition in relation to Śiva and the affective in-betweenness that characterizes it, as a way of being in the midst of the powers and vulnerabilities of ordinary personhood. Through its emphasis on unscripted encounter between the human and the divine, Kāraikkāl *pēy*'s poetry offers a porous human experience of affect to others. She demonstrated that through encounter, one could self-fashion a devotional subjectivity as a sustainable identity, separate and apart from inherited identity. Subsequent Tamil Śiva bhakti tradition, most prominently the three most famous male saints, learned much from Kāraikkāl *pēy*—the creation of a devotional subjectivity, the cultivation of affect as constitutive of the identity of servant to Śiva, and the necessity of exploration and talk about it. Yet in the practice of exploration the differences between her and the later saints are clear: the male saints performed pilgrimage to see Śiva, but they focused on named towns, many of which may have had institutional temples in which Śiva resided. When they do mention Śiva dancing at the cremation ground, as happens only infrequently, the mode is purely descriptive rather than conveying the discomfort of a fear-inducing immersive encounter.[22] Perhaps the challenges Kāraikkāl *pēy* described were later viewed as excess in a manner resembling Sara Ahmed's image of a "feminist killjoy," in which a willful woman is viewed by others as unhappy or as causing the unhappiness of others because of her spoken refusal to remain complicit with the social world, and her redefinition of what constitutes "happiness."[23] This is especially so if women's happiness is culturally defined as tied to marriage, a theme that is both suggested by and imposed on the works of female bhakti poet-saints such as Āṇṭāḷ and Mīrabāī, but ignored in Kāraikkāl *pēy*'s poetry. Kāraikkāl *pēy*'s affective embodiment of devotional participation as accessible to humanity, as immersive, and as discomfiting later became embedded in a canonical Tamil Śiva bhakti discourse that largely focused on a reassuringly paternalistic view of Śiva. That her words were also preserved in that canon allows us to contemplate her counterpoint, that an exploratory self-scripting is historically at the core of the lasting bhakti imagination.

NOTES

1 A brief and accessible introduction to this poet-saint is available online at Pechilis, "Karaikkal Ammaiyar," *World Religions and Spirituality*, April 13, 2016, www.wrldrels.org.

2 For a comparative discussion of poet-saint and biographer see Pechilis, *Interpreting Devotion*, 82–105; Pechilis, "To Body or Not to Body."

3 For a discussion on the choice of using "ghoul" as the translation, see Pechilis, "Story of the Classical Woman Saint."

4 Four poetic compositions are attributed to Kāraikkāl Ammaiyār: a poem in 101 stanzas, the *Aṟputat Tiruvantāti* (Sacred Linked Verses of Wonder); a poem in twenty stanzas, the *Tiru Iraṭṭai Maṇimālai* (Sacred Garland of Double Gems); and two hymns of eleven verses each on Tiruvālaṅkāṭu that were traditionally set to music, *Tiruvālaṅkāṭṭut Tiruppatikam* (Sacred Decade of Verses on Tiruvālaṅkāṭu, 1 and 2). In this chapter, I discuss verses from "Wonder," "Decade 1" and "Decade 2." A discussion of historical, literary, and cultural aspects of her compositions, as well as a list of Tamil sources that provide the text of her poems with commentaries, can be found in Pechilis, *Interpreting Devotion*.

5 Berger, "Mother," 47.

6 Seigworth and Gregg, "An Inventory of Shimmers," 2.

7 She usually uses the term *āḷ*. For use in the first-person singular, see vv. 7, 8, 11, 31 (reference to self in second person), 44 (*aṭiyēṉ*), 61; in the first-person plural, see vv. 3, 4, 12, 23, 91; and for reference to servants in the third person, see v. 40 (*toṇṭar*).

8 All translations are from Pechilis, *Interpreting Devotion*.

9 The term she uses for "any other" is *maṟṟoruvar-kku*.

10 Campantar 3.282.2 in Peterson, *Poems to Śiva*, 271; Appar 4.1.1–10 in Peterson, *Poems to Śiva*, 283–86; Cuntarar 7.1.1, 7.62.5 in Peterson, *Poems to Śiva*, 303.

11 Ramanujan, "On Women Saints."

12 Described as in *Mahābhārata* 13.128.13–18. See Kramrisch, *Presence of Śiva*, 298–300; Dhaky, "Bhūtas and Bhūtanāyakas."

13 On Kāraikkāl Ammaiyār and Buddhist cremation ground images and textual images of the cremation ground see Pechilis, *Interpreting Devotion*, 72–74 and 67–68, respectively. On Kāraikkāl Ammaiyār and Tantra see Pechilis, "Bhakti and Tantra Intertwined."

14 This discussion draws on Pechilis, "Bhakti and Tantra Intertwined"; Sanderson, "Impact of Inscriptions," 222–23. See also Sanderson, "Śaiva Age," 44. He refers to the use of the phrases such as "entirely devoted to Śiva" in inscriptions, competition for patronage, and indicates that "Jaina, brahmanical, and Buddhist literary evidence" can be found in "the longer version of this [2013] essay."

15 Sanderson, "Impact of Inscriptions," 212.

16 Sanderson, "Impact of Inscriptions," 212.

17 Sanderson, "Impact of Inscriptions," 212. He says that the earliest text of Mantramārga is Niśvāsamūla, 450–550 CE (p. 213).

18 Lorenzen, "Early Evidence for Tantric Religion," in Lorenzen, *Who Invented Hinduism?*, 26.

19 Gupta, "Tantric Incantation," 245. There is similar comparison to be made with the early Śaiva tantric text the *Brahmayāmala*; see discussion at Pechilis, "Bhakti and Tantra Intertwined." Many scholars date the *Devī Purāṇa* to 1000–1300.

20 See Pechilis, "Śiva as the Lord of Dance"; Pechilis, "The Siva Nataraja Image."

21 Coburn, "Structural Interplay," 88.

22 E.g., Campantar, 1.46.1–11, 1.134.5; Appar, 4.2.6, 4.80.1, 4.92.9; Cuntarar, 7.10.9. Kalidos, "Nāṭarāja" provides a discussion of the dancer in the male saints' hymns.

23 Ahmed, "Feminist Killjoys."

CHAPTER TWO

RELIGIOUS EQUALITY, SOCIAL CONSERVATISM

The Shiva-Bhakti Community as Imagined in Early Kannada Hagiographies

GIL BEN-HERUT

THE *vacanas*, short devotional poems associated with the early twelfth-century Shaiva devotees in the Kannada-speaking regions, are often read as protests against social discrimination. For example, Basavaṇṇa's famous *vacana* number 820 opens with the lines: "The rich will build temples for Śiva. What shall I, a poor man, do?"[1] This *vacana* presents temple worship as an exclusive and excluding arena available only to the rich. As an alternative for the poor who cannot build temples, Basavaṇṇa suggests in this *vacana* the practice of unmediated and personal worship through one's body. In a similar fashion, other *vacanas* attributed to the twelfth-century Shaivas from the Kannada-speaking region express resentment against discrimination based on social markers, pointing to the devotee's interiority as the sole criterion for spiritual advancement.

The protest-filled voice of the *vacanas* was used in the later history of the tradition, which came to be known as Virashaivism (from *vīraśaiva*) or Lingayatism (from *liṅgāyata*) as a tool for arguing against the social and political status quo. This is especially true in modern times, with social reformers and public intellectuals, Virashaivas and others, who refer to the twelfth-century devotional community using terms such as *egalitarian*, *democratic*, and *gender equal*, and present it as anticipating modernity and espousing progressive social values.[2] For example, Leela Mullatti's discussion of women's status in Virashaivism, based on her readings of certain *vacanas*, concludes with a statement about "the perfect equality given by Virasaivism to man and woman in their marital life."[3] The use of modern ideals for presenting the tradition, evinced not only in the realm of public affairs but also in art (novels, plays), percolates as well into critical scholarship. For example, the entry for *Liṅgāyat* in *The Oxford Dictionary of World Religions* states that Liṅgāyats adopted, among other things, the "denial of caste distinctions[,] . . . brahmanical superiority and authority, rites, and rituals. Women and men came to be regarded as equal."[4]

The practice of identifying in early Kannada Shiva-bhakti a voice that is egalitarian and committed to social change is anachronistic because the broad significations implied by these and similar terms are steeped in Western and modern value systems that are far removed from this tradition's cultural bedrock. The well-known scholar of Kannada literature Robert Zydenbos recognizes this problem in his memorable observation that "to write that Vīraśaivism has been 'democratic,' 'feminist,' or 'egalitarian' from the beginning, as some modern writers do, is somewhat like writing that nuclear weapons were used in the *Rāmāyaṇa*, as some other authors do."[5]

Zydenbos's admonition is a useful point of departure for examining the attitudes of this tradition toward ritual exclusion and social discrimination that we find in Kannada Shiva-bhakti sources other than *vacanas*. No doubt many of the *vacanas* we possess have early roots in the tradition, but we have access to them only as reformulated in writing by later agents such as the fifteenth-century Viraktas and modern Lingayats.[6] This is not true, however, for all early Virashaiva sources. Some early materials by and about early Shiva *bhaktas* were composed as written literary works, and one such narrative text actually goes back to the early thirteenth century or perhaps even beforehand. This work's early date and relative textual stability as well as its expansive portrayals of the lives of the twelfth-century figures enable us to ask to what degree it bears out present-day understandings of the twelfth-century Virashaiva community as "gender equal," "egalitarian," and "democratic." Or if not, in what ways does it diverge from such concepts?

THE EARLIEST HAGIOGRAPHIES ABOUT KANNADA SHAIVA SAINTS

The earliest source we have that deals with the lives of the Kannada saints is the *Śivaśaraṇara Ragaḷegaḷu* ("Poems in the *Ragaḷe* Meter for Shiva's Saints"). Written by the prolific and accomplished poet Harihara only a few decades after the emergence of devotionalism in the Kannada-speaking region, the *Ragaḷegaḷu* provides a rich picture of the tradition's origins. The stories about the local devotees that appear in this text portray a young devotional cult that embraced a variety of social attitudes, religious practices, and communal forms, some of which were considered traditional and mainstream. In this regard the *Ragaḷegaḷu* complicates the widespread and oversimplified understandings of the early tradition based on selected *vacanas* in their subsequently redacted form.[7]

The community of *bhaktas*, as it is imagined by the author, consists of poor people as well as rich, young and old, male and female, people hailing from the margins of society as well as from its center, whose trades include professions considered base and polluting as well as those considered prestigious and lucrative. The sheer diversity of the literary characters Harihara considers as model devotees attests to his inclusive, nondiscriminatory approach. Harihara explicitly argues for this sort of nondiscrimination by using terms such as *samaśīla* (literally, "equal conduct"), but the sort of equality implied by the stories themselves is far more complex than such a term would seem to imply.

Harihara's vision of nondiscrimination is in fact doubly bounded: first by the sectarian filter of exclusive belief in Shiva, since Harihara's social inclusiveness applies only within this fold and anyone outside it is ultimately rendered a threat[8] and, second, by the author's limiting of social nondiscrimination to the realm of worship practices. While Harihara's stories argue forcefully for freedom in ritual expression, total liberty in the realm of personal devotion, and comradeship among fellow devotees, the nonreligious social landscape as charted in the *Ragaḷegaḷu* remains conservative. It is replete with social asymmetries and hierarchical distance.

Although Harihara's stories about the Kannada saints exhibit an avid rejection of caste-based exclusion as it applies to the ritualistic arena, they do not imply a "denial of caste distinctions" in terms of labor divisions, group customs, and social roles. True, the *Ragaḷegaḷu* takes a number of occupations that are traditionally regarded as being lowly and purges them of the baggage of perceived pollution, but labor divisions as such are never challenged. Similarly, some of the stories in the *Ragaḷegaḷu* empower women with a certain independence, but this is usually limited to the religious arena; the general relation between men and women as depicted in these stories is far from anything that could be regarded as equal. And while some stories do contain rejections of Brahmanical supremacy—a major emphasis in more recent accounts of what the Virashaiva "revolution" involved—they also at specific points affirm certain Brahmanical practices and values.

Examination of work, gender, and Brahmanism shows that the nascent religious tradition later known as Virashaivism was not thoroughly egalitarian in spirit. Rather, it was making an effort to integrate innovative and radical devotional principles into conventional society. This new tradition was not invested in carving out an entirely new social sphere; rather, it appealed to as many spheres on the existing social spectrum as possible in putting forward its vision of Shaiva truth. In consequence of this rudimentary and pragmatic goal, the social terrain revealed in Harihara's stories is—in comparison to the ideal of a society composed of equals—quite knotty. We are forced to think about the imagined community of Shaiva devotees that appears in the *Ragaḷegaḷu* not as a coherent social entity but as a complex multiheaded creature.

Work

Work and work ethics in the Kannada Shaiva devotional milieu have often received scholarly attention in relation to one of the tradition's most famous slogans: *kāyakavē kailāsa*, "work itself is Shiva's heaven."[9] This slogan expresses the tradition's view that any work can have soteriological value—and even be a religious vocation—when one is wholly devoted to Shiva while working. More broadly, it conveys the tradition's conviction that it is anchored in this-worldly engagement. One Ragaḷe, or story from the *Ragaḷegaḷu*, that demonstrates this point tells about Kumbara Guṇḍayya, the pot maker who, after his daily visits to the temple, carries Shiva's image constantly in his mind while hammering away at pots in his backyard (fig. 2.1).[10] The devotee's focus on Shiva during his pot-making is so intense that Shiva himself descends from heavenly Kailāsa, dances to the banging sounds of his devotee, and finally lifts the devotee up to Kailāsa. By stressing Guṇḍayya's concentration on Shiva during his work, Harihara sends a vital message about the importance of any *bhakta*'s internal state during his or her work, a state which, when turned toward the god, can bring about spiritual liberation: the *bhakta*'s ascent to Kailāsa.

While Guṇḍayya's story does exonerate every type of work from ritual pollution in the most pronounced manner possible—the significance of which is difficult to overestimate in light of conventional attitudes in the classical South Asian imagination—it also has some conservative aspects. We can note, for example, the traditional and positive role kept in the story for Shiva's temple, which is not challenged as an excluding and elitist arena. This is quite different from what we hear in the *vacana* of Basavaṇṇa that was mentioned earlier. Indeed, throughout Harihara's Ragaḷes temple worship is affirmed as an efficacious and valid medium of worship. Unlike what one might think on the basis of Basavaṇṇa's words, the temple is depicted as being open to everyone and unhindered by the mediation of priests; the need for it to be challenged as such thus does not arise.[11] In addition, the narrator of Guṇḍayya's story does not comment on the social implications of the work of making pots, traditionally considered low on the social scale. He simply lets it be. In line with this, there is no devotee in the entire *Ragaḷegaḷu* who pursues an occupation different from that to which that devotee was born or for which he or she was trained. It appears that Harihara has little interest in the external social conditions of one's

2.1 "Work itself is Shiva's heaven," as demonstrated by Guṇḍayya the potter. Artist unknown, date unknown. Collection of the Vishwakalyana Mission, Bangalore, Karnataka. Used by permission of the Vishwakalyana Mission

work beyond a basic sense that all work has spiritual legitimacy and value.[12] The *Ragaḷegaḷu* stories do not convey any sense of rejection of hereditary, guild-like labor structures. A poor potter such as Guṇḍayya, even as an ardent *bhakta*, remains a poor potter, but such contingent, material, and social circumstances are rendered irrelevant in light of his absolute spiritual liberation. The revolution offered by this tradition is about infusing spiritual capital into one's work, not enhancing its social capital.[13]

The early tradition's adherence to a fixed vocational framework is also evinced in the naming pattern of Kannada saints.[14] Some of the most famous composers of *vacanas* and other saintly figures in the tradition are remembered in relation to their professions. This is the case not only with Kumbara ("potter") Guṇḍayya, but also Jēḍara ("weaver") Dāsimayya, Taḷavāra ("night watchman") Kāmidēva, Madivāḷa ("washerman") Mācayya, and many others.[15] The legitimization of any occupation in Harihara's corpus—and in the Kannada early imagination more broadly—is paradoxical. On the one hand, we have a total rejection of Brahmanical prejudice against certain occupations, since Harihara champions these very occupations. On the other, he precludes or minimizes the potential for endorsing social mobility by valorizing those same occupations. Inevitably, and conservatively, this has the effect of upholding existing and traditional labor divisions.

Gender

Discrimination against low-caste persons and against women is both entrenched in orthodox Brahmanical ideology and grounded in notions of ritual impurity, and the devotional attitudes of the early Virashaiva tradition toward women are as groundbreaking as those that concern a person's occupation—and are equally complex. The cadre of Kannada Shiva *bhaktas* and *vacana* poets is in fact heavily populated by female figures, and their relative independence and individual freedom speaks volumes about the progressive stance this tradition held in the past and still holds today with regard to women's status in society, their agency, and their right to speak in their own voices.[16] Harihara dedicates several stories in the *Ragaḷegaḷu* to women saints, carving out a new literary space for female figures. In each of them the female devotee's agency is plain to see.

In the Ragaḷe story about the famous Kannada female saint Mahādēviyakka, her unbounded devotion to Shiva propels her to transgress the limits of her prescribed role as virtuous wife, as would be dictated by traditional and normative writings.[17] Mahādēvi in the *Ragaḷegaḷu* is a woman who decides to leave her non-Shaiva husband, a powerful landlord, against his will and to live instead as a wandering renouncer devoted to the worship of Shiva. This radical change is dramatized by an equally radical change in her external appearance: she gives away her clothes and uses only her long locks of hair to cover her naked body.[18]

Despite this clear endorsement of female empowerment, however, it is difficult to read the representation of Mahādēvi and other women in this corpus as anticipating contemporary claims for gender-based equality.[19] Mahādēvi's success in maintaining her spiritual independence—even at the price of walking out on her marriage—is never fully accepted by the people surrounding

2.2

Mahādēvi as a secluded renunciant, after leaving her non-Shaiva husband. Illustration by Mugali Hudgi, date unknown. Collection of the Vishwakalyana Mission, Bangalore, Karnataka. Used by permission of the Vishwakalyana Mission

her.[20] Instead of spending time with fellow Shaiva devotees as she did before marrying, the only possible trajectory for Mahādēvi is to abdicate her social role as a married woman and become a renunciant (as in fig. 2.2), which is quickly followed by her ascent to Shiva's heaven.[21] Thus Mahādēvi's postmarital story is not about reintegrating into society in a new, transvalued way but about her inevitable, possibly also tragic, departure from it. It is a story about a form of female empowerment that flows directly from uncompromising devotion to her god but that exacts an unavoidable and enormous social toll.

A Ragaḷe with even more jarring implications when measured on the scale of social oppression against women and the protest that ought by modern standards to attend it is one about a poor female devotee called Nimbavve (literally, "sister acid-lime"), who decides to serve Shiva *bhaktas* by offering them her body, even while performing *pūjā* before a temple *liṅga*.[22] Although Harihara explicitly confronts the ethical issues that Nimbavve's devotional practice raises and forcefully argues for Nimbavve's agency and sense of empowerment, it is difficult to discard the idea that this story could also be read as legitimizing the sexual exploitation of deprived women. Throughout the corpus, then, gender appears as a field of struggle and compromise, even if it is also regarded as a field where liberation is possible.

Brahmans

The general antagonism toward Brahmanism attributed to Kannada Shivabhakti as we know it today can also be located in Harihara's stories, though—in a manner similar to his understandings of work ethics and gender—his treatment of Brahmans is complex and dialectical in ways that make it hard to call him anti-Brahmanical. The stories show a persistent mirroring of Brahmanical values, even when they are elitist and exclusive in nature. For example, Harihara tells about a non-Brahman devotee called Kallayya who masters Brahmanical scripture and wins theological debates not only against the paradigmatic, traditional, non-Brahman "others"—atheists (Lōkāyatas), Buddhists (Bauddhas), and materialists (Cārvākas)—but also against Brahmans.[23] Later in the text the same theme is pursued more elaborately when Kallayya's dog recites the Yajurveda in front of astonished Brahmans.[24] Despite Harihara's general lack of appreciation of the Vedas from a spiritual perspective, these incidents do point to his continual interest in them, even if for sectarian purposes only.

Apart from attitudes toward the authority of Brahmanical scripture, a stark rejection of Brahmanical identity, values, and practices in the *Ragaḷegaḷu* is brought to the fore only under two conditions: when Brahmans are labeled as Vaishnavas, and when Brahmans try to uphold purity-based canons of discrimination so as to exclude Shaiva devotees. Indeed, these two conditions always converge in the same characters.[25] But the corpus is also populated by "good" Shaiva Brahmans, and in this it is similar to remembered histories of other devotional traditions that celebrate the character of the Brahman *bhakta*, traditions like those of the Tamil Shaivas and the Marathi Vārkarīs.[26] Several protagonists in the *Ragaḷegaḷu* are simultaneously devout followers of Shiva and well-educated Brahmans working as high officials at court. Although their Brahmanical (and worldly) engagements run contrary to the idealistic devotionalism argued for in the stories, their Brahmanical DNA is not automatically denied by Harihara, nor does it preclude them from being "good" *bhaktas*. Rather, Harihara charts in these stories a path that Brahmans can follow in order to be considered "good" *bhaktas* without totally jettisoning their Brahmanical identity.[27]

It is possible that Harihara's target audience included Brahmans who, as he was, were searching for ways to participate in the emerging devotional cult while still preserving at least some of their Brahmanical ways. The *Ragaḷegaḷu* stories would seem to have offered them a way to maintain some aspects of their Brahmanness and Brahmanical background as long as they avoided trying to inflict Brahmanism—or Brahmanical restrictions—on those around them.[28]

CONCLUSION

In all three dimensions, then—work, gender, and caste—an analysis of the stories narrated in the *Ragaḷegaḷu* reveals a complex picture in terms of the social dynamics that must be taken into account if one asks whether bhakti is a vehicle for hegemonic power or an instrument of protest. In this earliest record of public memory in Kannada Shiva-bhakti, we find stories that do project harsh protest against any form of discrimination in the religious sphere, specifically in the ritualistic arena and in regard to personal forms of devotional expression. Yet hegemonic and conservative social structures outside this realm are not challenged. From a contemporary point of view, Harihara emerges as a conservative radical. He did not ask the "power or protest" question that we now do—or at least not at all in the same way.

NOTES

1 Ramanujan, *Speaking of Śiva*, 88.

2 Robert J. Zydenbos writes: "Only in most recent times have certain Vīraśaivas, who are active in the cultural and political sphere and who wish to project themselves as 'progressive,' hopped onto the anti-brahmin bandwagon in search of socio-political profits" ("Review: Vīraśaivism, Caste, Revolution," 531). For depictions of Virashaivism as egalitarian, see Ramaswamy, *Walking Naked*, 145–94; Ramaswamy, *Divinity and Deviance*; Schouten, *Revolution of the Mystics*; Ishwaran, *Speaking of Basava*; and Ishwaran, *Religion and Society*.

3 Mullatti, *Bhakti Movement*, 36.

4 Bowker, *Oxford Dictionary of World Religions*, 581.

5 Zydenbos, "Vīraśaivism, Caste, Revolution, etc.,"535.

6 Chandra Shobhi, "Pre-Modern Communities and Modern Histories."

7 My monograph on Harihara's *Ragaḷegaḷu*, *Śiva's Saints: The Origins of Devotion in Kannada according to Harihara's Ragaḷegaḷu*, argues for a reconsideration of our notions regarding a radical rupture with contemporaneous orthodoxy that is commonly associated with this tradition and questions the adequacy of using the terms *vīraśaiva* and *liṅgāyata* for this tradition before the fourteenth century.

8 Ben-Herut, "Arguing with Vaiṣṇavas, Annihilating Jains."

9 The expression is glossed in the *Vīraśaiva Pāribhāṣika Padakōśa* ("Vīraśaiva Lexicon for Technical Terms") as "doing work out of a feeling of complete surrender to Śiva" (Vidyāśaṅkara, *Vīraśaiva Pāribhāṣika Padakōśa*, 123). The textual history of the term is, in fact, quite complicated. See Michael, "Work as Worship," 617n2. See also discussions of the meaning of the term in Ishwaran, *Speaking of Basava*, 34–35.

10 See story in the *Guṇḍayyana Ragaḷe*. The stories from the *Ragaḷegaḷu* referred to in this chapter are taken from Harihara, *Nūtana Purātanara Ragaḷegaḷu*; and Harihara, *Śivabhaktimahimā Ragaḷegaḷu*.

11 Ben-Herut, "Things Standing Shall Move."

12 R. Blake Michael writes: "What existed was not a fully egalitarian society but a community of religious equals who continued to fulfill the tasks assigned [to] them by their occupations" ("Women of the Śūnyasaṃpādane," 368). Elsewhere Michael writes that "the Vīraśaiva-s permit a certain voluntary choice of occupation based not on birth but on preference" ("Work as Worship in Vīraśaiva Tradition," 616). This claim is not commensurate with the *Ragaḷegaḷu* stories.

13 I borrow the term *spiritual capital* from Verter, "Spiritual Capital."

14 Vijaya Ramaswamy makes a similar claim based on the *vacanas*. See Ramaswamy, *Divinity and Deviance*, 52–55.

15 See Devadevan, *Prehistory of Hinduism*, 40–41.

16 Leela Mullatti estimates that there were about fifty female saint-leaders in the early period of the tradition in Mullatti, *Bhakti Movement*, 7, 39–42. See also Champakalakshmi, "Caste and Community," 276; and Yaravintelimath, *Vacanas of Women Saints*.

17 Mahādēvi figures prominently in the larger South Asian cadre of devotional characters. Jack Hawley points to four central figures in a performance drawn together by the intellectual activist Madhu Kishwar, including Mahādēvi, in Hawley, *A Storm of Songs*, 335. Mahādēvi is highly venerated and commemorated by many communities in Karnataka today, and there are numerous publications, both in English and in Kannada, of her *vacanas*. See Akkamahādēvi and Basavarāju, *Akkana Vacanagaḷu*. For English translations, see Ramanujan, *Speaking of Śiva*, 111–42.

18 Her story is told in the *Mahādēviyakkana Ragaḷe*.

19 Vijaya Ramaswamy has produced a gender-based critique of female devotion to the male god based on readings of various *vacanas* in Ramaswamy, *Divinity and Deviance*, 28–33. Compare Glushkova, "Dharma and Bhakti," 181. R. Blake Michael's analysis of women's stories in the early sixteenth-century *Śūnyasampādane* points to a similarly asymmetrical treatment of women in Michael, "Women of the Śūnyasaṃpādane." On the need to develop multiple approaches to the question of gender in the context of South Asia, see Patton, *Jewels of Authority*, 5.

20 Vijaya Ramaswamy notes that Mahādēvi is suspiciously absent from lists of fellow devotees referred to by other female *vacana* composers, which Ramaswamy understands as an indication of a general disapproval of her unruly behavior (Ramaswamy, *Divinity and Deviance*, 43). R. Champakalakshmi makes a similar claim regarding the negative reaction to Mahādēvi by the people surrounding her, apparently based on readings in the *Śūnyasampādane* (Champakalakshmi, *Caste and Community*, 275–76).

21 The popular episode about Mahādēvi's association with the Kalyāṇa devotees (including Basavaṇṇa and Allama Prabhu) after leaving her husband is only found in later retellings, such as the fourth version of the *Śūnyasampādane* from the sixteenth century.

22 Her story is told in the *Nimbiyakkana Ragaḷe.*

23 *Hāvinahāḷa Kallayyana Ragaḷe*, vv. 191–94.

24 The episode appears in *Hāvinahāḷa Kallayyana Ragaḷe*, vv. 355–438.

25 Confrontations with insidious Vaishnava Brahmans receive the center stage in the *Kēśirājadaṇṇāyakara Ragaḷe*, the *Teluga Jommayyana Ragaḷe*, the *Basavēśvaradēvara Ragaḷe*, the *Bhōgaṇṇana Ragaḷe*, the *Śaṅkaradāsimayyana Ragaḷe*, the *Rēvaṇasiddhēśvarana Ragaḷe*, and the *Hāvinahāḷa Kallayyana Ragaḷe*.

26 Novetzke, "Brahmin Double."

27 See, for example, the episode about the Brahman Kēśirāja meeting another Shiva devotee, Teluga Jommayya, who is a hunter. The episode is told twice in the corpus (in the third chapter of the *Kēśirājadaṇṇāyakara Ragaḷe* and in the third chapter of the *Teluga Jommayyana Ragaḷe*). In it, Kēśirāja shares consecrated food with Jommayya. The food offered to the Brahman contains meat, and only after Shiva miraculously converts Kēśirāja's portion into vegetarian sweets does he start to eat it.

28 I thank Jon Keune for suggesting this terminological distinction (personal communication, 2016).

CHAPTER THREE

CASTE AND WOMEN IN EARLY MODERN INDIA

Krishna Bhakti in Sixteenth-Century Vrindavan

HEIDI R. M. PAUWELS

How politically correct is bhakti? Often it is hailed as ideological resistance to caste hierarchy and patriarchy. Does the ideology of devotion indeed work to liberate the masses, in particular low-caste people and women? Some scholars answer this in the affirmative,[1] and some Dalits themselves support this claim.[2] But others have blamed bhakti for providing religious sanction for a hierarchical and patriarchal status quo. Is it an elite attempt of upper-caste males to co-opt women and the masses by inculcating obedience?[3] Yet another option is to split bhakti in two camps: on the one hand, elitist *saguṇa* bhakti (worship of God with attributes, especially as one of the *avatāras* of Vishnu), and on the other, egalitarian *nirguṇa bhakti* (worship of God without attributes, more abstract).[4] Is there a good and a bad bhakti?

Homogenizing the many shades of bhakti into one or two archetypes works well for pedagogical purposes but hardly does justice to the vast gamut of different flavors. There are many bhaktis.[5] Currently prevalent self-understandings of different sects (*sampradāyas*) and the frequently assumed division between *saguṇa* and *nirguṇa* do not always hold true when compared to the earliest evidence. Therefore the first task is to understand which communities early modern bhakti authors felt themselves belonging to.

There is another caveat. The question of political correctness may not necessarily align with the concerns of the bhakti exponents themselves. It is anachronistic to hijack bhakti voices for the purpose of a particular agenda, be it colonial, nationalist, postcolonial, Marxist, conservative, feminist, fundamentalist, deconstructionist, or subaltern. Sometimes bhakti voices are impoverished when pressed into service to support contemporary agendas. Scholarship has a tendency to reproduce itself: some supposedly representative poems get all the airspace, and others are conveniently forgotten. And sometimes they are quoted out of context. Rather than hearing only what fits our agenda, we need to do full justice and restore agency to the authors (or singers) themselves. This means listening carefully to their voices as they speak or sing for themselves before we proceed to interpret them. We can ask our questions as long as in our answers we do justice to bhakti's own concerns.

It is not easy to hear bhakti voices as they echo through the humdrum of history. Many current misunderstandings of bhakti have been traced to and blamed on the first Western observers, whose views were colored by their own Christian prejudices. Yet these "Orientalists" were hardly the first to misinterpret others' viewpoints and see only what fitted their own agenda. Each generation of transmitters has added its own preconceptions. The individual bhakti voices come to us mediated through a range of agendas—some scholarly, some hagiographical—that have not yet been carefully mapped.[6] We should be alert so as to distinguish these different layers. Current editions of bhakti poetry cannot be taken at face value. Several were produced to proclaim the superiority of specific sects or in the zealous effort to construct a canon for Hindi, the national language. Some were based on manuscripts that were written down whole centuries after their presumed authors had died. Upon comparing manuscripts, historically as well as according to social milieu, one can map the changing messages over time.[7] All along, singers transmit the poems orally, adding their own layers of interpretation. In short, bhakti texts come to us filtered through the understandings of singers, scribes, and editors, each with its own context, its own speech situation. This is also true of the hagiographies in which such poems are often mentioned or quoted. Thus, before determining what *bhaktas* have to say to our questions, it is imperative to carefully establish their words and determine how they were interpreted over time. Only then will we be in a position to generalize about the bhakti movement as a whole.

Finally, when listening to bhakti voices, we must be aware of their formulaic character. The bulk of bhakti literature consists of songs that are built with formulas determined by rhyme and meter. How does this affect the message? What is a formulaic statement, and what is heartfelt? Formulaic elements are not necessarily insincere: each generation reappropriates the old ideals and fights its own battle for change. But we cannot take things at face value. Each poem needs to be understood in its relation to others, both previous and contemporary. The study of bhakti intertextuality has hardly begun.[8]

All this means that we are not yet ready to give a definite answer to our initial question about bhakti and power, but we can design a master plan that will eventually enable us to map the different patterns. Our primary aim is to allow individual bhakti voices to be heard. For each, we establish the trajectory of the original speech utterances, contextualizing as far as possible and speculating about where they may be formulaic. Then taking into consideration the transmission history of the sources, we record all angles from which our witnesses of the past are preserved, methodologically excavating the site of each bhakti voice. Finally, we map all these sites, laying out their interrelations with each other.

One such excavation concerns the degree to which sixteenth-century Krishna *bhaktas* in the Braj area who expressed themselves in Brajbhāṣā advocated hierarchical and patriarchal structure. A fruitful entry point is the sixteenth-century Vrindavan *bhakta* Harirām Vyās.[9] As it turns out, listening to Vyās's single voice changes the way we think about sixteenth-century Krishna bhakti overall.

Harirām Vyās, together with Hit Harivaṃś and Svāmī Haridās, was seen as part of the *rasik-trayī* ("triumvirate of connoisseurs") who shared a predilection for relishing (*rasa*) Krishna's love-play (*śṛṅgāra rasa vihāra*). All three were Brahmans who took up lifelong residence in Vrindavan, where they created inspired poetry in response to each other.[10] Vyās makes for a suitable case study for two reasons. First, he is one of few sixteenth-century Krishna *bhaktas* who composed hagiographic songs in praise of other *bhaktas*, including *nirguṇa bhaktas*.[11] Second, Vyās's prolific poetic output, collected as *Vyās Vāṇī*, is not limited to songs on the theme of Krishna's love-play (*śṛṅgāra rasa vihāra*) that were performed in the company (*satsaṅg*) of his like-minded *rasika* friends but also includes instructional poetry (*siddhānta*) intended for a broader audience. In several poems of the latter type, Vyās directly addresses the principal issues that concern us here: caste and women. He does so in colorful language; his poetry feels almost Kabirian at times.

A full manuscript study that allows Vyās's voice to be heard reveals that the vulgate edition compiled by his descendant Vāsudev Gosvāmī provides a fairly reliable text.[12] Nonetheless, for each poem I quote, I work here with the oldest available manuscript attestation.[13] I take care to distinguish between the text by itself and the hagiographical interpretations that attend it, and I speculate about the extent to which the ideas expressed may be formulaic or, rather, expressive of Vyās's individual voice.

BHAKTI TRANSCENDING CASTE

In his hagiographical poems in praise of *nirguṇī* saints, Vyās expresses his admiration, among others, for the weaver Kabīr and the cobbler Raidās. He makes it a point to stress that despite their supposedly low-caste professions, he ranks these sincere *bhaktas* higher than many who were thought to be high-caste. In the eyes of God, the former are preferred, no matter the latter's social pedigree. Bhakti transcends caste. In these songs, intended for a broad community of pilgrims visiting Vrindavan, Vyās is preaching a spiritual equality that we well might think of as projecting a *nirguṇī* ethos:

> Who ever found devotion by reciting [scriptures]?
> Pandits recite the *Bhāgavata Purāṇa* for money. There's no room left for Hari!
> Without reading Vedas or Purāṇas, Kabīr felt peace.
> Raidās gave up meat: he became a devotee, mounting the horse of grace. . . .
> Vyās says: Without belief, happiness is nowhere to be found. The snake of sorrow won't leave the heart. (V212-VB206)[14]

Vyās sees himself on the same side as Kabīr and Raidās, rather than aligned with contemporary Brahmans who recite the *Bhāgavata Purāṇa* for money. And the argument that the low-caste *bhakta* is better than the high-caste hypocrite is not limited to the exceptional case of these great saints. It holds good for ordinary people too. In several cases Vyās contrasts high-born disbelievers with devoted low-born *bhaktas*:

> Vyās [says]: leave godless Brahmans. Rather, be born in the womb of a dog-eater *bhakta*. (V201-J105; full poem translated later in this chapter)[15]

> Give up pride and find truth: Śyām dwells with the humble.
> Vyās [says]: Dog-eaters crossed [the ocean of existence to salvation] while high-caste Brahmans forgot about God and sank. (V225-J113)[16]

This may sound rather formulaic, but it is not only in theory that Vyās declares the lower castes full-fledged members of the bhakti community. He speaks out against the persistence of orthodox caste discrimination with regard to rules of food consumption. He preaches a radical shift of allegiance from the human social construct of caste, which forbids dining with fellow devotees, to an understanding of the community of God wherein all are appreciated for their devotion. In doing so, he uses the same vehicle for his instruction as Kabīr does—the pithy *dohā* couplet:

> Vyās: many low castes got across, absorbed in the name
> Mounting the boat of pride, crores of high castes drowned! (*dohā* 22)[17]

Vyās: to hell with the Brahman's sweets!
From Vrindavan's low castes beg for leftovers—and eat them! (*dohā* 25)[18]

This heartfelt concern comes to the fore in tirades against those who, while professing bhakti, would still discriminate on the basis of caste purity.[19] A Kabirian example gets at the heart of the hypocrisy:

Those who refuse to eat leftovers of *bhaktas*
Wear muzzles like pigs and dogs, sustaining the body with what's "kosher" and what's not.
Their bodies are hellish fires, because they despise God's people.
Impelled by the power of lust, they drink spit from some sexy girl's lips.
Flies may piss on their food, and still they'll avidly eat,
But when it comes to sipping the water that's washed some *bhakta*'s feet, they proudly refuse, they get angry.
God reaches for the food of a low-caste *bhakta*, but Brahmans stay far away.
At weddings they'll sit with Bājdārs and eat as Brahmans with the groom's party.
When meeting their sons, they'll kiss their snotty faces and be happy, stupid fathers!
But touching untouchable *bhaktas* pollutes them: they'll take an oil bath and change clothes.
In hot pursuit of God's *bhaktas*, God and the Ganges are restless to succeed.
Millions of sinners like Vyās fit in the dust covering the feet of just one holy man. (V154-J216)[20]

Words such as these do not refer to *bhaktas* of the past; they are interpellations in the present, an illocutionary act. To get his message across, like Kabīr, Vyās uses the shock value of irony and sarcasm. This outrage does not strike one as formulaic. To the contrary, the poem was so convincing that Vyās's hagiographers felt a need to contextualize it so as to deflect its scorn. They did so with stories of Vyās's anger at his purported patron, King Madhukar Shāh of Orcchā, who refused to eat *prasād* (food sanctified by contact with the divine image) from the hands of a low-caste person.[21] Read on its own terms, however, the poem seems rather to be directed against Brahmans who are more concerned with ritual purity than with bhakti. While such Brahmans seem to have been part of the real world of Vrindavan at the time, there is no room for them in Vyās's circle. Did Vyās's indignation at Brahmans hit too close to home, causing hagiographers to redirect it to his patron? If so, the hagiographers' concerns confirm that we are hearing an authentic voice here, one that was strong and problematic enough that it had to be muted or at least transmuted by later generations.

Vyās does not exclusively make use of negative rhetoric to make the point that bhakti is more important than *varṇāśramadharma*, the "classic" caste order as understood in Brahmanical texts. In an example of positive discourse, Vyās replaces traditional high-caste markers with bhakti ones:

> My caste is "Exclusive Devotee."
> My family deity is Radha, my hometown is Barsānā. I dine only with residents of Braj.
> My *gotra* is Gopāl, the rosary is my sacred thread. The peacock carries my hair-tuft, Hari's temple is the *tilak* on my forehead.
> The Holy Veda I recite is praise of Hari's name. Instead of sacred *kuśa* grass I raise drum and cymbal [to sing his fame].
> I trace my lineage along the Yamunā. My eternal duty is God's play. His leftovers and Rāsa are my mainstay.
> Serving Him determines what I do and don't do. My roots are in good company. In Vrindavan I'll always stay.
> My creed is the *Bhāgavata*, my prayer is Krishna's name. When it's time to perform the twilight libation, I say it over and over again.
> [Krishna's] flute is like a seer to me. His wishing tree cares for my wants. Vyās needs neither bless nor curse. (V93-J232)[22]

Here again Vyās makes the point that attention should shift from ritual purity to loving devotion. This poem is not formulaic; rather it creatively turns conventions upside down. Vyās systematically reinterprets the traditional ingredients of Brahmanhood by proposing bhakti substitutes. Here we have a challenge to orthodox Brahmanical practices coming from a man who is himself a Brahman. The first-person voice, repeated throughout in the refrain, makes it all the more poignant. One senses a personal journey behind the generic bhakti discourse.

A BRAHMAN REJECTING BRAHMANICAL AUTHORITY

Vyās does not stop with declaring Brahmanical paraphernalia superfluous: though himself a Brahman, he voices a general disdain for Brahmanical authority. I have elsewhere directed attention to a Kabīr-like poem in which he ridicules Brahmans who are nonbelievers. The word he uses is the same one used for "outsiders" by Kabīr, namely *śākta*.[23] In the following poem, Vyās makes fun of Brahmanical pretensions to religious authority, unmasking their sectarian differences as being inspired by mutual jealousy:

> Svāmīs, Bhaṭṭs, Gosvāmīs, they have set up different philosophies and styles of life,
> But never shall they love one another! The fire in their heart just doesn't get doused.[24]

Vyās, who himself has the epithet Gosvāmī, denounces his fellow *gosvāmīs* as corrupt. In another poem he says,

> They arrive singing and dancing–out of greed!
> No devotion can emerge in them, their passion and penance is all for show.
> They read hocus-pocus and meet with seductresses, taken in by the fleeting world.
> Lots of Svāmīs, innumerable Gosvāmīs. Even from Bhaṭṭs there's no release.
> Without true feeling they're all of them wailing. They're cheering with self-righteous anger.
> Vyās says: Without the grace of Rādhikā's enchanter, there never can be true love.[25]

This repeated lumping together of Svāmīs, Gosvāmīs, and Bhaṭṭs seems to fit with oral formulaic composition. Even so, however, the tone of the poems is anything but formulaic. Vyās's sneers at other Brahmans feel true to life. It is difficult to escape the impression that he is speaking of the Vrindavan of his time, which apparently attracted many pseudo-devotees of the type Vyās despised.

Vyās minces no words when denouncing Brahmans who use their high birth in the cause of what he calls extortion:

> Great sinners, craving gifts, use [their] Brahmanhood for extortion.
> Groping in darkness, fighting and dying, I'd rather have a million butchers!
> For instruction [they play] the role of Guru and Gosvāmī, but in their behavior all we see is meanness.[26]

Thus the Brahman Vyās, far from manipulating ideology to preserve his own elite position, was critical of the excesses of his Brahman contemporaries. It does not follow, though, that Vyās championed a progressive social agenda. Both Vyās's enthusiasm for low-caste *bhaktas* and his disdain for high-caste hypocrites is to be seen against the background of love for God. For him, empowerment of the lower castes is a spiritual matter. High-castes are likewise condemned by the sole criterion of bhakti.

To be true to the full picture that emerges from studying Vyās's voice, we must note one case in which Vyās lapses into orthodox rhetoric. In one early attested poem, he laments the evils of Kaliyuga, for which the only remedy is the name of God.[27] Vyās enumerates disapprovingly the many evils of the times, including the fact that "Brahmans are serving Śūdras and leaving the path of learning."[28] Yet even in this conventional description of the abuses and plights of the Kaliyuga, Vyās's overarching aim is to point his finger at Brahmans and Śūdras who do not qualify as *bhaktas*. The fact that he seems to favorably incorporate *varṇāśramadharma* at least as a rhetorical tool to display by contrast the depravation of the age suggests that Vyās's egalitarianism is in the end a spiritual one.

AMBIVALENCE ABOUT WOMEN

What about Vyās's views on women? First, it may be noted that he includes among the saints he praises the famous woman *bhakta* Mīrā, whom he sees as part of his bhakti family (V21-J21, V26-J26). Vyās does not differentiate between women and men, as long as they are *bhaktas*. Women can reach what is in his eyes the highest good, namely residence in the supramundane Vrindavan. This is not limited to the exceptional saint Mīrā, but also attainable for ordinary women, as we see in the following poem, specifically addressed to a woman:

> Listen to my plea, Vaiṣṇavdāsī:
> Smoldering in this body is hell: sickness, bile, and phlegm.
> To forget it, hang on firmly to God. Be smiling company, make happiness your home.
> Your marriage will grow stronger if you give your heart to God. Put your trust elsewhere and you're lost.
> Leave God, love any other, and the noose of Death is on your neck!
> A person who, lamp in hand, falls into a well becomes the laughing stock of the world.
> Above all, love Radha's husband, focus on him alone in enjoyment.
> The dust of his feet is Vyās's refuge. Reside in Vrindavan and find release.[29]

Whatever the identity of this Vaiṣṇavdāsī, Vyās urges her to turn away from physical love and put her faith first in God. He does not portray this as something antithetical to marriage. Rather, he promises a happy home for women who follow this advice. Women can have it both ways, it seems, because their devotion will also strengthen their mundane marriages.

In the hagiographies this song is interpreted as having been addressed to Vyās's own wife. It is contextualized by an infamous incident in which the two spouses quarreled. During a dinner for which Vyās had invited several *bhaktas*, his wife was serving the food. She poured the delicious creamy parts of the milk (*malāī*) on her own husband's plate, in that moment neglecting all others who were present. Vyās was upset by this preferential treatment and reportedly uttered "words that are not proper to say." Some hagiographers have it that Vyās chased his wife out of the house; others say that he himself left. In either case, the couple was reconciled only after a group of peace-seeking neighbors intervened. In most versions of this story, this reconciliation was achieved on the condition that Vyās's wife sell her jewelry to feed holy men: the hagiographers read the poem as Vyās's advice to his own wife to transfer her loyalty from her husband to holy men in general.[30] The song itself, however, seems more general and not particularly inimical toward women. Rather, he addressed them directly with what he considered to be good advice—the sort of thing he proffered to men in different circumstances.

Still, Vyās is hardly a champion of women's rights. He promotes the patriarchal view that a woman is to regard her husband as her God and that she is to give up her parental allegiance in favor of her in-laws:

> Sisters and children,[31] do not leave God.
> Shy away from company that brings ruin to the ways of [your/the] Lord.
> Don't get attached to parents, to your brother and [his] wife, to family, or to male or female friends.
> Choose the path of the holy; quickly scold those who deviate.
> Don't embarrass your guru; adorn yourself with words of praise.
> Vyās [says]: Leave godless Brahmans behind. Better to be born from the womb of a low-caste *bhakta*![32]

The hagiographers present this song as Vyās's last words, uttered on his deathbed. The women of his family ask in whose care he is leaving them. Vyās tells them to trust in God, to stay true to the guru's (his own) teaching, to associate only with fellow *bhaktas*. He generally gives conservative advice. On its own, however, the poem rather seems to address women outside Vyās's family because "sisters" is not the address used for daughters-in-law. The crux remains that women should work toward spiritual fulfillment from within their marriages. The family relations they are recommended to abandon (verse 3) belong to a woman's natal kin (*pīhar*), while the in-law relations (*sasurāl*) are tellingly absent. This reinforces the total identification of women with their husband's family rather than with their parental family. Women should uphold *pati gati*, which could be read as "the ways of the Lord" but more likely designates "their husband's honor" (verse 2). Conceivably the poem's last line could be construed as providing license for Brahman women to abandon heretic husbands, but more likely it gives voice to the sentiment that women should give up companionship with godless Brahman women. One again, if so, we have the familiar issue of the relative value of caste in the light of spiritual truth.

As in the case of caste, there is a single poem in the Vyās corpus that seems to display an unpleasantly conservative view of society—in this case something we today might call misogynistic:

> A woman who is not devoted to God—
> What's the use of her looks, skills, and beauty if she does not worship Śyām?
> She's equal to a harlot, a whore, a witch, a slut, a hussy!
> Day and night she's doing her make-up, she's just a pile of sensuality.
> She can't know the highest good, not in her dreams. She's blind, sporting in the noose of Death.
> With her there, her husband too will sink in lust. Better just be an ascetic.
> Keep a Shakta woman in the house and you'll never have any rest. You're sure to end up in hell.
> No holy man will set foot in such a house, so everyone will be ruined.
> Vyāsdās [says]: The man who is crazed for his wife is the laughing stock of the world![33]

This song would actually fit better within the context of the above-cited quarrel with his wife than the one the hagiographers quote. For one thing, Vyās actually uses "words that are not proper to say" (verse 3). Moreover, the point is made that holy men will not visit a man with a wife who is not a *bhakta* (verse 8). In any case, this poem presents the other side of the coin. Whereas Vyās may allow for God-fearing women to reach Vrindavan, those who are not religious ruin their house. Again, the touchstone of the individual's worth is bhakti alone.

To a certain extent Vyās's position with regard to women is comparable to what he feels toward people whose birth is "low," yet whereas he advocates admitting low-caste people (read "men") fully into the bhakti community, he refrains from doing the same for women. He reviles those who do not eat with low-caste *bhaktas*, but he never reproaches anyone for looking down on women *bhaktas*. While he stresses that low-caste *bhaktas* are good *bhaktas*, he is more guarded when it comes to women: only a good woman can qualify as *bhakta*. He surely is not a proto-feminist.

CONCLUSION

This case study of Harirām Vyās shows that we must modify some commonly held assumptions about bhakti. First, the perception that *saguṇa* and *nirguṇa bhaktas* have been seen as two distinct groups is contradicted by the evidence of Vyās.[34] At least this Krishna *bhakta* saw his activity as closely related to that of Kabīr and Raidās. Second, the thesis that *saguṇa* bhakti is socially conservative and elitist does not hold true in all cases. At least some *bhaktas* living in sixteenth-century Vrindavan—*saguṇīs* in the common understanding of the term—included low-caste *bhaktas* in their community. Though a staunch Krishna worshiper and himself a Brahman, Vyās felt the same disdain for caste purity in the light of spiritual truth, as did Kabīr. He too used sarcasm to reveal hypocrisy, in songs as well as in his pithy two-liners (*dohās*). This is not merely a matter of formulaic rhetoric. This Krishna devotee's invectives against haughty Brahmans feel true to life. Vyās also included women devotees in his community, but he was less concerned with the uplift of women than low-caste males. While explicit in his condemnation of women who do not follow the bhakti path, he is silent about similarly errant low-caste males. In both cases, however, there is a limit: he includes only *bhaktas* in his community, not low castes or women in general.

Further research is needed to establish whether Vyās was exceptional, or whether we can identify other *saguṇa bhaktas* with similar attitudes. In chapter 2 Gil Ben-Herut provided us with some important Shaiva points of comparison. We need more work along these lines. An important question that I have not even begun to grapple with is that of the reality check. Apart from the rhetoric in the texts, can we get at other data that might corroborate bhakti attempts at emancipation? Are there documents attesting low-caste *bhaktas'* upward mobility in a place like Vrindavan? What do the temple and sectarian archives tell us about the reality on the ground? Do we find historical changes? We do have evidence that royal interference caused one *nirguṇī* sect, the Dādūpanth, to exclude low-caste people from its ranks under pressure from Jai Singh II in the early eighteenth century, which indicates that they were included before.[35] Do we find other such cases where patrons' pressures prevailed over internally egalitarian impulses?

Finally, we need to take seriously that bhakti communities such as these are predicated on love for God. Does this mean they are limited to spiritual egalitarianism only? This seems to be the case also for the presumed revolutionary element in *nirguṇa bhakti*, and it is unlikely that *saguṇīs* would do any better.[36] In the end a message like Vyās's is not about reforming society but about turning one's heart toward God.

NOTES

This paper was first presented for the panel "Constructing Communities: Rhetorical Strategies in Medieval North Indian Hagiographies" at the annual Association for Asian Studies meeting in San Diego in 2000. I am grateful for comments by the audience, especially to William Pinch, and to Nita Kumar, who encouraged me to write up this paper.

1 Lele, "Bhakti Movement in India," 1–15.

2 Gupta, *Gender of Caste*, 25–6.

3 Guha, *Dominance without Hegemony*, 47–60.

4 Lorenzen, "Historical Vicissitudes," 1–32.

5 Hawley, *Storm of Songs*, 327–33.

6 An exception is Lutgendorf's work on political appropriations of Tulsīdās's work—conservative as well as progressive (Lutgendorf, *Life of a Text*, 340–439).

7 An exemplary study of the sixteenth-century Krishna *bhakta* Braj poet Sūrdās is Bryant and Hawley, *Sur's Ocean*.

8 An inspiring example in relation to Tamil classical and bhakti intertextuality is Ramanujan and Cutler, "From Classicism to Bhakti."

9 Vyās's birth date, either 1492 or 1510, is much debated. See Pauwels, *In Praise*, 264–68.

10 Whereas his friends came to be regarded as founders of separate sects, Harirām Vyās escaped institutionalization. His sectarian allegiance became a bone of contention from roughly a century after his death. See Pauwels, "Imagining Religious Communities."

11 Pauwels, "Imagining Religious Communities."

12 I designate this edition V in what follows. For more details on the manuscripts and the editions, see Pauwels, *Krishna's Round Dance*, 30–36; and Pauwels, *In Praise*, 24–30.

13 For most, that is the manuscript of *Vyās Vāṇī* dated 1737, preserved in a temple collection in Jhānsī (J). For others, it is the manuscript dated 1750, preserved in Braj Academy in Vrindavan (VB) or the one that is estimated to date from the period 1780–1830, preserved in Nimbārk Koṭ in Vrindavan (VN).

14 Pauwels, "Imagining Religious Communities." For the text, see Pauwels, *In Praise*, 99.

15 vyāsa bimuṣa brāhmana parihariyai, supaca bhakta kī kūṣi upajiyai.

16 taji abhimāna dīnatā jana kī, syāma rahata sacu pāyaiṃ; vyāsa supaca tāre kula bore, viprani hari bisarāyaiṃ.

17 vyāsa supaca bahu tari gae, eka nāma lavalīna; caṛhe nāva abhimāna kī, būṛe koṭi kulīna.

18 vyāsa miṭhāī bipra kī, tāmaiṃ lāgai āga; bṛṃdāvana ke svapaca kī, jūṭhana khaiyai māṃga.

19 It should be said that no *dohās* are included in the oldest manuscript of *Vyās Vāṇī*, but they are quoted in early anthologies. The same thoughts are also attested in the songs found in the early manuscripts. I quote from the edition by Gosvāmī.

20
jūṭhani je na *bhakta* kī ṣāta
tinike muṣa sūkara kūkara ke. abhaṣa bhaṣi poṣata gāta
jinike vadana sadana narkani ke, je hari janani ghināta
kāma vivasa kāṃmini keṃ pīvata, adharani lāra cuçāta
bhojana para māṃṣī mūtati hai, tāhū ruci soṃ ṣāta
bhaktani kauṃ caranodaka acavata, abhimānī jari jāta
svapaca bhakta kau bhogu grahata hari, vāhmana tāhi ḍarāta
vājadāra kī pāṃti vyāha meṃ, jeṃvata vipra varāta
bheṃṭata sutani reṃṭa muṣa lāgati, suṣa pāvata jaḍa tāta
aparasa hvai bhaktani chū chutihā, taila sacaila nhāta
hari bhaktani pāchaiṃ āchaīṃ ḍolata hari gaṃgā akulāta
sādhu carana raja mājha vyāsa se, koṭini patita samāta.

21 Pauwels, *In Praise*, 233 and 237.

22 For the text, see Pauwels, *In Praise*, 231–32.

23 Pauwels, "Hagiography and Community Formation," 22–23.

24 V142-J176: svāmī bhaṭṭa gusāṃī aginita, mati kari gati ācaraṇī; prīti paraspara karata na kavahūṃ, miṭai na hīya kī jaranī.

25 V144-J181: gāvata nāṃcata āvata lobha kaha
yāhī teṃ anurāga na upajatu, rāga vairāga sova kaha
maṃtra jaṃtra paṛhi meli ṭhagaurī, vasa kīnoṃ saṃsāru
svāmī vahuta gusāī aginita, bhaṭṭani pe na uvāru
bhāva vinā sava vilavilāta aru, kilakilāta kari tehū
vyāsa rādhikāravana kṛpā vinu, kahūṃ na sahaja sanehū.

26 V129-J190: dāna laina koṃ vaḍe pātakī, macalana koṃ vahmanāī
larana marana ko baṛe tāmasī, vārauṃ koṭi kasāī
upadesana kauṃ gurū gusāṃī, ācaranaiṃ adhamāī.

27 V172-J141: kalijuga syāma nāma ādhāra.

28 vāhmana karata sūdra kī sevā, taji vidyā ācāra, l. 7.

29 For the text, see Pauwels, *In Praise*, 224–25.

30 V282-J148; see Pauwels, *In Praise*, 220–22.

31 The second address, *beṭā*, can mean "son," but it may also refer to daughters, who are sometimes thus addressed to express endearment.

32 V201-J105; for the text, see Pauwels, *In Praise*, 226–27.

33 V283-J206; for the text, see Pauwels, *In Praise*, 224. I am following in translation the reading of V.

34 For other evidence, see Hawley, "Nirguṇ-Saguṇ Distinction."

35 Horstmann, *Der Zusammenhalt der Welt*, 7, 16–17.

36 Pande, *Medieval Bhakti Movement*, 98 and 122. For a personal interpretation of Kabīr's spirituality in relation to his revolutionary message, see Linda Hess's perceptive chapter on the topic in her book *Bodies of Song*, 345–98, and for more readings, 433n1.

CHAPTER FOUR

"ARE YOU ALL COMING TO THE ESPLANADE?"

Devotional Music and Contingent Politics in West Bengal

EBEN GRAVES

THE role of devotional music and song (*kīrtan* or *bhakti gīti*) in the Bengal region is commonly linked with the sphere of religious affect, but in recent years it has also served as a catalyst to assemble musicians in forms of public protest. A recent example of how musicians in West Bengal have redefined bhakti as a platform for political protest occurred with the formation of the Kolkata-based All India Kīrtan and Bhakti Gīti Artists' Association in state of West Bengal. This association's aims were publicly announced at its inaugural forum in September 2012. Its specific policy demands were directed toward the majority All India Trinamool Congress (AITC) party in West Bengal, focusing on policy initiatives that launched this party into power in 2011. The association's requests for attention to education through the establishment of devotional music institutes, improved healthcare facilities for musicians, and monetary stipends for performers clearly overlapped with the political platform of the AITC. However, to add moral heft to these demands, devotional musicians also articulated an ethical discourse that suggested how neglect of devotional music and musicians was tantamount to neglecting aspects of a shared national identity.

The role of music and expressive culture has long been recognized as an active ingredient in the formation of nationalist sentiment in South Asia in general and India in particular.[1] Sometimes it has also been recognized that bhakti can be essential to this process; particularly with regard to Maharashtra, scholars have considered how devotional images were redefined as they entered the political arena.[2] What has received less attention, however, is the question of how performers of devotional music themselves may become objects of political activism. That is what was seen in Kolkata in 2012, where the task of making legislative demands upon the majority party required a distinctive formulation of the relationship between music and expressive culture. By emphasizing devotional music's relationship to the Bengali nation, musicians at the Kolkata forum gave voice to a distinctive form of *regional* nationalism.[3] They did so in explicit ways through speeches, but they also used song performances themselves as a way to mobilize emotive power in the service of their political aims.

The society of devotional musicians assembled for the association's forum in 2012 represented a contingent political alliance. Though united under the banner of devotional music, the musicians present at the conference performed in different devotional song genres, shared diverse histories of performance, and expressed various conceptions of bhakti in terms of practice and theology. What, then, brought these musicians together in protest? The social mobilization represented at this forum was an attempt to form a *contingent political society*. In articulating the concept of "political society," Partha Chatterjee focuses on the various ways in which groups organize to interface with the state and "governmental agencies pursuing multiple policies of security and welfare."[4] What is distinctive about political societies, and a key component of how they differ from the elite sphere of civil society politics, is that they do "not always conform to what is envisaged in the constitutional depiction of the relation between the state and members of civil society," as Chatterjee has said.[5] To many, the idea that the state should support devotional musicians might well seem to stand outside the aims of proper secular governance. Apparently recognizing this straightforward objection, the moral rhetoric of association members did not seek to make devotional thought and practice the foundation for protest; rather, they focused on defining devotional music as a constituent part of the Bengali nation. Through this process musicians sought to give a common group identity to the diverse musics and musicians brought together under the association's umbrella and work "to give to the empirical form of a population group the moral attributes of a community."[6] The contingent political society represented at the association's forum drew from long-standing histories of devotional music in the Bengal region, and, at the same time, members of the association worked to envisage novel ways of interfacing with state-level governance in the political context of West Bengal.

CATEGORIES AND COMMUNITIES OF DEVOTIONAL SONG IN BENGAL

Studying the mobilization of musicians in an act of economic and social protest at this Kolkata event makes little sense without first understanding the landscape of devotional music in West Bengal and across South Asia more generally.

A key task in this respect is unpacking how the two terms used in the association's title—*kīrtan* and *bhakti gīti*—worked to build a moral community of musicians. In general usage both in West Bengal and throughout South Asia, the term *kīrtan* refers to devotional song. In West Bengal it most commonly refers to devotional song within the context of Gauḍīya Vaishnavism (Bengal Vaishnavism), a body of devotional knowledge and practice traced to the all-important Bengali mystic, Chaitanya (see chapters 12 and 13). Indeed, the term *Bengali kīrtan* is synonymous with *Gauḍīya Vaishnava kīrtan* in common usage.[7] If *kīrtan* implied this Bengali frame of reference and included musicians from the Gauḍīya Vaishnava sphere, the other term used in the title—*bhakti gīti* (devotional song)—functioned as a catch-all phrase to reference a larger constellation of devotional song idioms. In present-day West Bengal, *bhakti gīti* might refer to songs in praise of popular regional deities such as the goddess Durga, to the well-known Baul *gān* (Baul song), or to mixed forms of song and storytelling such as *Rāmāyaṇ gān* (songs on the theme of the *Rāmāyaṇa* epic). The inclusion of these two terms—*kīrtan* and *bhakti gīti*—in the title of the association was not happenstance. The word *kīrtan* referred to the Gauḍīya Vaishnava performers who comprised the majority of musicians present at the event, while the phrase *bhakti gīti* worked to include a range of other devotional musicians in the association's project of mobilization and protest.

It is important to appreciate that Gauḍīya Vaishnava practice since its inception—including musical performance—has been linked to themes of social mobilization and protest. Sacred biographies of the life of Chaitanya describe public *kīrtan* performances that were used to mobilize devotees in protest against the local government's prohibition of devotional music.[8] This was most clearly the case in a specific form of *kīrtan* that figured prominently during the life of Chaitanya—*nām kīrtan*, which features songs that repeat the names of Gauḍīya Vaishnava deities. Though some *nām kīrtan* performers were present at the forum in 2012, the majority of Vaishnava musicians represented there performed in a genre known as *padāvalī kīrtan*. This genre features the setting of devotional poetry to music and elaborates on the "divine plays" (*līlās*) of the three central deities of Gauḍīya Vaishnavism—Chaitanya, Radha, and Krishna; a related form of devotional performance in Bengal that uses song and storytelling to depict these divine plays is known as *līlā kīrtan*. A key characteristic of *padāvalī kīrtan* performance is a musical style where song texts are accompanied by long-duration meters (*tāls*) set to slow tempos from a repertoire of *tāls* unique to the Bengal region. In their appeal to a Bengali nation, an "imagined community"[9] that might support devotional music and musicians in West Bengal, those who spoke at Kolkata in 2012 drew upon notions of an intrinsic relationship between the Bengali nation and *kīrtan* music that date to the late nineteenth century, when Bengali elites saw *kīrtan* and the devotional practices associated with Chaitanya as a potential lodestar for an emergent Bengali national sentiment.[10] By the mid-twentieth century authors commonly suggested that the songs of Bengali *kīrtan* were responsible for "awakening the life of the Bengali nation."[11]

Of course, the Bengali national identity invoked in this way is not completely coterminous with an Indian national identity. Rather, it represents what might be called a form of *regional* nationalism that coexists with a pan-Indian identity and is defined according to a host of regional coordinates such as language, local forms of expressive culture, and shared history. Music's role in forming national solidarities has often been viewed within the frame of "cultural nationalism," a process of redefining and interpreting expressive practices that "stand for and 'create' the nation."[12] But what nation? Instead of emphasizing a pan-Indian identity, the association in Kolkata highlighted aspects of the Bengali nation in hopes of influencing the state-level majority party, the All India (but actually distinctively Bengali) Trinamool Congress. Massing together a large constituency of musicians through the mention of *kīrtan* and *bhakti gīti* was part of an effort to spark action on the part of this particular governmental party.

POLITICAL PLATFORMS AND LOCAL GOVERNANCE

Nearly every seat in Mahājāti Sadan Hall was taken when I arrived at the association launch in the early afternoon of September 12. A hum of excited conversation filled the large auditorium as musicians, devotional music enthusiasts, and members of the Kolkata-area media arrived. The curtain on the proscenium stage was drawn back to reveal senior musicians from throughout West Bengal such as Pandit Nimai Mitra, Saraswati Das, and Manoranjan Bhattacharjee. These well-known figures were seated behind a large table, flanked by dozens of other musicians. When the musicians came into view, a loud call resounded throughout the hall: "Nitāi-Gaura Hari-bol!" ("Chant [the names of] Krishna, Nitāi, and Gaura [Chaitanya]!") This devotional invocation, borrowed from the ritual sphere of Gauḍīya Vaishnava practice, was a clear marker that most audience members, whether performing musicians themselves or not, belonged to the Gauḍīya Vaishnava social domain.

Situated prominently behind the musicians on the stage was a large banner that proclaimed this group to be the All India Kīrtan and Bhakti Gīti Artists' Association. At the top of the banner, the association's mention of *kīrtan* recognized the fact that the majority of performers present on stage were *padāvalī kīrtan* musicians, while the terms *All India* and *bhakti gīti* appealed to a wider

4.1 The *padāvalī kīrtan* singer Saraswati Das performs at the Artists' Forum, Kolkata. Photo by Eben Graves

demographic base—the sort of group that might persuade policy makers from the majority AITC to take action on behalf of the association. Gaining the attention of political power brokers was crucial for most of the musicians present at this inaugural meeting. Working throughout West Bengal, they operate in a precarious live-music market where they are only remunerated for individual performances.[13] Performing in this gig economy undoubtedly offers economic opportunities, but the lack of institutional affiliation affects these musicians in various ways—not just the lack of fixed income but also, for example, the difficulty they have in obtaining a range of medical and insurance-related benefits. For many members, such problems are exacerbated by the fact that they come from a variety of caste backgrounds, as is common in the Gauḍīya Vaishnava social domain. One result is that these musicians have not benefited from special government programs designed to help the caste-defined poor—particularly, for political reasons, the rural poor.

What, then, did Association members demand so as to ameliorate their situation? The banner hanging behind the musicians on stage (fig. 4.1) specified the following:

1) Kīrtan institutes should be established in each district.
2) The artists should receive a stipend.
3) Health insurance should be arranged.
4) Concessions should be given on government-run transportation.
5) Housing should be constructed for needy artists under the Indira Housing Plan.[14]
6) Administrative arrangements (*praśāsanik byabasthā*).
7) Needy artists should be included in the BPL [below poverty line] list.[15]
8) Education should be arranged for the children of needy artists.
9) Life insurance should also be arranged for artists.

These demands articulated a platform that resonated with a major recent shift in West Bengal's political climate. In May 2011 a political alliance headed by the AITC under the leadership of Mamata Banerjee became the majority party in the West Bengal Assembly, which is the central legislative authority in West Bengal. The rise to power of the AITC swept away the long-standing dominance of the Left Front, a political alliance led by the Communist Party of India (Marxist) that had held power in West Bengal for thirty-four years. The Left Front alliance had become politically at risk because a number of its recent land-acquisition schemes had alienated its rural base. In an attempt to benefit from this estrangement, the AITC alliance led by Mamata Banerjee promoted a platform that was defined as "pro-people." It emphasized new policies such as improving education, upgrading healthcare facilities, and increasing employment for the rural poor.[16] Under the slogan of "Ma, Mati o Manush" (Mother, Motherland, and People), the AITC fashioned a rhetoric that was intended to connect perennial images of nationalism in South Asia—mother and motherland—to policy initiatives that would focus specifically on the people of West Bengal.

Within the context of these larger policy initiatives, the leadership of the AITC specifically included performers in the roster of state patronage, apparently recognizing the crucial role they might play in consolidating popular support for the newly regnant party. In her early years in power, Chief Minister Banerjee approved a change in the policies of the state's Backward Classes Welfare Department that would offer greater access to state aid for a variety of performing artists.[17] Somewhat later, the AITC offered organizational and financial support for festivals celebrating aspects of West Bengal's expressive culture, with Mamata Banerjee commonly attending and delivering inaugural speeches.[18] Yet the overwhelming majority of musicians represented at the association's inaugural meeting had not been beneficiaries of these various forms of support. Rather, state patronage had been directed at performers who specialized in Baul, Bhatiyali, Chhau, and Jhumur, among other genres. Support for these performers, who cluster in rural areas of West Bengal, was clearly linked with the party's focus on solidifying rural support in the domain of electoral politics.

MUSIC AS MOTHER IN BENGALI REGIONAL NATIONALISM

A variety of images and stories were invoked in speeches at the forum, creating a rhetoric designed to support the association's demands. Not surprisingly, imagery that resonated with the "Mother, Motherland, and People" slogan used by the AITC was featured throughout the meeting. In his prefatory remarks the moderator, Chinmoy Banerjee, highlighted an image that would be repeatedly stressed throughout the event: "This [devotional] music, which is spread throughout society in various forms, is a 'mother' music from which all music originated." Pausing for emphasis, he continued by questioning how this wellspring of devotional music with all its mothering power could be subjected to such neglect in present-day West Bengal.

In Bengal, where goddesses play a leading role in Hindu religiosity, the image of the nation as mother has a long history. As Jasodhara Bagchi has explained, it emerged in nineteenth-century Bengal as a rhetoric that framed the nation as a "sacrosanct space."[19] At the association's meeting in September 2012, however, this maternal imagery was supplemented by an appeal to the inherent musicality of the Bengali people. The well-known *padāvalī kīrtan* performer Suman Bhattacharya said in the course of a speech that preceded his song performance, "Those of us who have come here today are *kīrtan* singers, *bhakti gīti* singers, *Rāmāyaṇa* singers, *nām-saṅkīrtan* singers, . . . [and] Baul singers. These represent various types of song that are merged with the soil of Bengal. 'Bengali' means the Bengali nation, a music-loving nation, and this love for music is found in Bengalis from birth." Having established that context, Bhattacharya quickly returned to the policy request that retired artists should receive a monetary stipend. He cited the case of his *kīrtan* guru, Nilamani Das: "Nilamani Das used to receive an allowance of Rs. 500 per month. But for some unknown reason he stopped receiving that stipend. Now he has neither the strength to teach singing nor the strength to perform himself. . . . For that reason some arrangement should be worked out for artists in distress by this Artists' Association."

In her study of *rāṣṭrīya* (nationalist) *kīrtan* in western India, Anna Schultz considers how musical styles have the ability to become signs for novel political meanings that may exceed the devotional focus found in other performance contexts.[20] Much of this happens when specific musical styles evoke long-held emotional expressions of religious devotion in new contexts where the aim is to elicit a sense of national belonging. Music's work, argues Schultz, is often to be found in the "blurring of boundaries," where the musician is able to "alter meanings without the need to enlist more precise but less affectively potent semantico-referent speech."[21]

Clearly this happened at the Kolkata forum. Suman Bhattacharya's speech stressed the relationship between the various devotional musics represented in the association and the Bengali nation, but things became far more intense when he began to perform. One could sense this particularly as he sang the *padāvalī kīrtan* song called "Śyāmer muralī tumi ār rādhār nām loye bejonā," (You, flute of Krishna, calling Radha's name, do not make a sound).[22] In introducing this song Bhattacharya almost completely ignored its text and gave attention instead to its musical style, especially its accompaniment. Here the crucial element was the *tāl*, or meter, which was used to accompany the song. One of the defining characteristics of the *padāvalī kīrtan* repertoire is the manner in which musical time is structured through a unique repertoire of *tāls*. Though this term is found throughout the classical musics of north and south India, the repertoire and theory of *tāl* play a special role in Bengali *padāvalī kīrtan*. Bengali musicians commonly understand their repertoire of *tāl* to be a theoretically detailed system of ancient provenance, but, at the same time, they define the practice of *tāl* in *padāvalī kīrtan* as a cultural form linked specifically with the history of the Bengali nation. Suman Bhattacharya evoked this two-faceted understanding of *tāl* in what he said before he began to sing: "How amazing," he observed, that "this Ektāli Tāl is one thousand years old. This Ektāli Tāl exists in two types of song—one is south Indian classical music, and the other is Bengali *kīrtan*. . . . We can say with pride that our *kīrtan* is as rich as a classical music." Bhattacharya's emphasis on "our" in his introduction thus sought to define aspects of musical style as a form of a shared Bengali national identity, as can be observed in the portion of this song performance that has been uploaded to Vimeo for public viewing.[23]

The text of the song presents the image of a pained Radha, who fears hearing the sound of Krishna's flute since she believes it possesses a supernatural power over her. As Bhattacharya sang these words, the emotive imagery combined with the slow and plodding tempo characteristic of the musical style of *padāvalī kīrtan*. The musical style not only supported the devotional message of the song but became the medium for an impassioned call for Bengali national action. Audience members shook their heads in acknowledgment of his melismatic and virtuosic vocal passages and interjected loud rounds of applause during the performance. It was as if the music itself gave voice to his call for common action, though nothing in the lyrics directly made that connection.

"ARE YOU ALL COMING TO THE ESPLANADE?"

The speeches and performances at the association's opening meeting strengthened a relationship between devotional music and national values, but they did so in a relatively confined space. Ultimately the leaders' task was to expand that space so that it would be adequate to the political task that lay ahead. The conference organizer, the *padāvalī kīrtan* musician Siddhartha Sekhar Das, sought to inspire members of the association to do just that: "We shall first go to our Chief Minister, then we shall go to our Governor [of West Bengal]. . . . If our voice is not heard, then . . . what will be our next step? We, thousands of artists, shall arrive at the Maidan at Esplanade, [and] . . . we shall humbly appeal before the government, and tell them that our poverty should be ameliorated. We should be given recognition! Why are we neglected?" Concluding his speech, he implored the audience to respond to his call when he asked: "Are you all coming to the Esplanade?"

Kolkata's Esplanade is practically synonymous with popular protest in West Bengal. Adjacent to the Maidan, an expansive urban park in central Kolkata, the Esplanade has a strong association with power through its proximity to the governor's house and governmental offices.[24] The history of political rallies and protest in Kolkata cannot be told separately from the Esplanade area, as we can see in the story of the rickshaw-operator protests provided by Dominique Lapierre in his international bestseller, *The City of Joy*. Siddhartha Sekhar Das's call to rally on the Esplanade, then, was not only a request for mobilization at a specific place but was also a general call for members of the association to participate directly in political society.

The All India Kīrtan and Bhakti Gīti Artists' Association forum featured speeches and performances that attempted to connect the dots between different genres of devotional music, a shared sense of regional nationalism, and calls for active protest. Clearly the majority of musicians came from within the Bengali *padāvalī kīrtan* sphere, but a self-conscious attempt was made to include other devotional musicians under terms such as *bhakti gīti*. This was central to the task of creating a contingent political society. The organizers sought to assemble what Partha Chatterjee has called an "empirical form," a collection of individuals large and impressive enough to command recognition by the state government.[25] And they did so in specific terms by requesting musicians to assemble at the central Kolkata Esplanade.

Yet the most important political work they accomplished was arguably to be found in the music itself. Suman Bhattacharya's singing was able to confer the emotive force of bhakti, found in the stories of Radha and Krishna, upon the political domain. Performances, however, are short-lived, and as of January 2016 organizers of the association were still at work on their common task.[26] From suburban offices in the Kolkata metropolitan region, the association was ramping up its activities in hopes of having its requests heard during the pre-electoral season in West Bengal. The struggle is ongoing, and it seems the power of bhakti will be required for it to succeed.

NOTES

1 See, for example, Bakhle, *Two Men and Music*; Subramanian, *From the Tanjore Court*.

2 Novetzke, *Religion and Public Memory*, 193–204; Schultz, *Singing a Hindu Nation*.

3 For a study of music and regional nationalism in South Asia, see Dennen, "Third Stream, 149–79.

4 Chatterjee, *Politics of the Governed*, 37.

5 Chatterjee, *Politics of the Governed*, 38.

6 Chatterjee, *Politics of the Governed*, 57; emphasis in original.

7 See Mukhopadhyay, *Bāṅgālāra Kīrtana o Kīrtanīyā*.

8 See Mukhopadhyay, *Bāṅgālār Kīrtan o Kīrtanīyā*, ch. 13.

9 Anderson, *Reflections on the Origin and Spread of Nationalism*.

10 Bhatia, "Devotional Traditions and National Culture."

11 Mukhopadhyay, "Introduction," iii.

12 Turino, "Nationalism and Latin American Music," 175.

13 For more on the professional economy of devotional musicians see Graves, "Marketplace of Devotional Song," 52–86.

14 This program, named posthumously for the former prime minister Indira Gandhi, belongs to the Rural Development Ministry. Inaugurated in 1985, it gives subsidies and cash assistance to the rural poor for house construction. See "Indira Awaas Yojana—Guidelines," Government of India, June 2013, accessed January 22, 2018, http://iay.nic.in/netiay/IAY%20revised%20guidelines%20july%202013.pdf.

15 "Below poverty line" is an economic benchmark that determines eligibility for government assistance in India.

16 Chakrabarty, *Communism in India*, 98.

17 Chakraborty, "'Backward' Tag for State Folk Artistes."

18 A record of these speaking engagements can be found at "All India Trinamool Congress," accessed January 16, 2018, http://aitcofficial.org/.

19 Bagchi, "Representing Nationalism," WS-66.

20 Schultz, *Singing a Hindu Nation*, 193.
21 Schultz, *Singing a Hindu Nation*, 193.
22 This song is from the *līlā* known as "Baṅśī-Śikṣā," or the "Flute Instruction."
23 "Suman Bhattacharya—Padavali Kirtan (Khol—Rabin Sanphui)," Vimeo, accessed August 27, 2018, https://vimeo.com/199504818.
24 Chattopadhyay, *Representing Calcutta*, 46.
25 Chatterjee, *Politics of the Governed*, 37.
26 Uddalak Mukherjee, "Music from the Margins," *Telegraph* (Calcutta), January 12, 2016.

CHAPTER FIVE

ALL THE VALMIKIS ARE ONE

Bhakti as Majoritarian Project

JOEL LEE

THE goal of this chapter is twofold: to sketch an historical argument and to make a theoretical proposal. The historical argument is that the Arya Samaj, a major reformist Hindu organization born in North India in the last quarter of the nineteenth century, made a decisive intervention in the public representation of a vast swath of the Dalit population in the 1920s and 1930s, forging a novel link between the composer of the Sanskrit *Rāmāyaṇa* and the communities collectively known as the "sweeper castes" in the colonial period. That the Arya Samaj's Valmiki was soldered together from disparate traditions as part of a contested Hindu majoritarian project less than a century ago is a historical datum that goes unrecognized by a great deal of sociological and religious studies scholarship, to the detriment of our understanding of Dalit lifeworlds and the history of religion in South Asia.

The theoretical proposal sought to be advanced here is that we consider the degree to which affective dispositions, or emotional orientations, constitute the substantive grounds of belonging in many of the historical communities in which we are interested. That is, we would do well to tunnel our way beneath the paradigm of *imagined communities*—with its cognitive shading of things—to get to the *felt* community, the *visceral* community, the boundaries of which are regulated by embodied affects like *ghṛṇā*, or revulsion.[1] To ask who feels *ghṛṇā* for whom is to trace the contours of a felt community. One could likewise map belonging in such communities through patterns of relations of *prem*, *dīntā*, or *ghamaṇḍ*—love, meekness, pride. Of course, the success of an imagined community is precisely its transformation into a felt community, the working or massaging of an idea of membership into the viscera of would-be members.[2] But it does not always work that way. Some communities are imagined, hoped for, represented in song and poetry and census data and scholarly essay without ever taking root in the affective experience of ostensible members. Such is arguably the case with those Dalit castes now known as Valmikis or Balmikis and their relation to the Hindu community. To consider disjunctures between the imagined and the felt—for example, when the idea of inclusion runs athwart the embodied disgust of *ghṛṇā* and fails to overcome it—is, perhaps, to throw new light on the caste question that haunts bhakti studies.

At the center of this chapter's historical narrative is an influential text entitled *Śrī Bālmīki Prakāsh*, published by the Arya Samaj in the 1920s. This text emerged in the long shadow of the decision made by British colonial administrators to classify "untouchables" as Hindus by default in the decennial census, a policy that contradicted prevailing sociological common sense among Hindus, Dalits, and others in the late nineteenth century.[3] The castes that supplied virtually all of the sanitation labor across North India, for example, described themselves as the Lāl Begī *qaum*—*qaum* signifying a nation or religious community—and contrasted themselves in frankly oppositional terms to Hindus, Muslims, and Sikhs in their liturgical songs. The enumerative politics of the first three decades of the twentieth century—driven by colonial policy—raised the stakes of how the multipolar socioreligious landscape was represented, as political power would now hinge, for the first time in the history of South Asia, on the capacity of groups to mobilize numerical majorities. After the Partition of Bengal in 1905, the Muslim League and the Indian National Congress began to argue with each other and the colonial state over whether Dalits should be counted in the census as Hindu, Muslim, or something else. The more radical Arya Samaj took a different approach and set out to create facts on the ground. They did so by promoting *shuddhi*, a "purification" ceremony by which members of the "depressed classes," first in small numbers and later on a mass scale, were ritually refigured as Hindu. In the early 1920s a team of Arya Samaj activists led by Ami Chand Sharma set out to conduct *dharm prachār* (preaching of religion, proselytization) among the Chuhras, the most populous of the sanitation labor castes, who alone constituted more than 10 percent of the total population in politically crucial swaths of the Punjab. As part of this Hinduizing effort, which was centered on Lahore and Delhi but later spread, Ami Chand Sharma composed *Śrī Bālmīki Prakāsh*. Internal evidence suggests that the tract was composed in 1928, though this may represent its second edition. It went through at least three editions and circulated widely and intensively; a 2006 reprint is easily available today.[4]

Sharma begins the narrative of *Śrī Bālmīki Prakāsh* thus:

A Ram Sevak (servant of Ram) rises every dawn, bathes and reads Shri Balmiki's Ramayan. One day as he read the text, the multifarious virtues of Shri Balmiki's Ramayan came to his attention, and . . . he began to think about who it was who had put into writing in this world the glorious virtues of Shri Ramchandar in the Ramayan. His heart replied: Shri Maharishi Balmiki ji did so. Forthwith his heart genuflected before Shri Balmiki ji and from his lips fell the words:

> Had he not been revealed in the world, Balmiki the God,
> Where would such a beneficent book as the Ramayan have come?

As he was singing the above song, a Balmikiya who was passing by heard Balmiki ji's name and stood nearby. He folded his hands and began to entreat the devotee, "Maharaj! The bhajan you are singing is to which Balmiki ji?"

The Ram Sevak replied, "What, brother, have there been many Balmiki jis?"

Balmikiya: I am not learned, but I have heard that in the Bhaktamal two Balmikis' stories are told. The people of the Granth Sahib say there were seven Balmikis. Why, is this untrue?[5]

Here we may pause to note some distinctive features of the text. First, perhaps defying our expectations for an Arya Samaj document, we find ourselves not in a milieu of Vedic cerebralism but rather in a world of entreaty, handfolding, and genuflection; of hearts that speak and bow before saints; of *bhajan* singing and Nabhadas's *Bhaktamāl*—in other words, a world of bhakti affectivity and textuality.

We also find ourselves confronted—as Sharma did by his Dalit interlocutors—by skepticism about the singularity of Valmiki. Are there other Valmikis besides the composer of the *Rāmāyaṇa*? Who are they?

A number of scholars have pointed out that the literary traditions of South Asia are in fact littered with discrete and unrelated figures who happen to share the name Valmiki.[6] Some of the more obscure Valmikis include a Vedic grammarian mentioned in a Yajurvedic text and a *suparṅa* bird-of-prey, a winged eater of serpents, mentioned in the *Udyogaparvan* of the *Mahābhārata*. The *Rāmāyaṇa*, of course, features the virtuous Bhārgava Brahman who curses a Nishāda hunter in meter and hosts the banished Sita. Centuries later, in the *Skanda Purāṇa*, the name Valmiki is attached for the first time to the ancient trope of the reformed highway brigand—a trope that gets hung on characters as diverse as Anguli Mala of Buddhist legend, Nāmdev of the Marathi bhakti pantheon, and Sunan Kalidjaga, popularizer of Islam in Java.[7] The conjoining of these two initially separate narrative figures—the rhyming rishi and the repentant robber—gives us what we might call the modern standard Valmiki or the Amar Chitra Katha Valmiki.

There is also the *chānḍāl* Valmiki, or rather Bāl Mīk or Bāl Nek. In my research I have drawn together a corpus of some forty or fifty—depending on how you count them—sacred songs and stories that circulated orally among the sanitation labor castes in the colonial period, a few of which are still told today. One of the main protagonists of this oral tradition is Bāl Mīk, a swineherd and magician of Ghazni who facilitates the miraculous birth of Lāl Beg, the *paighambar* or prophet of these castes. This Bāl Mīk, often described in the oral tradition as a *chānḍāl*, is an antinomian figure who supervises intercaste marriages and manifests himself as a leaking carcass that refuses to disappear until Banaras Brahmans agree to relax civil disabilities imposed on sweepers. In this oral corpus there is no mention of the *Rāmāyaṇa*, of Sanskrit, of the bird-killing Nishāda, of Sita or Lav or Kush or indeed of any element of the Valmiki portrayed in the *Rāmāyaṇa* itself. The reformed bandit trope does make one appearance in the oral corpus—one, again, out of forty or fifty—but here Bāl Mīk is more a serial killer of Brahmans than a highway robber, and it is Guru Nanak who persuades him to abandon homicide as an occupation.

Setting aside relatively obscure Valmikis, then, we will concern ourselves with three narrative figures who go by one or another variant of that name: Valmiki 1, the Bhārgava Brahman composer of the *Rāmāyaṇa*; Valmiki 2, the repentant robber-turned-ascetic, who is grafted onto Valmiki 1 from the *Skanda Purāṇa* onward; and Bāl Mīk—to call him Valmiki 3 would be a distortion of the sources in which his story is told—the *chānḍāl* swineherd of Dalit oral tradition. My contention is that before 1928, there is only a tenuous thread connecting the *chānḍāl* Bāl Mīk to Valmiki 2 and no evidence that anyone saw the *chānḍāl* Bāl Mīk as bearing any relation to Valmiki 1.[8]

In fact, there is positive evidence that bhakti publics[9] understood Valmiki 1 and the *chānḍāl* Bāl Mīk to be different, even contrastive, figures. The first textual appearance of the *chānḍāl* Bāl Mīk, to my knowledge, is in Priyadas's commentary on Nabhadas's *Bhaktamāl*, the *Bhaktirasabodhinī*. In this early eighteenth-century text Priyadas writes of *ubhay Bālmīki*—that is, *both* Balmikis—and proceeds to tell their two distinct stories: one of a sage (*rishi*) whose song is known throughout the world and one of a rustic sweeper who finds favor with Krishna.[10] Bhagwan Prasad Rupkala, in his commentary on the *Bhaktamāl*, published in 1910, further elaborates the distinction by giving the two separate entries in his table of contents, "Mahārṣi Śrī Bālmīkijī" and "Dūsre Śrī Bālmīkijī."[11]

Thus—returning to our Arya Samaj tract—when the Dalit character asks the Ram Sevak to *which* Valmiki is he singing a *bhajan*, he does so on good authority. It is the Ram Sevak who is at pains to demonstrate that the multiple Valmikis and Bāl Mīks of tradition are actually one, rather than the other way around. In the rest of the tract, then, as the Ram Sevak contends that the only actual Valmiki is the composer of the *Rāmāyaṇa*, and that the sanitation labor castes are descended from his *chānḍāl* disciples and should therefore adopt his name and identify themselves as Hindu in the next census, he is in fact attempting a historically unprecedented fusion of previously distinct figures.

Now why does Ami Chand Sharma make this move, and how—given the warranted skepticism of his audience—does he go about bridging the chasm between the swineherd of Ghazni and the Brahman sage? The "why" question has a relatively straightforward answer: by positing the isomorphism of Valmiki and Bāl Mīk, Sharma supplies the Chuhras with a genealogy construable as Hindu. Again, in the colonial period the Chuhras were prevailingly known as Lāl Begīs, an autonomous religious *qaum* whose members largely had Muslim or Islamicate personal names. The question of their official religious categorization was unsettled; most ominously from the Arya Samaj's point of view, the Uttar Pradesh census commissioner in 1901 understood Lāl Begīs to be the third largest sect in Islam after Sunnis and Shias.[12] Shifting the emphasis from Lāl Beg to Bāl Mīk and providing a Hindu pedigree for the latter was a crucial step toward reframing all of this.

But how could Sharma, the Arya Samajist author, pull off such a feat of counterintuitive genealogy? Given the potential of the reformed brigand trope to unite a despised and an admired category of person within a single biography, one might expect that Sharma would attempt to deploy Valmiki 2 as the bridge figure. Certainly this has become the default, commonsense explanation in the eight decades since the Arya Samaj's campaign took root. But in fact Sharma eschews this approach, declaring the entire brigand trope to be calumny, wrongly imposed on the unimpeachably virtuous Valmiki 1. Sharma has no use for the folklore wordplay that has the sinner's recitation of *marā marā marā* unwittingly transform into the pious repetition of Ram's name, nor is he interested in the robber-turned-ascetic being covered by a termite mound. There are several reasons for this, including the long-standing textual association between the reformed brigand and the "tribal" Bhīls (who are utterly unrelated to the sanitation labor castes), but a full discussion of these reasons would draw us far from the point at hand.

Instead, Sharma seizes on the one place in the bhakti canon where the *chāṇḍāl* Bāl Mīk appears, the one narrative site where these two distant communities—Lāl Begīs and broadly Vaishnava *bhaktas*—glimpse each other dimly. This is the story that Priyadas tells in his *Bhaktamāl* commentary, the one Rupkala puts under the heading "Dūsre Śrī Bālmīkijī." Here is how Sharma tells it:

> One time the Pandavs held a sacrifice. In order to test its completeness Shri Krishna hung up a conch that would sound of its own accord when the sacrifice was complete. If it did not sound, then it was understood that the sacrifice was incomplete. All the preparations for the sacrifice had been completed; the Brahmans and sages had already taken the gifts presented to them, yet the conch did not sound. Raja Yudhishthir said to Shri Krishna "Maharaj! The conch did not sound. The sacrifice is incomplete, what can be the cause?" Krishnaji replied, "King! Some devotee of mine remains without food from your sacrifice." Yudhishthir said, "Where shall we search for him?" Krishna said, "Search everywhere! He will be found." Arjun and Bhimsen began searching and in the stable they found Shri Balmiki. . . . Shri Krishnaji took all five of the Pandavs to Shri Balmikiji and said to him "Maharaj, come [to our] home." He replied, "Maharaj, I am a *chāṇḍāl*, you people become polluted [*braṣṭ*] upon seeing me. For this reason I did not go to your place." Krishnaji said "O great sage! To me even a *chāṇḍāl* devotee is very dear [*bahut pyārā hai*], therefore please come and make complete the sacrifice of the Pandavs."
>
> Shri Balmikiji came to the house of the king. Krishna gave Draupadi the order to make the food. With great love Draupadi prepared thirty-six kinds of dishes. Having served the plates she placed one before Shri Balmikiji. All five of the Pandavs stood in attendance upon him. Shri Balmikiji ate all the food in a few mouthfuls. Seeing Balmiki take lentils, vegetables, halwa, pudding, and the rest, and mix them together, a feeling of revulsion [*ghṛṇā*] arose in Draupadi's heart that this man is indeed base [*nīch*]. Balmikiji finished his meal, yet still the conch did not sound. Then the Pandavs said to Krishnaji, "Maharaj! The conch still has not sounded." [Krishna said,] "Ask Shri Draupadiji." Draupadiji said "I felt revulsion toward the great sage; that is why the conch did not sound." . . . Draupadiji again prepared food and with pure feelings

> served it, at which point the conch sounded and the Pandavs' sacrifice was complete. Shri Balmikiji, praise be to your devotion [*bhakti*] and humility [*dīntā*] which destroyed the pride [*ahaṅkār*] of haughty Brahmans and made the devotees rejoice.[13]

There is a great deal one could say about this story and its divergent tellings. In terms of providing coherence to the new genealogy, this story offers no more, perhaps less, than the reformed robber trope would have. To avoid logical contradiction Sharma simply asserts a few lines earlier in the tract that Valmiki is no less Brahman here than ever but that he calls himself *chāṇḍāl* simply to drive home the point about bhakti being inclusive. What makes the story so fit for the Arya Samaj's project, then, is not the theoretical ballast it gives to Bāl Mīk's new Hindu lineage but rather its allegorical purchase on the situation at hand, the Hindu majoritarian project of the 1920s and 1930s, and its insight that for community to matter, it must be anchored in embodied affects. These two points need to be elaborated.

It is difficult to miss the resonance of the story of Bāl Mīk's inclusion in the Pandavs' *yagya* (Sanskrit *yajña*) with the experience of Ami Chand Sharma, other Arya Samaj activists, and the tens of thousands of Dalits inducted into the house of Hinduism by *shuddhi* in the 1920s. The Pandav brothers, who had neither heard of nor had any business with the *chāṇḍāl* who lives out in the stables, found themselves suddenly in need of him to accomplish a political end, a *yagya*. They ultimately achieved their goal by going to him, persuading him to join them, and interdining with him amid much fanfare. This is an almost perfect parable of the logic and practice of Hindu majoritarian inclusion as the Arya Samaj, and subsequently Gandhi's Harijan Sevak Sangh, set about it.[14] Like Bāl Mīk, the Chuhras and other "depressed classes" in the 1920s and 1930s were suddenly and aggressively told that a community who until a moment before wanted nothing to do with them now *needed* them and moreover that they now *belonged* to that community. The magical conch announcing the formation of a Hindu *rāṣṭra* could not be sounded without them. In the words of Congress and Arya Samaj leader Swami Shraddhanand, "The uplift of the untouchables and their assimilation in the Hindu polity is the very plinth on which alone the edifice of free India can be constructed."[15]

The story also provides an allegory of the emotional labor involved in creating a bhakti community. With insight into the psychology of exclusion, Sharma concludes the story with an overt appeal to the pleasure, to Dalit ears, of narratives that "destroy the pride of haughty Brahmans" (never mind that Draupadi and the Pandavs are Kshatriyas; Sharma ignores such details when convenient). More than a theology or ideology, it is an emotionology that the story offers its Chuhra audience,[16] a model of affective relations that features the socially dominant solicitously serving the *chāṇḍāl* and declaring him *pyārā* (dear). Of course the emotionology modeled also celebrates Dalit meekness and compliance, the correlate of the political quiescence and acceptance of *savarṇ* (i.e., privileged caste) leadership that the Arya Samaj and its Congress allies explicitly encouraged through their social uplift institutions.[17]

Most vividly, though, what the story emphasizes is the *ghṛṇā*, the disgust, that Draupadi must overcome in order for the new community to be produced. As we know from the hagiographies of Ravidās and Tiruppān Āḷvār and any number of caste-stigmatized *sants*, radical acts of inclusion do not just go off without a hitch. Imagined communities do not simply materialize; rather, they advance haltingly, with spasms of reaction. Draupadi's back and forth struggle with her own *ghṛṇā*—a learned, embodied, visceral guardian of a socioreligious boundary—dramatizes the gulf between the imagined community and the felt community of Hindus in the early decades of the twentieth century. It allegorizes the effort of other Arya Samaj activists of the period—like the author of *Patitoddhār*, an Arya Samaj text of the same period—to convince Hindus to uproot the *ghṛṇā* they feel toward Chamārs and Bhangīs, and to redirect it, instead, at Muslims.[18]

But dissolving and reconstituting dispositions anchored in the viscera is hard work. Indeed it often fails.[19] Sharma's influential account of Bāl Mīk at the Pandavs' sacrifice provides an aspirational model for overcoming *ghṛṇā* and the achievement of a Dalit-inclusive community of *bhaktas*. Yet, as the subsequent social history of the sanitation labor castes bears out, this aspect of the Arya Samaj project remains not felt, only imagined.[20]

NOTES

1 Connolly, *Why I Am Not a Secularist*; Miller, *Anatomy of Disgust*; Reddy, *Navigation of Feeling*; Rosenwein, *Emotional Communities in the Early Middle Ages.*

2 Anderson, *Imagined Communities*, 141–54.

3 Lee, "Recognition and Its Shadows"; Lee, "Jagdish, Son of Ahmad."

4 Prashad, *Untouchable Freedom*, 91–99.

5 Sharma, *Śrī Bālmīki Prakāś*, 11. Shifts in tense are in the original. The translation is mine.

6 Goldman, "Vālmīki and the Bhṛgu Connection"; Leslie, *Authority and Meaning in Indian Religions*; Sahdev, "Adi Kavi Valmiki"; Sahdev, *Maharishi Valmiki.*

7 Geertz, *Islam Observed*, ch. 2; Leslie, *Authority and Meaning in Indian Religions*, chs. 3–4.

8 The only exceptions here are British colonial administrator-folklorists like Richard Greeven, who, upon encountering Lāl Begī oral traditions in the 1880s, speculated that, "absurd as it may appear," the Bāl Mīk of sweeper lore must be Rishi Valmiki and that the sweepers had simply "forgotten" the connection (Greeven, *Knights of the Broom*, 67).

9 Novetzke, *Religion and Public Memory*.

10 Rupkala, *Śrī Bhaktamāl*, 148–58.

11 Rupkala, *Śrī Bhaktamāl*, 2. See also Nirmal Dass, who notes in his translation of *Ādi Granth* verses that "The *chandal* Valmiki should not be confused with Valmiki the Brahmin, the author of *The Ramayana*" (Dass, *Songs of the Saints*, 266).

12 Burn, *Census of India 1901*, 96.

13 Sharma, *Śrī Bālmīki Prakāś*, 17–18.

14 Versions of this parable continue to be told today, in all manner of media. The Hindi film *Lagaan* (2001), in which a protonationalist struggle against the British is only able to succeed when the Indian (cricket) team compels a Dalit character named Kachra ("Trash") to join them, is a case in point. As with the *chāṇḍāl* Bāl Mīk story, the narration of this act of inclusion takes no cognizance of the Dalit character's agency—the question is never asked whether he wants to join the Indian team. He simply *must*.

15 Jordens, *Swami Shraddhananda*, 163.

16 Stearns and Stearns, "Emotionology."

17 Lee, "Recognition and Its Shadows," ch. 4.

18 Sharma, *Patitoddhār*.

19 For a fine illustration of this point, see Orwell, *Road to Wigan Pier*, 127.

20 See Jaoul, "Casting the 'Sweepers'"; Lee, "Recognition and Its Shadows"; Lee, "Jagdish, Son of Ahmad"; Prashad, *Untouchable Freedom*.

MEDIATIONS

CHAPTER SIX

THE POLITICAL THEOLOGY OF BHAKTI, OR WHEN DEVOTIONALISM MEETS VERNACULARIZATION

CHRISTIAN LEE NOVETZKE

In a concept note circulated for the conference that preceded this volume, my coeditors asked the question "Is bhakti a language of power or of protest?" This is a very provocative question. Bhakti informs a vast literature, but does it constitute a language? If we think of a language as a symbolic system oriented around expressing something, it does seem right to call bhakti a language. Bhakti forms a symbolic system for communicating the sentiment of devotion, and like other languages it has its own dictionary.[1] But if bhakti is a language, it implies a set of interlocutors. A social component is a prerequisite for a language, so bhakti is a language only if it is social.

Something about power is also implied. Every language is a system of power and is fundamentally about empowerment—but in bhakti's case, the empowering of whom? Bhakti can reinforce prevailing social norms, but it can also empower the nonnormative or counternormative, the antinomian, disruptive, and quixotic. It is this latter set of descriptors that we so often associate with bhakti; many have argued that bhakti is a weapon of the weak. As such, bhakti often contests dominant practices of caste, gender, and sect, even if it sometimes reinforces those practices as well.

Yet protest is its own form of power, and power is agnostic. It flows alike to the dominator and the dominated, though in unequal measures. We see this in the history of bhakti. Certain socioreligious movements may have begun as a kind of protest directed against the dominant order only to later routinize many of the same normative features of society that it once clearly opposed. It is not just the words one uses but what those words do in the world, to people and for them as well. Bhakti has always had powerful words, but do those words also have powerful social effects?

One place where the power of bhakti is visibly expressed is in the many moments of vernacularization in India, where bhakti is ubiquitous and essential. Something powerful is happening when a new literature emerges in a regional language, and bhakti is there at the start of almost all regional literatures on the subcontinent, even if bhakti may not always be the sole or primary force compelling literary creation in a regional language. As the preeminent historian and philologist of Sanskrit Sheldon Pollock has pointed out, vernacularization is always a political event.[2] This is true whether it takes form in the emergence of new literatures in medieval India, which Pollock has studied, or in new modes of democratic engagement in contemporary India, as Thomas Blom Hansen and Lucia Michelutti, among other political anthropologists, have shown.[3] The role of religion in both these contexts, medieval and modern, is well known. And as Hansen and others point out, "devotionalism" in one form or another remains important even in the ideologies of vernacular democracy that dominate contemporary Maharashtrian politics. Vernacularization is about the political—the negotiation and distribution of power in society, from court to market to home and everywhere in between—and bhakti is often deeply involved when vernacularization takes place.

The term *political theology*, an idea getting a new lease on life in the academy, is one way to conceive of this nexus of religion and vernacularization. Carl Schmitt's work is the most easily recognizable harbinger of this idea in Western modern thought. He argued that political theology stands for the notion that "all significant concepts of the modern theory of the state are secularized theological concepts."[4] The essence of his insight is that over time theological ideas become governmental and social principles. This is hardly unique to Schmitt, and my use of this term does not follow his usage into realms of jurisprudence or sovereignty or his retrograde (and disturbing) concept of the political. Hegel, Nietzsche, Marx, Kant, Weber, and many others understood that at the heart of modernity nestled Christian theological concepts restated as politicized, rationalized ethics. I use political theology in this wider sense, outside the confines of Schmitt's abhorrent politics.[5] The utility of political theology as a term is that it helps us trace a particularly influential intellectual genealogy in the course of which religious ideas come to inform seemingly secular bodies of political theory and ideology but do not necessarily lose their theological character in the course of doing so. Indeed, the side-by-side enactment of the secular and the sacred is what gives a political theology its gravity. It is a challenge to secularization theory but not a capitulation to an entirely postsecularist position.

The political and social theorists mentioned above are particularly concerned with relatively recent developments—the nineteenth century and onward, and more in Europe than elsewhere in the world. But the kinds of things that feature in their analyses can also be seen many centuries before and a half a world away. Too few scholars of bhakti have been interested in tracing what sorts of political theologies might underwrite modern concepts, or at least presage them in some way, imparting political ideas that resonate with equality, liberalism, sovereignty, or freedom—ideas that then exceed and transcend their theological origins but never entirely escape them. Some may avoid such a move because it smacks of fundamentalism or essentialism; others may be convinced that such a task is anachronistic and ahistorical. Yet I hold on to the idea that political theology is useful for examining what happened when religion met social power in the Marathi-speaking regions of western India in the thirteenth century. This is evident in three distinct textual units: early Marathi inscriptions from the Yadava dynasty; the first work of Marathi literature, the *Līḷācaritra*; and the "jewel" of early Marathi literature, the *Jñāneśvarī*. Taken together, these show that vernacularization in Maharashtra carried within it a sort of bhakti that aimed in the direction of political outcomes.

BHAKTI IN THREE MODES

One of the first mentions of bhakti in Marathi appears in an inscription dedicated by the Yadava royal court to the important Vaishnava temple at Pandharpur in 1190 CE. The inscription was made as the Yadavas formed the first generation of their sovereign dynasty, and it is one of their oldest surviving inscriptions. The text is brief. It tells us that the Yadava ruler Bhillama donated some funds to what is described as a "small temple" (*lān maḍu*) to Vitthal, the future Pandharpur temple we know now.[6] The word *bhakti* does not appear here, but a strong connection is made between royal beneficence and the worship of Vitthal, the local and regionally significant form of Vishnu who reigns at Pandharpur. But even without the term *bhakti*, the inscription remains importantly related to bhakti and vernacularization in two critical ways. First, within a few centuries this temple was to become the center of the Varkari devotional tradition, even though it is not likely the Varkaris existed at this point in time and the inscription predates the lifespan of even the earliest Varkari *bhakta* by at least a century. Second, after these Varkari bhakti figures did emerge, they became the key agents of vernacularization over the next several hundred years. All this suggests that some sort of bhakti public actually did surround Vitthal and this small temple at the point when our 1190 inscription emerges. The upstart Yadavas evidently hoped to acquire the social capital associated with the place. History suggests that they did indeed make an important contribution to planting the seed for the Varkari bhakti tradition, though as a sovereign dynasty they themselves would not survive to see this new vernacular literary-religious movement flourish.

The next related donative inscription comes at the height of Yadava rule under Ramchandra in 1273, and bhakti is an important and explicit concept here. This inscription begins in Sanskrit with an invocation of the *bhaktajana*, the "people of devotion" who with "bristling hairs and eyes filled with happy tears" worship Vitthal. The donors named in the inscription are those "who look after the joy of Vitthal's attendant *bhaktas*."[7] Then the inscription shifts to Marathi. In that mode it invokes the donors as the *bhaktimāli*—doyens of bhakti. Following shortly after this bilingual inscription we have the appearance of seven slates, on which are inscribed the names of hundreds of people who gave amounts small and large for the building of Pandharpur; they also attest to donations made by King Ramchandra and his famous prime minister Hemadri. Taken as a group, these inscriptions indicate that a thriving and politically powerful (not to mention wealthy) bhakti public surrounded Vitthal by 1273. The hundreds of donors' names suggest the deep interconnections that existed between political and economic fields and the realm of bhakti.

The last of our three inscriptions comes in 1311, well after the battles in which the Yadavas were subdued in 1294 and just before the full extinction of the dynasty in 1313. This last inscription seems to be all about bhakti; through bhakti it expresses a political hope. Although it is not certain who made the donation recorded, there are signs that it was offered during the last year of the rule of Ramchandra. The donation is in honor of Vitthal, who is described as "he who supports the *bhaktajana*." As for the donor, he is described only as a *bhakti kiṅkar*, that is, a servant of bhakti. The inscription's conclusion is important. It reads: "Those who defend *dharma* forever are the Maharashtrian devotees [*parivaṇḍe marāṭhe*] of Vitthal, the lord of the land [*kṣetra*], and they will be fortunate." This swan song of the Yadavas leaves me with the sense that although they lost hope for political power, they dearly wished to be remembered.

This inscription offers a way that the Yadavas could remain in public memory, and in the process, the inscription supplies a new and enduring idea of the political imagination of a regional linguistic and cultural ethnicity that is here described as "Maratha." This is not the Maratha that would evolve into a caste block within the course of two hundred years but something more elemental—a connection of language, place, and religion, and all these tied to a political unit, the Yadavas. Here a Maratha is a person who speaks Marathi and who worships Vitthal, or rather, for whom Vitthal is the lord of the land.

Fast-forward six centuries and we hear something surprisingly familiar. In 1950, when the eminent sociologist Irawati Karve traveled with the Varkaris, pilgrims going to see Vitthal, she wrote, "I found a new definition of Maharashtra: the land whose people go to Pandharpur for pilgrimage."[8] And so in 1313 one last act of the Yadavas was to issue an inscription that joined together a region, a polity, a language, and bhakti itself, all intertwined with the idea of being Maratha, being Maharashtrian. Bhakti then takes the form of a symbolic system invoking the diffused power of the demotic, power inhering in the people of a region in general. Here devotion to Vitthal is also devotion to Marathi and devotion to the land on which Marathi speakers dwell. This is not the power of a single mighty king or family, but the power of a public defined by language and region; it is not explicitly differentiated by caste, class, or gender. The rudiments of a political theology take shape at this point. It coalesces around the idea that a bhakti public is also a political public—independent of a royal court or other governing force yet capable of being recognized by that force and being made the subject of its appeal. The efforts of contemporary Varkaris—those who live on in our own day—to remain above the fracas of politics can be seen as being historically rooted in just this moment.

The time frame of these three inscriptions brackets the period of Yadava power in the region. This is also the period of the emergence of Marathi literature, the literary vernacular moment. The first extant literary text in Marathi is the *Līḷācaritra* of 1278. It was completed a few years after the second of the three inscriptions just mentioned. This is a work I would describe as conveying sacred historical realism. It is the key hagiography of the founder of the Mahanubhav religion, a Gujarati Brahman named Chakradhar, yet as a record aiming to precisely and exactly record the life of Chakradhar, it is deeply etched by a concern to clearly convey historical facts. In the *Līḷācaritra* bhakti generally refers to a way of worshiping or adoring in public—doing bhakti, as it says, or having *bhakti darśan*. Once again we hear of *bhaktijana*, but what is meant this time is Chakradhar's first followers. These *bhaktijana* are the "devoted people" who follow him. This is the general use of the word in the *Līḷācaritra*, and its connection to the earlier usage seems to indicate that bhakti was conceived as a social thing, whatever else it might be—something that brought people together in public contexts of worship. This sense of bhakti is also what we see in the 1311 inscription at Pandharpur, where bhakti forms a cultural field that is socially capacious yet delimits its scope to those who speak Marathi, who live within the geographical region of spoken Marathi, and who are devoted to Vitthal.

The very act of creating the *Līḷācaritra* in Marathi is considered an act of bhakti—devotion to Chakradhar and the other sacred figures of the Mahanubhav religion. The rationale for the use of Marathi (as opposed to Sanskrit, which might have been expected) to preserve the life of Chakradhar is an extension of the historical realism of the text—Marathi was the spoken language of Chakradhar, his followers, and their social context. Yet there is also a social ethics attached to the use of Marathi. This is apparent in an exchange recorded in another early Mahanubhav text, the *Smṛtisthaḷa*. The *Smṛtisthaḷa* tells us that the early Mahanubhavs who were compiling the *Līḷācaritra* debated which language they ought to use. Given that the majority of followers were Brahmans, one follower proposed they use Sanskrit, but the eldest of the devotees countered that to do so would "deprive the elderly women" among the followers.[9] There is a somewhat different political theology of bhakti here than we saw in the inscriptions. To deprive anyone of the ability to gain access to Chakradhar's life and words is considered something contrary to the bhakti that motivates the creation of the *Līḷācaritra* text. A nascent kind of social equality around gender lurks in the decision among the first Mahanubhavs to use Marathi rather than Sanskrit.

The third mode in which we encounter a political theology of bhakti in early Marathi texts comes with the composition around 1290 CE of the *Jñāneśvarī*. It is quite different from the others. The *Jñāneśvarī* is the transcription of an orally performed commentary on the *Bhagavad Gītā* in Marathi; it is attributed to the *sant* Jnandev (ca. 1275–96 CE). It is also regularly cited as the first great work of Marathi literature. Here, I should note that the *Jñāneśvarī* does not mention Vitthal or Pandharpur, even though it became associated with the worship of Vitthal and with Pandharpur in the centuries to come. Yet the *Jñāneśvarī* comments extensively on bhakti as it addresses the treatment of bhakti in the *Gītā*. Thus bhakti is a concept deeply integrated into the *Jñāneśvarī*, even though it is not bhakti to Vitthal.

In the *Jñāneśvarī* we see a connection between bhakti and critical engagements with the social inequalities of caste and gender. In this text bhakti seems to serve as a marker of the places where social barriers to hearing the word of Krishna dissolve. The text tells us that it will tear down the levees of Sanskrit that unjustly confine the salvational waters of the *Gītā*. It tells us that the Vedas are miserly texts that refuse to share in the profit of salvation because they are written in Sanskrit and therefore restrict access along gradients of caste and gender. And the text explicitly names its target audience as *strīśūdrādika*—women, low castes, and others.[10] Yet the *Jñāneśvarī* is also a place where we hear arguments about how to deal with a world of social inequity. Bhakti offers an otherworldly solace for this-worldly pain. Bhakti in the *Jñāneśvarī* is an idea that provides free access to the salvific words of the *Gītā* and also provides a way to bear the social injustices of everyday life.

In the *Jñāneśvarī* there is a balance between these two disparate functions that bhakti provides, and it far outlasts this early Marathi text. Here we find a two-pronged ethical theology that will later become transformed into a political theology. To some, it may seem a paradox: How can there be spiritual parity without its social counterpart? But this is what we have—an emulsion I have called "sonic equality." By this term I mean the conviction—a social conviction—that all people are equally entitled to hear words of salvation in their own everyday language, but simultaneously I mean the admission that this does not necessarily require everyday social order to change. Jnandev must transpose the Sanskrit *Gītā* into the Marathi *Jñāneśvarī* because salvation's promise is only actualized in the vernacular—in Marathi, the language accessible to everyone in the region despite caste and gender distinctions. Yet the *Jñāneśvarī*, especially when it engages with bhakti, does not go on to call for complete social equality. The idea of equality here is limited to the sonic realm; full social equality still remains a distant hope. The *Jñāneśvarī* is fully aware that there could be such a hope, however. We hear it in its famous "Pasāyadān," its prayer for grace, which asks:

> May the wicked drop their crooked acts and keep good company,
> And may a sense of friendship develop among all beings.[11]

The *Jñāneśvarī* thus ends with a hope for a more equitable future. And in subsequent years, under the influence and public memory of the Varkari religious tradition, Jnandev came to be regarded as a champion of social equality, a figure who lived among, dined with, and worshiped with "women, low castes, and others." The limited theological ethics of sonic equality were to be replaced by a fuller sense of social equality, the result of a trajectory that develops into a consistently articulated political theology.

The reason this could and did happen has to do with bhakti's relationship to vernacularization. I see vernacularization as the use of the trope of the everyday in a shared discursive and public field. Its full expression may be in a regional literature like Marathi, but there are precursors in the representation of nonelite speech in Sanskrit contexts through Pali and Prakrit modes of address that claim to vocalize the demotic world. These Prakrits (the word connotes "natural speech" or "unrefined speech") give us a prototype of vernacularization. In them the everyday invades the language of an elite male high-caste world: Prakrits are very often the medium by which women, low castes, and others converse in Sanskrit dramatic texts. And we have many other texts—the *Gītā*, the Purāṇas, Buddhist texts, and so on—that declared their message open to all, even if the language of their medium was not actually open to all. Vernacularization is the linguistic realization of the quotidian aspirations of these texts. As with the modes in which Jnandev's public memory came to transform the perception of his social ethics, so too vernacularization as an ongoing process involves something much deeper than the simple use of a regional language. Vernacularity absorbs the very character of regionality, causing vertical social relations to be embraced within the quotidian world where the elite and nonelite meet. In this way, vernacularization implicitly espouses a political theology of everyday life—the idea that theological concepts, when transferred to the quotidian world, come to embody central questions about everyday social relations. It would be naïve to imagine that the process of distilling the Sanskrit cosmopolis into vernacular literary media, as the *Jñāneśvarī* does, might not also entail a social critique. I would argue that when seen in its true and full dimensions, vernacularization is to be understood as the process of social critique that is implied and enacted when idioms of power are transferred into the field of everyday life.[12]

In this way the *Jñāneśvarī* returns us to the inscriptions we have considered, and it provides us links to the *Līḷācaritra* as well. While the *Jñāneśvarī*, the *Līḷācaritra*, and the inscriptions do not all three share a single object—the worship of Vitthal, for example—they do share a common subject: bhakti. And they all locate bhakti in the field of everyday life, the vast world of the *bhaktajana*. The world of the everyday lends bhakti its power and is the source of its protest because it is a field in which the function of vernacularization—the transference of the idiom of power into everyday life—is most acutely seen in the Marathi context.

CONCLUSION

Was an enduring political theology drawn out of these three early uses of bhakti? Indeed, the *parivaṇḍe marāṭhe* of our last Marathi inscription within a few centuries would come to be a powerful force in the region's political life. From the seventeenth century onward, the Maratha Empire inaugurated by Shivaji (ca. 1627–80), whose mother was of Yadava lineage, fashioned itself as a realm within which bhakti and vernacular politics could coalesce, forming a nascent regional chauvinism with Shivājī as its principal emblem.[13] But there's more to bhakti than any one region—one *deś*—can hold. These engagements with bhakti in Marathi compelled a public debate about social injustice to happen, particularly around caste and gender, in relation to the *strīśūdrādika*.[14] This public debate, beginning in the thirteenth century, constituted a kind of nascent public sphere in the vernacular where the common good was discussed, even if unequally and haphazardly. This may not be the public sphere of Jürgen Habermas, with its well-established bourgeoisie and institutions of civil society, but I argue that it was a public sphere nonetheless. It endures as a link from the time of the Yadavas and their inscriptions—through the creation of the *Līḷācaritra*, the innovations of the *Jñāneśvarī*, and centuries of Marathi public memory—right down to the present day. This link is forged through the idiom of bhakti, which was the defining idiom of early Marathi literary creativity, and has remained central to Marathi literature in the centuries since that time. The political theology at the heart of Marathi bhakti remains vibrant today.

When bhakti met vernacularization in the thirteenth century, the argument of spiritual access to all led to something else, a political theology that transferred the idea of a bhakti public and of sonic equality into a field of discourse in Marathi that focused on the question of the common good. Though this idea was initially couched in terms of an equal access to the word of salvation, its natural expression was in a regionally intelligible language. To many who use it and to some of its principal ideologues, this language seems to exist in order to create a sphere of sonic equality—the idea that everyone should be able to hear the words of salvation in their own everyday language. In its first elaboration, this message may have been meant only to encompass the salvation of the soul, but in time its importance outgrew this theological restriction. The political theology of bhakti is the way sonic equality, a theological idea, catalyzed social equality, a political idea. Bhakti, at some point, came to imply an ethics regarding the salvation not just of all souls but of the soul of moral society itself.

NOTES

1 Callewaert and Sharma, *Dictionary of Bhakti*.

2 See Pollock, *Language of the Gods*, 423.

3 Hansen, "Vernacularization of Hindutva"; Hansen, *Saffron Wave*; Hansen, *Wages of Violence*; Michelutti, "Vernacularization of Democracy"; Michelutti, *Vernacularisation of Democracy*.

4 Schmitt, *Political Theology*, 36.

5 I am referring to Schmitt's affiliations with the Nazi Party from 1933 to 1936. Though he was expelled and though there have been recent attempts to appreciate aspects of Schmitt's legacy despite his work for the Nazi Party and his formulation of the führer concept, the pall of Nazi violence hangs over his work.

6 For more on all these inscriptions, as well as citations, see Novetzke, *Quotidian Revolution*, 93ff.

7 Novetzke, *Quotidian Revolution*, 95ff.

8 Karve, "On the Road," 22.

9 Deshpande, *Smṛtisthaḷa* 15, 73.

10 See *Jñāneśvarī* 11.8–10, 18.1446–49, in Dandekar et al., *Śrī Jñāneśvarī.*

11 *Jñāneśvarī* 18.1773, in Dandekar et al., *Śrī Jñāneśvarī.*

12 Here I am indebted to the insights of Sheldon Pollock, who argues forcefully that vernacularization is always about power's transfer into new literary and social realms. See Pollock, *Language of the Gods,* chap. 6 (223ff).

13 See Hansen, *Wages of Violence*, 20–27.

14 Novetzke, *Quotidian Revolution*, xiii, 15, and 237ff.

CHAPTER SEVEN

BHAKTI AS ELITE CULTURAL PRACTICE

Digambar Jain Bhakti in Early Modern North India

JOHN E. CORT

A MAJOR theme within bhakti literature and practice has involved criticism of and resistance to forms of domination within Indian society. Some of the stars of bhakti literature and performance, many of whom are also among those who have most often been translated into modern languages, come from subaltern social locations: Ravidās, Kabīr, Mīrābāī, Āṇṭāḷ, Akka Mahādēvi, Nāmdev, Muktābāī, Janābāi, Chokhāmeḷā, Tukārām—the list goes on. Tied to the perception of bhakti as primarily a literature of protest are several other generalizations: it is the language of the uneducated or undereducated "common people" rather than scholars trained in Brahmanical learning; it is a literature of the spoken vernacular rather than the elite classical Sanskrit; it is a sung verbal tradition rather than a written one.

But this is not the whole of bhakti. Many of the earliest extant bhakti hymns are elaborate Sanskrit and Prakrit *stotras*, composed by poets trained in all the complexities of classical poetics.[1] Other important bhakti texts are long, elaborate narratives, such as the *Bhāgavata Purāṇa* and other Purāṇas as well as devotional versions of the epics, in Sanskrit, Prakrit, Apabhramsha, and all the vernacular languages, in which the deeds of the god in question are often framed in an attitude we can characterize as bhakti. Still other important texts are extensive Sanskrit theological treatises, in which bhakti is deeply theorized using all the elite intellectual tools of Indian philosophy. For example, even during the heyday of the composition of bhakti literature in Brajbhāṣā, we find Sanskrit and vernacular treatises authored by learned Brahmans and other intellectuals, and these texts are essential for an adequate understanding of bhakti in early modern Braj and North India.[2] Further, many if not most of the vernacular traditions give evidence of extensive learning in those languages, as the training of a vernacular poet could be no less rigorous than that of a poet in a classical language.[3]

An example of early modern North Indian bhakti literature and performance that problematizes a too-easy equation of bhakti with subaltern locations is the extensive literature in Brajbhāṣā, Ḍhūṇḍhārī, and other vernacular languages, and also in Sanskrit, composed by Digambar Jains in North India in the early modern period. Bhakti was just one of a number of genres in which these authors wrote. Separating bhakti from other literary genres can paint a misleading picture of the work of bhakti authors. While bhakti in many settings has been a language of protest, consideration of this literature leads to a more complicated and multifaceted portrait of bhakti as a mode of religiosity, literature, and cultural performance that spanned the full range of social locations in classical, medieval, and early modern India.

Jainism is often stereotyped as a religious tradition focused on asceticism, but scholarship over the past several decades has shown that bhakti has been an integral part of the tradition for two millennia.[4] Jains were widely found in northern and western India in the early modern period. Some of the better-known Jains were successful merchants and bankers, while others filled a more modest economic niche as shopkeepers and moneylenders in cities and villages. Śvetāmbar Jains tended to pursue lives as traders and merchants. Digambar Jains were frequently engaged in livelihoods that depended on literacy. While not all Jains were wealthy, most of them lived at a material level noticeably above that of most Indian peasants and urban workers. Whether they were merchants, shopkeepers, or bureaucrats, a degree of literacy was essential for most Jains. Many of the Digambar Jains of early modern North India were part of what I. P. Gupta, in the context of sixteenth- and seventeenth-century Agra, has termed "a professional class." This social stratum, located between the courtly nobility and the rural and urban laboring poor, consisted of "officials attached to different departments for administration or defence . . . [and] teachers, scholars, astrologers, priests and other religious functionaries, writers, copyists, calligraphists, translators, physicians, surgeons, lawyers, engineers, builders, poets, musicians and master-craftsmen."[5] Jains were rarely among the political or cultural elite. There was almost always a fairly clear divide between the Jains and both the rulers (whether operating from Persianate or Rajput conceptions of sovereignty) and the intellectuals most closely associated with courts (Persianate litterateurs, Brahmans, bards). Jains, especially Digambar Jains, served important roles in the administration of many courts. Bhaṅvarlāl Jain listed fifty-four Digambar Jains who served in the Kachavāhā court of Amer and then Jaipur between the seventeenth and twentieth centuries, and Kastūrcand Kāslīvāl added information about Digambar Jain ministers in the courts of states such as Nagaur, Bharatpur, Diggi, Sikar, Kota, Bundi, Sikar, and Alwar.[6] But this did not translate into inclusion in the circles of the political and cultural elite. We can see this by the social and spatial location of the Jains in both sixteenth- and seventeenth-century Agra and eighteenth- and nineteenth-century Jaipur. The neighborhoods inhabited by Jains, and therefore also their temples and other institutions, were centrally located, but they appear invisible in the Mughal and Rajput accounts of their courts.

THE TRAINING OF A DIGAMBAR BHAKTI AUTHOR

In a process that has yet to be explored adequately, the late sixteenth and early seventeenth centuries saw a profound shift in the Digambar literary cultures of North India. Throughout the medieval period, literary production among Digambar Jains in North India was almost exclusively in the hands of domesticated monks known as *bhaṭṭāraks* and their disciples. By the mid-seventeenth century, the situation had changed drastically, and the majority of Digambar authors were laymen. While some of them were professional intellectuals bearing the title of *paṇḍit*, clearly this title was also applied as an honorific to men who gained their livelihoods from other occupations but who were respected for their learning and literary skills. These authors are nearly invisible in the archives maintained by the ruling and cultural elites for whom they worked. In these sociopolitical elite circles, Mughals tended to patronize Persianate authors, and Rajputs to patronize Brahmanical and bardic authors. Within their own sphere, however, the Jains produced thousands of texts in almost all the elite languages and in almost all possible genres—including bhakti.

The early geographical center of this transformation of Digambar Jain literary production was the Mughal imperial capital of Agra. Founded as a capital by the sultān Sikandar Lodhī (Lodi) in 1505, it became the center of the Mughal imperium under the emperors Babar (Babur), Humāyūṃ (Humayun), and Akbar. Large numbers of people migrated to the city. Among them were significant communities of Jains: Śvetāmbar Jains, who came as merchants and traders from further west in what is now Rajasthan and Gujarat, and Digambar Jains, who came from cities and small towns of northern and central India both for business and to work in the imperial government as clerks and middle-level officials. The city contained a large number of Jain temples and other religious institutions; an account from 1594 listed forty-eight Digambar temples in the city.[7] The literary skills that the Digambar Jains brought to their employment soon spread to specifically religious compositions. Most of the literature composed by Digambar Jains in Agra was in the vernacular. Nemicandra Śāstrī discusses eighteen lay Digambar authors who wrote in Agra between the 1610s and the 1770s.[8] In the words of Śāstrī, "If one were to remove the contributions of the literature of Agra from the history of Hindi Jain literature, what would be left would be worthless."[9]

Unfortunately, our knowledge of the intellectual training of these Digambar laymen is scant. One finds many references to an author's teacher or teachers, but we have no record of a specific curriculum. For our best example of the education of a Jain author, we must turn to one who was born into a Śvetāmbar family, and only later in life moved into a world of spiritual pursuits that included Digambars as well. This is one of the most famous of the early modern Jain authors: Banārsīdās (1587–1643). He left us an account of his life in his *Ardhakathānak*, from which we can learn something of the education of a Jain poet in early seventeenth-century North India.[10]

As a child in Jaunpur he was sent by his father to school with an unnamed Brahman *paṇḍit* for a year at the age of eight to learn to read and write. Banārsīdās said that in that year he became proficient in his studies. Five years later, he decided to expand his learning and studied under another Brahman, Paṇḍit Devdatt. He learned astrology (*jotis*) and studied a text on mathematics, the *Khaṇḍasphuṭa*. He also demonstrated a growing interest in literature. He studied two Sanskrit textbooks that were essential for writing metrical verse: the *Nāmamālā* on synonyms and the *Anekārtha* on words with multiple meanings. He studied literary aesthetics (*alaṅkar*), and because his interests especially lay in the contemporary secular love poetry known as *rīti*, he studied the *Laghu Koka*, a Sanskrit textbook on erotics. Around this same time he also studied with a Śvetāmbar monk, Bhāncand, and his lay disciple Rāmcand. As part of these studies, Banārsīdās composed a text on Sanskrit grammar called *Pañcasandhi*. He engaged in the formal study of textbooks on orthoprax Jain rituals such as bathing an icon (*sanātar*), meditation (*sāmāïk*), and confession (*paḍikaunā*), and memorized many verses (*silok*) on various ritual topics. He also learned the necessary hymns (*aston*) for these rituals; it is safe to assume on the basis of both Śvetāmbar ritual culture and Banārsīdās's own later compositions that he memorized devotional hymns in Sanskrit, Brajbhāṣā, and Prakrit. He studied two textbooks on vernacular metrics, the *Chandakos* and the *Srutabodh*. Finally, he learned to recite correctly (*paḍhai suddha*), an essential skill for a poet in a culture in which poetry was mostly either sung or recited publicly.

Banārsīdās's literary and performative skills were well known. In 1611, when he was still a young man, he gained a reputation in Agra for his singing, and groups of ten or twenty men would gather to hear his singing of Qutban's *Mirigāvatī* and Manjhan's *Madhumālatī*, two great classics of Hindavi Sufi literature. In 1614 or 1615 he became friends with Cīnī Kilic Khān, the local governor in Jaunpur. Cīnī Kilic was interested in literature, and so Banārsīdās taught him the *Nāmamālā*, the *Chandakos*, and the *Srutabodh*.

Banārsīdās's literary output gives evidence of his significant training and erudition. He has left us three long Brajbhāṣā texts: his aforementioned autobiography, the *Ardhakathānak*; the *Samaysār Nāṭak*, a verse version of Kundakunda's Prakrit *Samayasāra*, one of the foundational texts of Digambar doctrine for which Banārsīdās relied on a later Sanskrit commentarial version and a sixteenth-century Brajbhāṣā version; and the *Banārsī Vilās*, a collection of nearly five dozen shorter texts compiled by his friend and colleague Jagjīvanrām in 1644, the year after Banārsīdās's death. In addition to the *Samaysār Nāṭak*, many of his texts were direct or indirect translations from the Sanskrit: the *Sahas Aṭhottar Nām*, a hymn giving 1,008 names of the Jina, designed for devotional recitation; the *Suktimuktāvalī*, a translation of the Sanskrit *Suktimuktāvalī*, a twelfth-century poem of *nīti* (moral wisdom) and Jain devotion and practice; and the *Param Jyotī Stotra* (also known as the *Śivmandir Stotra*), a translation of one of the most popular Jain Sanskrit devotional hymns, the circa-twelfth-century *Kalyāṇamandira Stotra* of Kumudacandra.

Banārsīdās was also skilled in Brajbhāṣā poetics. He composed his own *Nāmamālā*, a lexicon of synonyms based in part on earlier Sanskrit models. Many of his shorter Brajbhāṣā works show a fascination with difficult verse forms. His works also show a deep familiarity with Jain doctrine. The range of his compositions included many that allow us to bring him into a discussion of bhakti. In addition to his translation of a Sanskrit devotional *stotra* into Brajbhāṣā, he wrote several shorter devotional texts, such as his *Ajitnāth ke Chand* ("Verses to [the Jina] Ajitnāth"). On the whole, he inclined more toward Adhyātma, an inner form of Digambar spirituality that shared much with *sant nirguṇ* sensibilities.

Banārsīdās was at the fountainhead of a stream of many dozens of lay Digambar poets over the next two centuries. For roughly a century after Banārsīdās's death in 1643, the main center of this literature was Agra. The two most important poets and intellectuals from Agra were Dyānatrāy (1676–1726) and Bhūdhardās (fl. 1724–49).

Dyānatrāy was involved in a religious study circle (*dharmsahailī*, *sailī*) led by one Mānsiṃh Jauharī, an otherwise unknown lay Digambar intellectual.[11] He was also taught in this circle by the Digambar author Bihārīdās. Dyānatrāy later moved to Delhi, where he learned poetry and Digambar spirituality (Adhyātma) in a circle led by one Sukhānand. Dyānatrāy was a prolific poet. He composed the liturgies for many *pūjās*, extended rituals performed in temples and involving offerings to Jina icons. The subject matter of these *pūjās* covered many fundamental aspects of Digambar Jain theology, cosmology, and philosophy, and ever since, his *pūjās* have been a principle means by which Jains learn these subjects. His *Carcā Śatak* was a textbook that treated many of the same subjects in brief form. More than three hundred of his *pads* are extant, and many of them are still widely sung today. These also cover a wide range of topics, from devotion to the Jinas to the full extent of Jain doctrinal topics. Some of them are *updeśī*, songs that "instruct" the audience in Jain philosophy and metaphysics. Others are *adhyātmik*, in which he urges the audience to pay attention to *bhed-jñān*, "knowledge of the difference" between pure soul and impure matter and body. This central teaching of Digambar *adhyātma* bears many similarities to the *nirguṇ* bhakti of the *sants*. Still others are intended to be sung in the temple while worshiping icons of the Jinas, celebrating the salvific message of the Jinas. Finally, he translated from Sanskrit into Brajbhāṣā the *Ekībhāva Stotra* by the eleventh-century monk Vādirāja, a hymn that Dyānatrāy in the last verse of his translation termed a "boat of bhakti" (*bhagati jahāj*).[12]

Bhūdhardās was equally learned.[13] From two brief contemporary references, we know that he gave regular sermons in the Syāhgaṅj temple in Agra.[14] His contemporaries said that Bhūdhardās combined devotion and worship with expertise in grammar and Jain scriptures. This is a pattern repeated in the literary and cultural output of most of the Jain authors of this period. The evidence of Bhūdhardās's texts confirms his renown as a scholar. Many of his shorter compositions are verse primers on fundamental Jain doctrines.[15] In his prose *Carcā Samādhān* he addressed 139 potential doubts in the minds of his readers. In it he cited about 85 Digambar texts. He devoted the 107 verses of *Jain Śatak* to exploring various topics in devotion, renunciation, and morals.

His most popular text has remained his *Pārśva Purāṇ*, a long verse telling of the life of the twenty-third Jina. At the end of the text he explained that he told the biography of Pārśva in the vernacular after examining many previous versions, which presumably included texts in the Jain classical languages, so that his contemporaries could have access to the story. He also confessed his intellectual limitations in a statement of humility such as is found in many Indian texts, but I think that we can read in Bhūdhardās's detailed listing of the knowledge and training he said he lacked an indication of what in fact he *had* studied to be a learned poet:

I have not studied the *Amar Koṣ* (dictionary of erotics), nor have I seen any vernacular prosody (*piṅgal*).
I have not memorized any verse (*kāvya*), nor have I studied the Sanskrit grammar (*sārsutī*).
I lack knowledge of syllables (*acchar*), conjunctions (*sandhi*) and compounds (*samās*).
I made this in the vernacular, for the sake of reflecting on dharma.[16]

As with both of his Agra predecessors, he translated Sanskrit devotional hymns into Brajbhāṣā: the *Jinacaturviṃśatikā* by the medieval poet Bhūpāla, a praise hymn addressed to all twenty-four Jinas, and Vādirāja's *Ekībhāva Stotra*, his translation of which he termed a "garland of bhakti" (*bhaktimāl*).[17]

Bhūdhardās was the last of the great Digambar poets from Agra. During his lifetime the Mughal Empire was in a period of contraction. In the first half of the eighteenth century, the center of Digambar Jain intellectual life in North India shifted from Agra to Jaipur, which was founded in 1727 by Sawai Jai Singh II. Jains had a significant presence in the Kachavāhā court long before the founding of the new capital, but they eagerly took advantage of the new opportunities provided by Jai Singh, coupled with the decline of Agra and other Mughal centers. Jai Singh needed trained intellectuals and administrators for his expanded government, and he needed merchants to help fuel the economic growth of the kingdom and its new capital. Digambar Jains were prominent among the people who shifted to Jaipur from the Mughal heartland. The Jaipur Digambar community produced a long series of well-trained intellectuals in the eighteenth and nineteenth centuries, such that it became known as a "second Kāśī," that is, a second Banaras.[18] Kastūrcand Kāslīvāl has written, in what may not be an exaggeration,

> In the initial one hundred years after its founding, there were more intellectuals in this city than anywhere else in Rajasthan. It seemed as if there was a contest here to compose Hindi texts. Wherever one looked, *paṇḍit*s were writing one text after another. People had such enthusiasm for creating literature that they gave it special effort, and gave unprecedented support to its propagation. Jain intellectuals wrote vernacular commentaries on narrative epics, story epics, *purāṇs*, and doctrinal texts. In addition, they wrote fine spiritual and devotional literature. For this reason, between VS 1800 [1743 CE] and VS 1940 [1883 CE] Jaipur can be said to have been the foremost city in India in the creation of literature.[19]

Dozens of Digambar authors were active in Jaipur in the eighteenth and nineteenth centuries. They studied both Sanskrit and vernacular language, and they composed texts and commentaries on doctrinal, narrative, and devotional themes. Looking at their education and their compositions shows a pattern similar to that of Agra in the preceding century and a half. In the interests of brevity, however, let me refrain from a detailed investigation of the Jaipur authors and summarize the basic argument that emerges from looking at the literary centers of Agra and Jaipur.

BHAKTI AS ELITE CULTURAL PERFORMANCE

Starting in the early seventeenth century, dozens of Digambar Jain laymen in the cities and towns of North India engaged in writing texts in the vernacular. Many of them were also reasonably fluent in Sanskrit, occasionally writing in the language but more often translating from it. Their compositions covered the full range of doctrinal topics. In addition, many of the lay authors composed dozens and hundreds of shorter vernacular *pads* on a range of topics. Many elaborated on basic aspects of Jain doctrine and cosmology. Others were focused on the need to turn inward and focus one's spiritual quest on realizing the pure soul buried beneath the karmic dirt accumulated by lives of ignorance and foolish behavior. Still others focused outward and sang of the Jina in a spirit of deep devotion.[20] Many of these laymen were well-educated and gave public sermons in the intellectual and spiritual assemblies that met regularly at Jain temples. They were not poorly educated, socially disadvantaged subalterns.

The composition and performance of bhakti texts was an expected part of a larger literary, intellectual, and ritual life among Digambar Jains. Vernacular language and Sanskrit went hand in hand. The translators of Sanskrit texts consistently lamented what they described as a declining ability to understand the classical tongue, hence the need to "make it simple" for their contemporaries, but the large number of authors who engaged in translation indicates that Sanskrit fluency was fairly common among Jain litterateurs. Further, bhakti and doctrinal study also went hand in hand. Digambar poets were expected to produce texts in both areas. Bhakti as a mode of religiosity and literature was embedded in the intellectual lives of these Jain communities. Bhakti was not a language of subaltern protest; it was part of the Digambar Jain religious and intellectual establishment.

It could be argued that the Jains provide a distinctive exception, and that most bhakti literature and performance did not emerge from such relatively privileged social locations. But there is an extent to which all locations of bhakti are distinctive. If we do not take into account the full range of social locations of bhakti throughout the history and geographical extent of South Asia (and now globally), we are guilty of adopting a presupposition of bhakti that unduly limits its many and varied expressions. The title of the Yale conference—Exploring Bhakti: Is Bhakti a Language of Power or of Protest?—implied that bhakti is one thing. I argue that the title more properly should be plural: Exploring Bhaktis: Are Bhaktis Languages of Power or of Protest?

Furthermore, once we accept the need to cast our net as wide as possible in order to understand bhaktis more fully, we see that throughout the histories of South Asia there have been many examples of bhaktis in similar elite intellectual, social, and ritual settings. Medieval Tamil bhakti poets such as Vedāntadeśika composed bhakti hymns in Sanskrit, Prakrit, Tamil and Manipravalam.[21] The Gauḍīya and Puṣṭimārgīya Vaishnava communities from Orissa in the east to Gujarat in the west depended on Sanskrit bhakti theologians to spread and authenticate their messages.[22] In early modern Gujarat, the Swaminarayan (Svāmīnārāyaṇ) tradition established its orthodox bona fides by generating a rich theological and devotional literature in the elite languages of Sanskrit and Brajbhāṣā, at the same time that it generated vernacular texts in a range of contemporary languages.[23] Many other examples could easily be added.

In conclusion, bhakti was—and is—a mode of religious literary, ritual, and social expression found in all strata of Indian society. It can be a subaltern site of protest against social and theological hierarchies; it can also be an elite site in which all the skills of elite aesthetics and intellectual inquiry are combined with expressions of devotion. Perhaps it is not going too far to say that there is no such thing as bhakti. There are bhaktis.

NOTES

1 Gonda, *Medieval Religious Literature in Sanskrit.*

2 Okita, *Hindu Theology.*

3 Allison Busch's *Poetry of Kings* is an excellent study of the training of authors in early Hindi during the same period that my chapter explores. While she focuses largely on "secular" poets, much of her analysis applies equally to "bhakti" poets.

4 Cort, "Bhakti in the Early Jain Tradition"; Cort, "Singing the Glory of Asceticism."

5 Gupta, *Urban Glimpses of Mughal India*, 66–67.

6 Jain, "Jaypur ke Jain Dīvān," 332–39; Kāslīvāl, *Khaṇḍelvāl Jain Samāj*, 195–220.

7 Cort, "Tale of Two Cities," 40.

8 Śāstrī, "Āgrā meṃ nirmit Jain Vaṅmay."

9 Śāstrī, "Āgrā meṃ nirmit Jain Vaṅmay," 553. All translations in this chapter are by the author.

10 My discussion here repeats material in Cort, "Making It Vernacular in Agra," 75–76. Chowdhury, *Banarsidas*; Lath, *Half a Tale*; and Petit, *Banārasīdās*.

11 Cort, "Dyānatrāy"; Jain, *Hindī Jain Bhakti Kāvya*, 278–87.

12 Dyānatrāy, *Ekībhāva Stotra* 26, in *Mahāvīr Vandanā*, 310.

13 Śāstrī, *Mahākavi Bhūdhardās*; Jain, *Hindī Jain Bhakti Kāvya*, 335–49.

14 Daulatrām Kāslīvāl, *Puṇyāsrav Kathākoś* 15, quoted in Kāslīvāl, *Mahākavi Daulatrām Kāslīvāl*, 66; and Bra. Rāymall, *Jīvan Patrikā*, in Bhārill, *Paṇḍit Ṭoḍarmal*, 334.

15 For one example, see Cort, "Cosmic Man and the Human Condition," 34–47.

16

> amarakoṣa nahiṃ paḍhyo maiṃ na kahiṃ piṅgala pekhyo
> kāvya kaṇṭha nahiṃ karī sarasutīsoṃ nahiṃ sīkhyo.
> acchara sandhi samāsa jñāna varjita vidhi hīnī
> dharma bhāvanā hetu kimapi bhāṣā yah kīnī. (Bhūdhardās, *Pārśva Purāṇ* 9.328, p. 163)

17 Bhūdhardās, *Ekībhāva Stotra*, concluding *dohā*, in *Mahāvīr Vandanā*, 316.

18 Jain, *Hindī Gadya*, 16.

19 Kāslīvāl, "Prastāvnā" to Gārg, *Pārśvadās Padāvalī*, *do-tīn*.

20 Cort, "God Outside and God Inside."

21 Hopkins, *Singing the Body of God*.

22 Okita, *Hindu Theology*; Redington, *Vallabhācārya on the Love Games*.

23 Williams and Trivedi, *Swaminarayan Hinduism*, 131–232.

CHAPTER EIGHT

LOVER AND YOGI IN PUNJABI SUFI POETRY

The Story of Hir and Ranjha

MANPREET KAUR

THE devotional expanse of bhakti embraces many varieties of religious practice. The swell and spread of bhakti throughout the Indian subcontinent in the early modern period was fundamentally dependent on what we might call a commensal attitude among many religious modes, including Sufi and yogic ones, and this pattern of partaking of one another's essence persists today. Both in early modern poetry and in contemporary performances the great *bhakta* Mirabai becomes a female yogi—a yogini—when she follows her lover-prince Krishna. When he takes up the "yogic garb," she does too.[1] The tropes are stirred together in a different way in Punjabi Sufi poetry. Here a young woman called Hir (fig. 8.1) falls in love with the flute-playing herder boy (like Krishna!) called Ranjha, and once again Hir and Ranjha become yogis (Punjabi: *jogī*) as they pursue their love.[2] Thus a persistent question arises: If none of these domains—bhakti, Sufi, yogic—is airtight, then what does it mean to recognize their specific linguistic, literary, and performative qualities while at the same time enjoying the ways in which they commingle?

THE *JOGĪ* EPISODE IN THE *QISSĀ* OF HIR

"Call me Dhido Ranjha, let no one call me Hir!," says the heroine midway through her love story, demanding to be called by the name of her beloved.[3] This widely remembered pronouncement marks Hir's distinctly defiant stance in the world of the Hir-Ranjha narrative, where identities are expressed in terms of clan names and natal places.[4] At one level, she claims the right to name and thus own herself; at another, she performs the ultimate denial of self,

8.1 *Heer*, by the Pakistani painter Abdur Rahman Chughtai (1894–1975). This female protagonist continues to inspire artists across Punjab as the epitome of love and beauty. Courtesy of Chughtai Museum Lahore, represented by Arif Rahman Chughtai

representing an adherence to the Sufi path. This pronouncement is delivered as part of a lyric form called *kāfī*—a short strophic poem with a simple refrain. It is attributed just as often to Shah Hussain (d. ca. 1591) as it is to Bullhe Shah (d. 1758), two Sufi poets of the Punjab. The latter was also a contemporary of the Sufi Waris Shah (d. 1798), the preeminent teller of the Hir-Ranjha narrative as it appears in the *qissā* form, a long epic romance told mostly in verse, employing various meters. Waris Shah's *qissā* is titled simply *Hīr* (1766). The earliest extant textual evidence of both Shah Hussain and Bullhe Shah's verses date to the late nineteenth century, making it difficult to ascertain whether the above quoted *kāfī* existed before Waris's *Hīr* was composed or came about after the work had attained its celebrity. Whatever the case may be philologically speaking, Hir goes on to say in the *kāfī*, "Ranjha is in me, and I, in Ranjha. . . . I am nowhere; there is just him, entreating himself."

In a kindred transformation of the self, Ranjha becomes a *jogī* so that he may make the journey to Rangpur, where his beloved Hir has been residing since her unwilling marriage to a Kheḍā clansman. But the episode of Ranjha becoming a *jogī* involves an arduous journey. He is required to go to Tillā Jogiyāṅ, the seat of the Nath Yogis, to take on this identity. Both the *kāfī* and *qissā* genres employ the trope of Ranjha as a *jogī*, but it is in the longer formulations of the *qissā* tradition that the episode of Ranjha's transformation is detailed.

The name *qissā* is etymologically related to the term used when God says in Sura 12:3 of the Qur'an, "We *relate* to you the best of stories."[5] These words appear just before Allah narrates to Muhammed the story of Yūsuf, the biblical Joseph. It is no wonder that the story of Yūsuf and Zulaikhā—the wife of the biblical Potiphar, who was so enraptured by Joseph—is a favorite among the storytellers of the Islamic tradition, and the expressive tradition around this story shows how the "prophetic narrative is completely reshaped as poetic romance."[6] At the conceptual commixture of *adab* (literature) and *kalām* (theology), the genre of *qissā* flourishes in Punjab in the early modern period as a favorite means of presenting an allegory: here Sufi devotion is depicted through stories of exemplary love. This love blossoms in the form of several love-legends, both oral and written. In addition to the Yūsuf-Zulaikhā pair we have Sassī-Punnūn, Sohnī-Mahiwāl, Shirīn-Farhād, Lailā-Majnūn, Sāhibān-Mirzā, and no less important than any of these, Hir-Ranjha.[7] Each tale bathes in the rich pool of references that the others establish. For instance, descriptions of Ranjha working as a cowherd for Hir's father (so that Ranjha can see Hir daily) call to mind the image of Mahiwāl (literally, "one of the herdsman clan"), which is so potent that it tempts Sohnī to cross the perilous Chenab River daily. That river, in turn, is the same one that affords Ranjha his first chance to see Hir, in consequence of which he utters, "Ah! My Beloved." This image of Ranjha—a flute at his lips as cattle graze in the background—resembles that of Krishna. It is in this densely intertextual environment that Waris Shah wrote his Sufi epic romance *Hīr*.[8] While the resemblance between Mahival and Krishna works instantaneously by simple association, the resemblance connecting Ranjha to the figure of a *jogī* takes quite some narrative effort to achieve. It comes later in the story.[9]

When the love affair is discovered, Hir's clan attempts to quash it by marrying their daughter to a young man from the Kheḍā clan. A year passes. It is then that she coaxes Ranjha, through a letter, to become a *jogī* so that he can visit her. At first Ranjha resists, but descriptions of Hir "turning to dust" in her

8.2 *Young Ranjha*, by the Pakistani painter Abdur Rahman Chughtai (1894–1975). Ranjha is almost never visualized without his flute, as in this famous painting. Courtesy of Chughtai Museum Lahore, represented by Arif Rahman Chughtai longing for him (*viraha*) nudge him in the right direction. He goes to Balaknath, who in this narrative is pictured as the primary disciple of the pioneering yogic guru Goraknath, and seeks this yogic transformation from him. The center called the Goraknath Tillā, or simply Tillā Jogiyāṅ (literally "the mound of the yogis"), to which Ranjha heads so as to have this encounter, is considered historically to be one of the first centers established by the Gorakhnathi or Kanphata (pierced-ear) yogis, the Nath Yogis.[10] But the word *tillā*, which appears in this name, also appears in the names of all Punjabi locations where Sufis were believed to have carried out their forty-day penance (*chillā*).[11] Obviously the homonym plays a role in achieving this *jogī*-Sufi association. The path to Tillā Jogiyāṅ, the highest peak in the salt-range mountains of the region, is meant to provide an arduous penance.

The figure of Balaknath—and the presence of *jogīs* in general—was no doubt a dominant force in the Punjab during Waris Shah's time. By this time in the eighteenth century there existed several centers of yogic practice and initiation in the region, but the reference to the original Tillā Jogiyāṅ itself, which allows Ranjha to be placed directly in the lineage of Balaknath, is surely deliberate.[12] The episode with Balaknath exemplifies all the motifs that occur when an ordinary person is transformed into a *jogī*, as typically recorded in the *premākhyān* genre: the teacher attempts to dissuade the student, the student persists and proves his determination to become an initiate, and then the act itself is done. By the end of this sequence, Ranjha is a *kānphaṭa jogī*.

The conversation involving Ranjha, Balaknath, and Balaknath's disciples at the *tillā* consists of a battle of wits, flavored with local idioms, punchlines, and the like. While Waris Shah may not be asserting some sort of sectarian victory as he develops this conversation, he is certainly eager to represent the Sufis well. Theological dialogues of this nature and literary representations of them did indeed proliferate in Punjab in the eighteenth and preceding centuries—between Sufis and yogis, yogis and Sikhs, Sikhs and Sufis, and so forth. They also serve as important background for the tale Waris Shah is trying to tell.

SIDHAGOṢṬI AND OTHER DIALOGUES

Accounts of theological face-offs are a staple in the Indic tradition broadly speaking. Often such accounts are framed as dialogues that could have occurred in a public seminar, yet the dialogues themselves are set to rhyme. The poetic devices chosen for this literary task add affect to the theological persuasions represented in the content. For Punjab, Nanak's conversation with the yogis in a work called the *Sidhagoṣṭi* (Conference with the Perfected Ones) serves as an interesting point of comparison for what we see in Waris's *Hīr*.

The *Sidhagoṣṭi* is structured as a progressively clarifying round of questions and answers. The questions have a beseeching quality about them, while the answers are inevitably compelling: this is hardly an ordinary conversation. Its seemingly canned aspect is easy enough to understand in view of the fact that this "record" exists as a part of the *Gurū Granth Sāhib*, but it is also true that the text plays with the tension between fact and persuasion.[13] While the Sikh *janamsākhī* (literally "witness of life") tradition remembers this moment as part of a journey (*udāsī*) by Nanak to Gorakh Khatari, the *Sidhagoṣṭi*, which actually enters the scriptural canon, reverses things. Guru Arjan, who is remembered as the author of *Sidhagoṣṭi*, represents the *jogīs* as visiting the court of Guru Nanak instead. This second location signals that readers should expect to encounter here a certain familiar set of tenets and conventions of the Sikh faith, which the Guru repeats in front of the *jogīs*.

The words uttered at the beginning of verse 33 of the *Sidhagoṣṭi*, "nāmi rate sidh goṣti hoī" (attuned to the divine Name, *Sidhagoṣṭi* is attained), suggest a conversation not with the *siddhas* but among Sikhs themselves. Thus Sikh disciples in Nanak's assembly (*sangat*) who have been pursuing the simple (*sahaj*) path of uttering the divine name (*nām*) become the actual *siddhas* who are destined to reach the state that Nanak, the true *siddha*, has already attained. Throughout the text, in a similar way, the dialogue constitutes a chance to take metaphors from the yogic world and appropriate them in a Sikh mode. For instance, Nanak says the following in response to a question posed by the attendant *siddhas* in verse 10:

> antari sabadu niraṁtari mudrā haümai mamtā duri karī
> kāmu krodhu ahaṁkāru nivarai gura kai sabadi su samajha parī
> khiṁthā jholī bharipuri rahiā nānaka tārai eku harī
> sācā sahibu sācī nāī parkhai gur kī bāt kharī

> Let the inner word be your [yogic] pose. It's the piercings sustained
> from the inner word that let you renounce ego and attachment.[14]
> In comprehending the Guru's word, you forsake lust, anger, and
> self-absorption.
> Let your pouch and cloak be the realization of God's oneness.
> As God is true, so is his name—consider this pure saying of the
> Guru.

By implying that it is a preoccupation with external accoutrements that keeps a *jogī* from achieving true knowledge, these verses record the pleasure of affirmation that comes from appropriating *siddha* speech. The journey that living beings make through this phenomenal world, during which both Yogis and Sikhs seek the ultimate truth, is described multiple times as an attempt to cross an "unfordable ocean." This is the predicament described in both Nath Yogi and Sikh texts, but from the perspective of the *Gurū Granth Sāhib* only the Sikhs know the right way to deal with it, hence within the logic of the *Sidhagoṣṭi* text theirs is the winning side. A parallel thing happens within the Chishti Sufi milieu. When Sufi-yogic interactions are recorded in texts such as those we find in the *malfūẓāt* genre (discourse with saints), only the Sufi knows how to be victorious.

Translations of concepts and texts across sectarian boundaries may also be seen as a "dialogic" activity in this broad literary landscape. When the yogic idea of *akālpurakh* is given a new context in the Sikh scriptural corpus, or when Indic texts like *The Pool of Nectar* (*Amṛtakuṇḍa*) are translated in such a way that they enter Islamic contexts, we have acts of translation that are not to be understood simply as being motivated by a desire to prove the superiority of one's own position. Simultaneously we have a more basic fact—a comparativist's curiosity.[15] This curiosity is intellectual, spiritual, and creative. While a doctrinal text such as *Sidhagoṣṭī* may present the yogic attitude as a version of spiritual practice that is eventually bested by the Sikh mode, the love legend chosen by Waris Shah does not participate in such an overt act of ranking. It picks the figure of the *jogī* as an ally that moves the plot forward, not as an "other" that must be vanquished.

TO BE OR NOT TO BE A *JOGĪ*

As soon as Ranjha's metamorphosis into a *jogī* is complete, instead of staying at the *tillā* and practicing renunciation as an initiate into the tradition must, Ranjha divulges to Balaknath that he undertook this challenge only for the sake of Hir and must leave for Rangpur to find her. Is Ranjha then a *jogī* after all? The first person who sees Ranjha after this episode, a herdsman, sees through his disguise immediately! What then does this garb mean for Ranjha, and what does it do for Waris? Perhaps it enables Waris to retrace the narrative terrain that had been laid out by one of his literary predecessors. Waris Shah was not the first to introduce the figure of the *jogī* into the story of Hir and Ranjha. Damodar Gulati provides us with the first extant written account of this love legend, known to us as *Hīr Dāmodar* (ca. 1600). While several differences between Waris and Damodar do exist, in both cases Ranjha takes on the garb of a *jogī* only for ulterior motives.[16] In neither case is he able to follow through; he is incapable of the life of a *jogī*. This is not only because he has been completely spirited away by Hir's *ishq*, her love; his character is just not suited for hardships. Being a rich Jat, he is, in his own words, "an opportunist," while yoga (*jog*) is akin to "drinking iron."

In Waris Shah's version of the story, none of this is hidden from Balaknath: he knows that Ranjha possesses no unwavering intent. It's only "an unhappy circumstance," he surmises, that has brought Ranjha to the *tillā*. Yet Balaknath humors him and lets him have the accoutrements of the *jogī* no matter what he intends to do with them in the end. Perhaps he too, like Hir, is mesmerized by Ranjha's beauty—something of which his own disciplines accuse him. Or perhaps this episode has a more formal significance. The yogis are not bested but recognized as powerful models. A Sufi poet skillfully asks the leader of the yogis if he may borrow not simply the physical garb of a yogi but the literary garb of the metaphor of yogi, to which the leader Balaknath agrees. Henceforth, Ranjha's quest may be likened to that of a yogi.

And that brings us to a final consideration, also of an intersectarian or interreligious nature. This is the intermixing of the otherwise distinct figures of the *jogī* (one adept in yoga), the *faqīr* (a Muslim ascetic), and the *darveṣ* (an itinerant Sufi). The seemingly muddled language of Waris Shah's *Hīr* explores these differing titles, but to what end? Consider the following passage, in which Ranjha speaks to Balaknath: "*Jogīs*, leaving the world, have become *faqīrs*, for the world has too many traps."[17] Similarly, to dissuade Ranjha from taking up the life of a yogi, Balaknath explains just how arduous it is going to be, albeit in Sufi terms. He says, "By controlling the reins of the horse of patience (*sabr*) through meditation (*zikr*), a *bhujangī* has to kill his *nafs* (lower self)." When Ranjha reaches Rangpur, he tells the pestering girls there that "tigers, snakes, *faqīrs*, cranes, and sparrows have no country they can call their own" and then goes on to proclaim, as if in the same breath, "My caste is that of a *jogī*; I recognize no relations nor family. He who keeps country and caste in mind is a man of the world, not a *darveṣ*."[18] In passages like these it seems that all modes of asceticism converge in the service of Ranjha's universal appeal. He is at once *jogī*, *faqīr*, and *darveṣ*, while all the while he is simply an *āshiq*, that is, a man on the love-journey of *ishq*. Here the title *jogī* simultaneously loses its specific relevance and gains a richer sense by being placed among a set of terms that suggest the wider world of which it is part. For Waris Shah the term *jogī* means something regional—Punjabi—instead of being defined along specific sectarian lines, whether within the Hindu domain or in its relation to ascetics and itinerants who happen to be Muslim or Sikh instead. After all, becoming a *jogī* will allow Ranjha not only access but also due regard when he arrives at the Kheḍā settlement in Rangpur.

This also makes sense in relation to the larger contours of his narrative. Waris Shah is speaking to and of a particular region within the larger Punjab, and his Hir-Ranjha tale assumes and reinforces what Farina Mir calls the "spatial armature" provided by five narratively articulated locations within it.[19] We have Ranjha's village Takht Hazara, Hir's natal village Jhang, Hir's in-laws' home at Rangpur, the Chenab River where their love blossoms, and Tillā Jogiyāṅ, the site of Ranjha's apparent transformation. But there is something further. This is also the region within the Punjab that Waris Shah's *panj-pīr* (the five mentors whom the characters of his *qissā* often invoke) inhabit and help to define. From Pakpattan in the north (the principal site associated with Farid) to Sehwan (Lal Qalandar) in the south and on to the legendary realm of Khwaja Khidr, we encounter a network of well-traveled roads, and these give an element of definition to the range of diverse, if connected, spiritual outpourings and influences that they encompass. To this spiritual armature then, if we may call it so, the trail to Tillā Jogiyāṅ is added. The shared nature of that network is affirmed when Balaknath himself, while letting Ranjha leave, seeks the blessings of the *panj-pīr* to aid Ranjha in his future strivings.

It is this extended spiritual armature that allows us to appreciate the full range of meanings that emerge when Hir sings of her desire to become a yogini in the following *kāfī* attributed to Shah Hussain:

sajan bin rātāṁ hoiyān wadhiyāṁ
rānjha jogī, main jogiyānī, kamlī kar kar sadiyāṁ
mās jhure jhur pinjar hoyā, kadakan lagiyān haḍiyāṁ
main ayāni niyoh ki jaṇā, birhoṅ tanawan gaḍiyāṁ
kahe husain faqīr sāṁī da, laṛ tere main lagiyāṁ

The nights have become long without my beloved.
Since Ranjha became a yogi, I am a yogini. Everywhere people call me crazy.
My flesh is all wrinkled, my bones are a creaking skeleton.
I was too young to understand love, and now as the nights swell and merge,
Says Hussain, the Lord's mendicant, I play host to that unkind guest—the guest of separation.

In this moment of self-articulation, Hir asserts that she has already adopted, in her distinctively feminine way, whatever masculine function Ranjha may take on—here, that of a *jogī*. Yet look at what the acts of a female yogini do: they leave her with wrinkled flesh and creaking bones. This picture of someone who is doing severe ascetic penance goes directly against the typical representation of ideal feminine beauty, which Hir so powerfully represents. As in the case of Mirabai, the Indic trope of representing separation (*viraha*) as an affliction allows for this, making withered beauty its own sort of trope.[20]

Taking on the *jogī*'s attire, or taking on *jog* itself, has become a metaphor through the popularity of Waris Shah's *Hīr* and can be invoked as instantaneously as the figure of Krishna had been in the image of the flute-playing cowherd Ranjha. The mere mention of being a *jogī* is enough to offer transformational power. It gives access to new worlds and possibilities, making proximity possible in separation, and perhaps more than proximity—union (Sufi *tawhīd*). In the end, thus, we have a narrative that does far more than simply using the figure of the yogi as a contrasting device that serves to throw the realm of love, its opposite, into high relief. No, the two mix in far more complicated ways. The amplitude of narrative space allows them not just to coexist but to interpenetrate.

CONCLUSION: THE POWERS OF BHAKTI AND BEYOND

How do we situate these broader-than-bhakti connections in regard to what is normally thought of as bhakti? Consider two sets of verses from Bullhe Shah:

> It is he who is the flute, he who is Krishna, he who is the lord of the Yadavs. . . .
> He has shaved his head and has entranced me in love. He wears cowrie shells in his ears.[21]

> How wonderfully Krishna has played his flute.
> Flute player, herdsman, Ranjha, your notes are shared with everyone. Your delights are my time of gloom. It is you who have mingled my tune with yours.
> Flute player, you call yourself Krishna. You perform so many beautiful hymns. My eyes cannot see you. What a tangled game you have set up.[22]

Kāfī 66, the first I have quoted, makes it plain that the one who has "shaved his head" and "wears cowrie shells"—features we have come to associate with Ranjha in that moment when, dressed as a *jogī*, he arrives in Rangpur—is actually to be understood not as Ranjha this time, but as Krishna. *Kāfī* 104, the second, performs a similar magic, but in the reverse direction: here Ranjha, the flute player, calls himself Krishna. Hearing verses such as these, we see how one master transformation—from Ranjha to *jogī*—has paved the way for many further transformations, at least as they are perceived by his beloved. In the eyes of Hir, whose eyes Bullhe Shah inhabits, the *jogī* who is Ranjha can turn back into the more pleasing form of Krishna. Thus the worlds of bhakti love and the *qissā* feed upon one another.[23]

Scholars have long debated how these multivalent expressions work, emphasizing the nature of authorship, the phenomenon of influence, or the fact of intersectarian relationships. In Bullhe Shah's case, it has been said that a certain "portability" allows him (or multiples of him) to speak to devotees of multiple traditions and sectarian identities.[24] In regard to the image of the yogi, however, we confront instead an ever-widening expressive field of metaphors that work precisely because they retain their specific sectarian charge. The Nath Yogi who stands behind this master metaphor is never forgotten. Krishna's flute becomes even more beguiling precisely because when it sounds, it is as if Ranjha is playing it by the Chenab. Similarly, while the theological import of a "typical" Sikh or Sufi text is to undercut appearances, the appeal of this transgressing *jogī* comes precisely from the misleading appearances that emerge from the central elements of his dress—the ashes, the cloak, the earrings. Finally, as Ranjha completes his narrative journey and comes to be identified in the same moment as both *jogī* and Krishna, he becomes not only Hir's true beloved but one of the magnetic poles of an ever-generative trope of Punjabi literature. This trope is replayed endless times, with countless turns of phrases. Hir models herself in the multitudinous moods of love for Ranjha. The fact that both Krishna *and* Ranjha are implicitly also the archetypical Nath Yogi, shifting back and forth in Hir's field of desire, allows us to identify her as heroine along with Mirabai, while at the same time keeping the two distinct. Such acts of simultaneous stability and transformation are a main feature of what gives literature—and bhakti—its power.

NOTES

1 Hawley and Juergensmeyer, *Songs of the Saints of India*, 139; original in Caturvedī, *Mīrābāī kī Padāvalī, pad* 117.

2 To respect their familiarity in Punjabi, I give these names without diacritics. They are pronounced Hīr and Rānjhā, respectively.

3 Shackle, *Bullhe Shah*, 249.

4 Farina Mir's work on the colonial material archive of the Hir story has convincingly shown the centrality of local and natal affinities and regional identities in the Punjabi literary imagination. See Mir, *Social Space of Language*.

5 Emphasis mine. In addition, Sura 28 of the Qur'an is called Al-Qasas, i.e., "The Stories," a term derived from the same root.

6 Shackle, "Between Scripture and Romance," 158.

7 Usborne's prose translation, *Adventures of Hir and Ranjha*; Sekhon's verse translation, *Love of Hir and Ranjha*.

8 Sufi meanings embedded in the *qissā* genre may also be best appreciated in a wider intertextual context, inclusive of sister-genres like the Indic *premākhyān* and earlier Persian *masnavī*. All of them employ tropes such as *sifat* (praise), *sarāpā* (head-to-toe descriptions), etc. For an analysis of Hindavi Sufi romances, see Behl's *Love's Subtle Magic*.

9 In his essay "Transition and Transformation in Varis Shah's *Hīr*" in Shackle and Snell, *Indian Narrative*, 241–46, Shackle attributes this "transformation" to Waris Shah's poetic skill.

10 Briggs, *Gorakhnāth and the Kānphaṭa Yogīs*, 102.

11 Small shrine-like locations such as the one near Hussein Tekri, those in Faridkot, and those within the premises of the Ajmer Sharif Dargah of Moin ud-din Chishti are all called "Farid tillā" and all point to the idealized significance of penance perfomed by Baba Farid early in the Chishti tradition.

12 Present-day Sialkot (or, the town of the Sials) is located about 125 miles by road from Tillā Jogiyāṅ.

13 The *Sidhāgoṣṭi* is a set of seventy-three verses composed in *rāmkalī rāga* and compiled in *Śrī Gurū Granth Sāhib*, 938–46.

14 The word *mudrā* may work with a double meaning here, both to designate a pose, as in dance or perhaps yoga, and as the Punjabi word for earrings worn in pierced ears.

15 To understand the authorship questions surrounding the *Dasam Granth*, see Singh and Mann, *Granth of Guru Gobind Singh*. Ernst, "Muslim Studies of Hinduism?," 173–95, provides a detailed taxonomy of the *Pool of Nectar* texts, as does the same author's "Islamization of Yoga," 199–226.

16 See Ghaffaar's translation of Damodar, *Heer Damodar*.

17 Verse 259, following the Gurmukhi edition of *Hīr*, edited by Shah Hasan.

18 Verses 264 and 311–14 in the Shah Hasan edition.

19 Mir, *Social Space of Language*, 136.

20 Mirabai beseeches Krishna, whom she identifies with the figure of a wandering yogi, in the following way:

> Yogi! Do not go! . . .
> I shall make a pyre of aloe and sandalwood—light it with your own hand;
> When I am burnt to a heap of ashes, smear them onto your body.

Notice the image of the body turning to ashes. This forecasts the moment of union that occurs when those ashes are smeared on the yogi's body. The translation is by Snell in *Hindi Classical Tradition*, 107 (original in Caturvedī, *Mīrābāī kī Padāvalī*, *pad* 46). For a discussion of the human body as detailed from the perspective of Sufi understandings of Islam, see Kugle, *Sufis and Saints' Bodies*, 2007.

21 Shackle, *Bullhe Shah*, 121, 66:2 and 66:4.

22 Shackle, *Bullhe Shah*, 181, 104:1–3.

23 Poem 66 is also more Braj-inflected than the other *kāfīs*. Later poets such as Khwaja Ghulam Farid also refer to Mohan and Manmohan, familiar terms in

Brajbhasha, and prefer the Braj *muralī* to the Punjabi *vanjhulī* when speaking of the flute.

24 Rinehart, "Portable Bullhe Shah," 53–87. Compare Hawley's chapters on "Author and Authority" and "Mirabai as Wife and Yogi," in Hawley, *Three Bhakti Voices*, 21–47, 117–38; and Asani's "At the Crossroads of Indic and Iranian Civilizations: Sindhi Literary Cultures," in *Literary Cultures in History*, ed. Pollock, 612–46.

CHAPTER NINE

ILLUMINATING THE FORMLESS

God, King, and Devotion in an Assamese Illustrated Manuscript

PHYLLIS GRANOFF

THE British Library is home to an illustrated manuscript of an Assamese verse rendering of the first chapter of the Sanskrit *Brahmavaivarta Purāṇa*.[1] The *Brahmavaivarta Purāṇa* celebrates the divine powers and deeds of Krishna and Radha. The Assamese manuscript, consisting of 210 folios, each measuring 24.5 by 64.5 centimeters, includes 400 paintings and is unquestionably one of the most splendid products of the Vaishnava devotional movement in Assam to have come down to us (fig. 9.1).[2] It illustrates the complexity that can lie behind the creation of a devotional poem and its visual representation. In this manuscript we can see diverse influences, in India from the contemporary textiles of Muslim courts in the Deccan to Jain manuscripts from distant Gujarat, and beyond India, to medical illustrations from Tibet. The complexity of this manuscript is not just in its visual language, however; in the additions that the Assamese author made to the Sanskrit text he has also produced a multifaceted document that is both devotional text and political statement, a hymn to god and the king, Purandara Sinha, for whom he composed his poem.

The composition of bhakti texts in Assamese begins in the fifteenth century with the great Assamese religious leader Śaṃkaradeva (1449–1568) and his followers.[3] Śaṃkaradeva's literary output was prodigious; he translated into Assamese major Sanskrit texts such as the *Bhāgavata Purāṇa* and *Rāmāyaṇa* and composed numerous dramas in Assamese on Vaishnava themes. His many devotional poems remain central to the liturgy of Assamese Vaishnava ritual today. Śaṃkaradeva also wrote a treatise on devotion to Krishna, the *Bhaktiratnākara*, which is a compilation of verses from the *Bhāgavata* and other Purāṇas, embellished with his own Sanskrit commentary. Śaṃkaradeva's

9.1 *Brahmavaivarta Purāṇa*, Folio 142b, illustrated by Durgārāma Betha, 1836. British Library, used by permission of Granger

contributions to Assamese religion and culture were not limited, however, to these remarkable writings. In the many texts that describe his life and deeds, Śaṃkaradeva is also depicted as a pioneer in creating visual representations of the life and deeds of the god Krishna. One of his major works was a woven silk tapestry depicting scenes from the life of Krishna. Commissioned by a prince in 1565 CE, it took a year to complete and was the start of a long tradition of silk weavings on the life of Krishna. Śaṃkaradeva is described as superintending every aspect of the tapestry's production. Fragments of this so-called Vrindavani Vastra, probably an altar cloth, may still exist; many examples were preserved as the cloth backing to Tibetan tankas.[4]

The study of manuscripts like the Assamese *Brahmavaivarta Purāṇa* is complicated by two factors. One is undoubtedly beyond remedy; this is the rarity with which such manuscripts have been preserved. The second is potentially surmountable; so many illustrated manuscripts are held in the Vaishnava monasteries or *sattras* and remain inaccessible. In any case, however, it seems clear that the British Library *Brahmavaivarta* manuscript is exceptional both in its style and quality. It is written on the usual material employed in Assam, *sāñcipāt*, a writing material prepared from the bark of the aloeswood tree. The manuscript is dated 1836 CE and unusually names both the scribe, Jādurāma Chāṅgakākatī, and the painter, Durgārāma Betha. In fact there are clearly two different hands discernable in the written text. This Assamese version of the *Brahmavaivarta*, composed by a poet named Durgācārya, is known only from this one manuscript.

At the end of each chapter the poet has added fulsome praises of his royal patron, and the illustrator has provided royal portraits and scenes from courtly life. The quality of the painting and the presence of so many verbal and visual depictions of the king suggest a royal audience. Indeed the poet at the end of the royal panegyrics often directly addresses the court, calling upon them to listen to the deeds of Krishna and recite his name.

The closest parallel to the *Brahmavaivarta* manuscript is an illustrated manuscript of the *Dharmapurāṇa*, also in the British Library.[5] Made a century before the *Brahmavaivarta*, this manuscript similarly opens with a verbal and painted portrait of the king who was the poet's patron, but the body of the text quickly takes over. Praise of the king occurs again only at the end of the text. This highlights the unusual nature of the *Brahmavaivarta*, in which so much attention is given to the royal patron in words and paintings.

Like most if not all handwritten manuscripts, the *Brahmavaivarta* manuscript is not free from mistakes. Some folios repeat the text of the immediately preceding folios and have been entirely crossed out. Sometimes the text and illustration are out of sync; a folio may mistakenly repeat the text of an earlier folio, and is therefore a mistake, but the illustration is correct in that it corresponds to the text that the folio should have had. Illustrator and copyist are thus clearly working independently of each other.

Often the details of the descriptive passages of the text are not depicted in the illustration. For example, although the text describes the god Śiva as five-headed and naked, in the illustrations the god has one head and is clothed in a tiger skin. He also does not carry the attributes named in the text, the trident, ax, and rosary. Similarly, the Goddess of Learning, Sarasvatī, in her illustration does not correspond to her textual description; in the text she has her usual attributes, the lute or *vīṇā* and the book, but in the illustration she is without them. One can assume that these depictions of Śiva and Sarasvatī correspond to visual images that were well known to the illustrator, who retains a great degree of independence in his work.

The manuscript illustrations for this *Brahmavaivarta* are incomplete. Several folios have the illustrations barely sketched in, while others have only the text, with the area designated for the illustration still blank. These incomplete folios tell us that the text was written first, with space carefully left for the folio to be illustrated later. One cannot help but conclude that the failure to complete the manuscript is a reflection of the sad fate of the ruler who figures so prominently in the text, King Purandara Sinha, who was deposed for a final time shortly after this manuscript was made.

By carefully comparing text to image and Assamese text to the Sanskrit original we can learn much about the practice of different types of translation in late medieval India. There are two tasks of translation at work in this manuscript. The first is the translation from Sanskrit into Assamese, and the second is the translation of the written text into visual images. When the Assamese rendering differs from the Sanskrit text it is difficult to know for certain if this is a choice of the translator or if the translator had a slightly different Sanskrit version than the published Sanskrit text that we have today. Purāṇas are notoriously labile texts. Translations of Sanskrit texts into vernacular languages exhibit a wide range in their fidelity to the source text.[6]

I highlight two distinctive features of this manuscript as a translation. The first is the abundant references to current politics and the long royal panegyrics, accompanied by illustrations. The royal panegyrics and paintings of the king and his court transform the purely devotional source text into a text of devotion to the king as well as the god Krishna. In addition, the text is further localized in Assam by the poet, when he supplies the specific names of Assamese tribal groups where the Sanskrit text had only generic terms. The second feature that stands out is in the translation from text to image. The illustrator takes great pains to render visible what is abstract in the language of the text.

This is particularly striking in the illustrations of the creation narratives. Two significant aspects are the attention to the unique Assamese setting of this manuscript, specifically to the king and his court, and the ways in which the painter has concretized the abstract language and concepts of the text.

PURANDARA SINHA AND HIS COURT

The nineteenth century was a tumultuous time in Assam. There was an invasion by the Burmese in 1816 and then by the British. Purandara Sinha had ascended to the throne of Assam in 1818, but his rule was short-lived. He was ousted by a pro-Burmese faction. Although he was restored to the throne in 1832, he was able to rule for only six more years before he was again removed from the throne. The manuscript, written in 1836, thus belongs to the brief period when Purandara Sinha ruled over Assam, his reduced territory no doubt in a situation of deep insecurity. One of the praise sections to the king even prays that he might recover his kingdom. This wish is perhaps optimistically positioned at the end of a long description of various powerful mantras that grant all of one's wishes. Every chapter of the Assamese text in this manuscript ends with a praise of the king and an illustration of his many activities, including his leisure pursuits.

The manuscript begins with two sections that are not found in the Sanskrit text, a short hymn to Krishna and a much longer account of King Purandara Sinha and his ancestors.[7] Only once this has been completed does the poet begin his actual verse rendering of the *Brahmavaivarta Purāṇa*. This dual opening tells us at once that Durgācārya's poem is many things: a vernacular rendering of a Sanskrit devotional text, a royal panegyric, and a potent prayer to Krishna that cannot be disengaged from the poet's fervent desire for the welfare of the Ahom dynasty.

The glorification of King Purandara Sinha and his lineage employs formulaic language clearly derived from Sanskrit panegyrics found in both inscriptions and literary texts in medieval India. The list of kings begins with Rudra Sinha. He is likened to the epic heroes Duryodhana in his pride and Karṇa in his generosity. The moon of his glory still shines. He ruled from the city of Ratnapura, where all the subjects lived happily. His son was Rājeśvara Sinha, who was like unto Indra, king of the gods, and in beauty to Kāma, the god of love. In figure 9.2, King Rājeśvara Sinha is shown seated in his palace. A servant seated behind him holds a fly whisk while two figures sit slightly bowed before him, one of them holding a flower. Outside the palace sit retainers with swords and shields. The illustration is remarkably detailed, an excellent example of the refinement and skill of these paintings. It is night, and the moon and stars shine at the corner of the painting. Great care has been taken in rendering the palace walls, with their finely wrought decorations of swirls and flowers. The painter has also differentiated the retainers by skin color, as if to emphasize that the king ruled over all of Assam with its many different peoples. The poet continues describing Purandara Sinha's ancestors, and the painter depicts each of them in carefully individualized portraits.

The poet reserves his most lavish praise and ornate language for the description of his patron Purandara Sinha. In one section he offers a series of elaborate metaphors to describe the glory of this king, which reaches even to the heavenly realm and thence to every place in the universe, where it remains forever. The metaphors rely on several tropes that are standard in Sanskrit poetry. The first is that glory is white; the second is that rivers are feminine. This king's glory is said to be a flock of white doves that fly to the city of the gods, where they rest on the breast of the heavenly river, the Goddess Ganges. They swallow up all the pearls that make up her necklace until their stomachs are full and then fly throughout the universe, spitting out the pearls that they have swallowed. These pearls become the stars that shine eternally. The illustrator, not to be outdone by the poet, has just as vividly given us a pictorial metaphor. In the poem, the birds, ladies, and stars are readily understood as part of an extended figure of speech that magnifies the king's all-pervasive fame; but the painter faced a challenge in making the viewer grasp that the birds, ladies, and stars of his painting have an extended meaning that supplants the literal. It took him two illustrations to do this, on folios 6a and b. Both of these folios have two illustrations; a smaller illustration at the left, illustrating the metaphor, and a larger illustration at the right, depicting the king in his palace. The first folio sets the scene; it depicts the River Ganges, with three lovely heavenly maidens bathing in it. Their translucent garments have been painted with great care. Above each of the ladies is a flowering plant; this painter delights in painting flowers, to which he always imparts a sense of motion in their curving leaves. A curtain of clouds frames the scene and echoes the undulating waves of the river. In the second illustration of the metaphor (fig. 9.3), we see the birds spitting out the pearls that they have gathered, thereby creating the stars, and metaphorically scattering the fame of the king throughout the universe.

In each of these folios the painter gives his viewers a clue that we must look beyond the concrete figures of the river, the birds and the pearls to the king himself if we are properly to read this illustration. He does so by juxtaposing an even larger illustration of the king with the illustrations of the metaphor.

9.2 *Brahmavaivarta Purāṇa*, Folio 3b. King Rājeśvara Sinha seated in his palace. British Library, used by permission of Granger

9.3 *Brahmavaivarta Purāṇa*, Folio 6b. Praise of King Purandara Sinha comparing his fame to white pearls. British Library, used by permission of Granger

But in the second illustration, in which the birds spit out their pearls (fig. 9.3), he does something more. The king sits in the top story of his palace, as is customary in the royal illustrations. He is accompanied by his usual retinue but one of the retainers does something unusual. Instead of looking at the king or another figure in the palace, one retainer who is seated in front of the stairs leading to the king's chamber turns away from the king to look outside the illustration and across the text at the painting of the ladies and the birds. It is almost as if he has heard the poet's words and wants to see for himself how the king's fame spreads like the stars across the heavens. This subtle gesture brilliantly draws the text and the illustrations together, helping to close the gap between the written words and the painted image.

This is not the only example of a painted metaphor. In the actual opening of the *purāṇic* text, following the long genealogy of Purandara Sinha, we are told that the sage Vyāsa composed the *Purāṇa* by milking the goddess Sarasvatī, as one might milk a wishing cow. He uses the Vedas, which are like her calf. In figure 9.4, we see the sage Vyāsa milking a cow while a calf looks on. The figures are set in an almost surreal landscape with a giant butterfly and fantastically colored bird flying above them. Like the metaphor of the birds and pearls, this one too relies on images that were well known: that the Goddess of Speech is like a fabulous cow that can be milked by the learned. But if the words of the text are readily understood, that was not necessarily the case with the illustration, which may very well have been a picture of someone milking a cow. But again, the painter has guided the viewer to the correct interpretation of the milking scene as metaphor. The illustration on the next folio depicts the *purāṇic* reciter, Sauti, telling the story of Krishna to the sages assembled in the forest, letting us know that the "milk" was the sacred text that is about to commence.

Not all the metaphors in the poem are illustrated. Each chapter of the poem closes with a praise of the king, and these praise passages are enlivened by carefully chosen metaphors that are themselves strikingly visual. In one passage the king's glory is likened to the Ganges River, something we have already met, but the metaphor is given a different twist. The infamy of the king's enemies becomes the Yamunā River, which is described as dark in classical Sanskrit poetry. They meet in battle, which is likened to the holy place Prayāga, the confluence of the Ganges and the Yamunā in present-day Allahabad. Valiant heroes bathe in the waters of the battleground and gain heaven, just as those who bathe at Prayāga do (folio 52b).

The illustrations of the king and his court are similar, with often subtle variations. Two show the king with his falcons, similar enough that having seen one we find the other familiar, but different enough to retain our attention.

9.4 *Brahmavaivarta Purāṇa*, Folio 10b. Vyāsa composes the *Purāṇa*, milking the goddess Sarasvatī as one milks a cow. British Library, used by permission of Granger

9.5 *Brahmavaivarta Purāṇa*, Folio 82b. Capturing elephants for the king. British Library, used by permission of Granger

Elephants figure often in the royal illustrations; one even shows the capture of elephants (fig. 9.5). The keeping of elephants was a royal prerogative. Given the role of the British in Assamese affairs, it is not surprising to find British officers depicted as in this folio. In addition to the praise poems and illustrations at the end of each chapter, in an unfinished section of the manuscript, the poet has even provided a summary of the history of Assam around the time of Purandara, detailing the invasion of the Burmese and the chaos that resulted (folio 200).

While it is not unusual for a poet to praise his patron, the amount of attention lavished on the king and his court in this manuscript is distinctive. I have given here only a sample of the illustrations and the poetry, but hopefully they are sufficient to make clear that this is a text of devotion to both king and god, a celebration of kingly as well as divine deeds.

GIVING FORM TO THE FORMLESS

We have already seen how the painter of this manuscript delighted in rendering concrete the abstraction of metaphors. He did so by depicting not the abstract quality, the fame of the king or the process of creation of the text by the Vedic sage, but by painting the concrete entities with which these abstractions were compared: white birds, the act of milking a cow. There are several places in the text, however, where the painter tackled head-on the problem of representing that which is beyond representation. The first examples are at the opening of the manuscript, in the praise poem to Krishna. The poet praises the god as the ultimate reality in language with which we are familiar from Vedānta philosophy: God is existence, consciousness and bliss; He consists of pure knowledge; God is the cause of everything but himself without cause; He is one without a second. Krishna is not the material cause, the *pradhāna*, or the individual soul, the *puruṣa* of the Sāmkhya. The poet goes on with a list of what Krishna is not; Krishna is neither existent nor nonexistent. Krishna as the absolute reality and ground of all existence is beyond the realm of speech and thought, without characteristics. This absolute is what remains after all else is negated; it is known from the Vedas only by means of denying what it is not. It is on account of ignorance of this ultimate reality that the world appears to exist, like the illusion of a snake in a rope, like a mirage of water in the hot shining sun of midday. Krishna is radiant light, pure, bliss. The poet's devotion in this prayer is as much to this formless absolute as it is to the forms that emerge from the absolute as the prayer progresses.

The painter surely faced a challenge in translating what is beyond form into visual imagery, which by definition seems to demand form. But he has not shied away from the task. Here is what he has done. He has depicted God as the formless absolute reality as a luminous mass; its sentience is conveyed by the fact that this glowing entity is also a seeing eye (fig. 9.6).

There are other places in the text in which the painter has lent visual form to such abstract notions of the divine. In another passage in the text that describes the formless absolute, the absolute is described as pure light, round in shape, as bright as a million million suns that blaze at the peak of the hot season. In figure 9.7, instead of the seeing eye, the painter has given the large orb a bright red center. That this is the sun in the sky is made clear by the small cloud border to its side. As if to illustrate the creative potential of the absolute, the painter has given us a disk that pulsates with energy. It casts off its rays, streaks of white and red, in every direction. Again we see how the painter has used swirling vegetation to convey motion. The painter's sun is perhaps an even more powerful rendering of the abstract absolute than the words of the text. The striking visual image seems to confirm that the absolute cannot be conveyed by words at the same time as it suggests that it can be known by the painterly imagination.

The text has several accounts of how creation proceeds, beginning with this absolute that splits into Krishna and Radha. In one account Krishna was struck by the god of love and let his semen fall. Embarrassed in the presence of the other gods, he cast his sperm into the waters. After a thousand years it turned into a child. This is the Virāt, the support of all things. It lay there in the waters. From its ear wax arose two demons, who attacked the god Brahmā. Vishnu killed them, and their fat became the earth. The myth is familiar; the illustrations surprise. Virāṭ is an idea, the abstract support of the universe, and the painter indicates as much, giving it some form, the head, and abstract shapes for the rest of the body. The demons are of course fully developed, and we see them walking out of the water, which is a translucent covering of the back of the brown demon (fig. 9.8). This painter in fact excels in painting demons, who often add a comic touch to the illustrations.

Like this one, many of the illustrations accompany the myths that the *Purāṇa* retells. Hopefully the manuscript will be published someday in full. This is a unique manuscript, and I have only touched on its riches. It is a text of devotion to god and king. Even the devotion to Krishna that has inspired the text is twofold; it is devotion to an ultimate formless reality and to the Krishna of myth and images. And it is a remarkably creative synthesis of written word and visual image. This is not a workshop production; there is an animating intelligence behind the sophisticated painted images that make them distinctive among illustrations to *Purāṇa* texts.

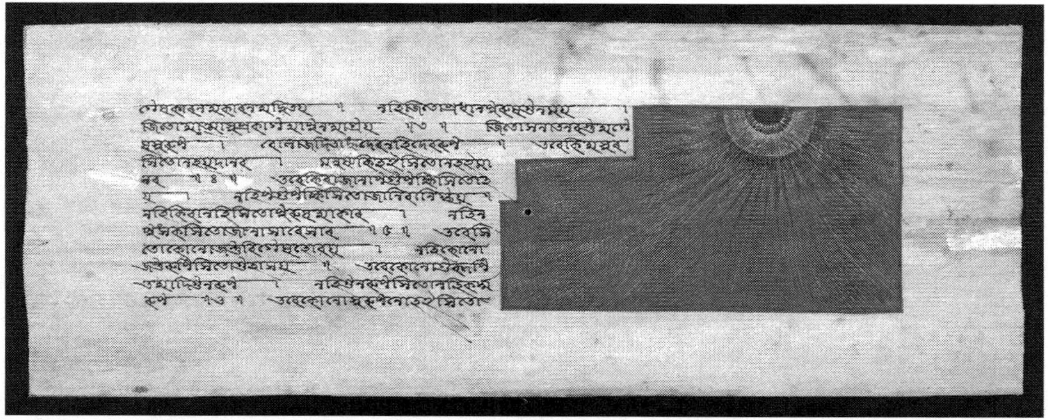

9.6 *Brahmavaivarta Purāṇa*, Folio 1b. The highest reality as consciousness. British Library, used by permission of Granger

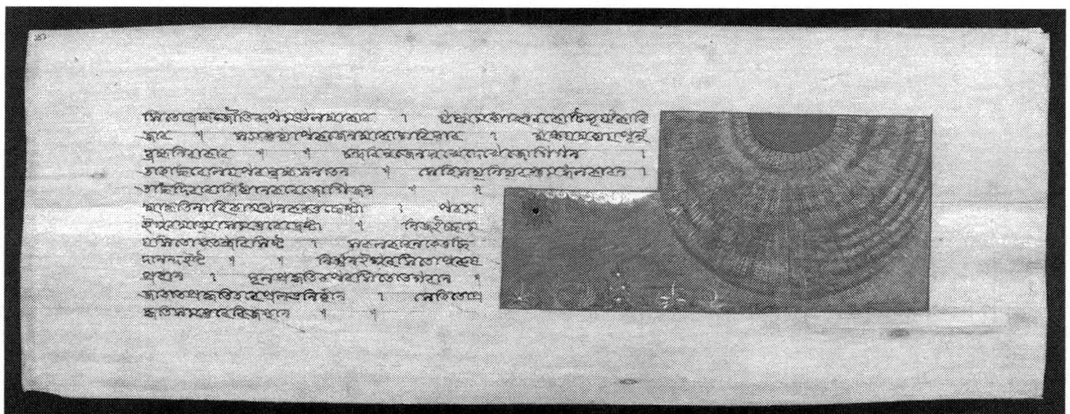

9.7 *Brahmavaivarta Purāṇa*, Folio 181a. The formless absolute as light. British Library, used by permission of Granger

9.8 *Brahmavaivarta Purāṇa*, Folio 34a. Creation. British Library, used by permission of Granger

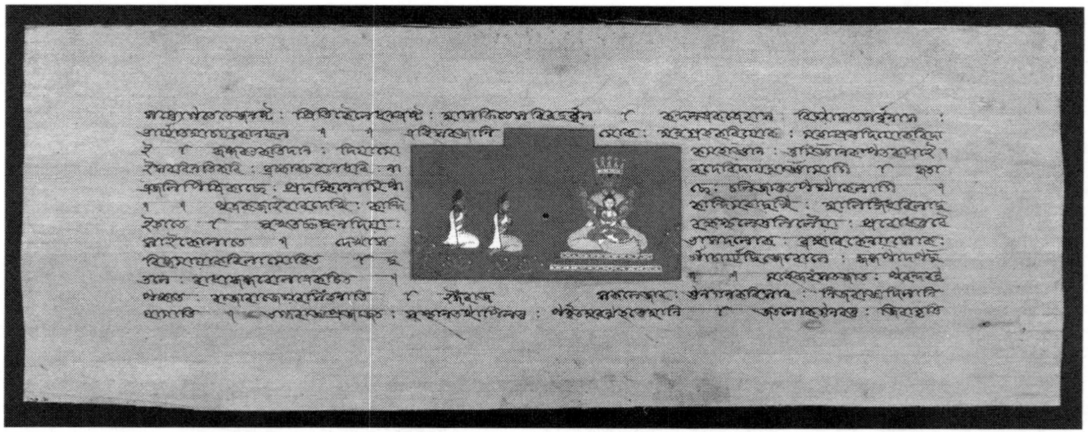

9.9 *Brahmavaivarta Purāṇa*, Folio 164b. Nārada in the lap of Brahmā. British Library, used by permission of Granger

Anyone familiar with Assamese manuscript paintings will be struck at once by the singularity of this manuscript. There is nothing even remotely like it in the corpus of Assamese painting. What then might have been its sources? Śaṃkaradeva is said to have made a tapestry depicting the deeds of Krishna, and this may be an important clue to some of the sources of the painting in this manuscript. The exuberance of the floral patterns in the manuscript are reminiscent of textiles. The use of flowers and animals to fill in the background is also associated with textiles and painting from Gujarat.[8]

The flowers in our paintings are not the only echo from distant lands. An illustration of diseases on folio 128b is remarkably close to similar illustrations in Tibetan medical manuscripts. We know that there was considerable Tibetan interest in Assamese textiles; several recovered fragments thought to be Śaṃkaradeva's original Vrindavani Vastra were found as tanka backings in Tibet. The depiction of diseases on this folio suggests Assamese interest in things Tibetan as well. And we need to keep in mind that the Assamese considered Tibet as under Assamese control; the Tibetans are one of the many tribes of Assam listed in the creation stories in this Assamese version of the *Brahmavaivarta*.

The parallels to the textiles open up further possibilities. Rosemary Crill noted that most silk weavers in India trace their origins back to Gujarat. She noted that the migration of weavers from Gujarat can explain certain technical features of weaving in Assam. The connection to Gujarat is intriguing. A schematic representation of Krishna's world, Goloka, is strikingly similar to Jain cosmic diagrams so familiar from large paintings in Gujarat and the many illustrated texts that describe the cosmos. It is difficult not to recall Jain manuscripts in which such cosmic diagrams abound. An equally striking reminder of Jain illustrations is on folio 164b, in a story about the sage Nārada. Brahmā holds Nārada on his lap. Anyone who has ever seen a Jain *Kalpa Sūtra* manuscript from Gujarat, I think, could not fail to make the connection between this tiny Nārada and the image of the Jina on Indra's lap (figs. 9.9 and 9.10).

This manuscript is a remarkably complex document. It belongs obviously to pan-Indian devotional art as an illustrated *Purāṇa* and to both *nirguṇa* and *saguṇa bhakti*; it is also a political statement, a praise of Assamese kings at a time when their rule was threatened and would indeed soon end. Artistically, it is similar to textiles, and through textiles and the Gujarati community of weavers, to Jain manuscript illustrations. Assamese textiles were treasured in Tibet, and I believe we can also discern the influence of Tibetan illustrations here. I hope the sheer beauty of this manuscript will lead others to explore its many secrets.

9.10 *Kalpa Sūtra*, undated, from Patan, Gujarat. The Jina Mahāvīra in the lap of Indra. Brooklyn Museum 1994.11. Used by permission of the Brooklyn Museum

NOTES

1 Or. 11387.

2 The manuscript has been discussed and partly illustrated by Losty, *Art of the Book*, 140–41. He has also illustrated a few folios in Losty, *Krishna*. One folio is given prominence as the cover illustration of this booklet. L. D. Barnett wrote a brief description of this manuscript and the manuscript of the Assamese *Dharmapurāṇa* when they first came to the British Library in Barnett, "Two Illustrated Assamese Manuscripts." My account of the reign of King Purandara Sinha, the royal patron of the manuscript, follows Losty, *Art of the Book*, 140.

3 Neog's *Early History of the Vaishnava Faith* remains the main source of information about Śaṃkaradeva and his work.

4 Crill, *Fabric of India*, 89, plate 65; Crill, "Vrindavani Vastra." The British Museum held an exhibit focused on the Vrindavani Vastra from January 21 to August 15, 2016.

5 Or. 11386.

6 This is of course not unique to Indian texts and can be observed in Europe as well, where, for example, German translators in the Middle Ages would often embellish their French original. Starkey, *Reading the Medieval Book*, 40.

7 The Sanskrit text I have used is Apte, *Brahmavaivartapurāṇa*.

8 Crill, *Fabric of India*, 157.

CHAPTER TEN

BHAKTI AS RELATIONSHIP

Drawing Form and Personality from the Formless

DAVID L. HABERMAN

HISTORICALLY bhakti has been translated into English as "devotion" and has not infrequently been understood in terms of faith, particularly in earlier writings that betray the dominance of Protestant perspectives in the comparative study of religions. The historian of religion Rudolf Otto, for example, wrote of Hindu bhakti: "The similarities present here are so important that it is tempting to consider this religion, viewed from the outside, as a sort of duplicate on Indian soil of that religion which emerged from Palestine and which we call Christianity. . . . the spiritual inheritance which has come down to us Protestants through Luther and the Reformation is *the doctrine of salvation by faith alone*."[1] The assertion that bhakti is a Christian-like spiritualized faith that has little to do with action was supported by many other early scholars and can still be heard today. But what is left out of this seemingly irenic comparison? Bhakti—at least in the form of Braj Vaishnavism—is better seen as the pursuit of a *relationship* through particular *cultural practices*, specifically those that involve worshipful interaction with *embodied forms* of divinity. To represent bhakti as "faith alone" falls far short of the reality.

A crucial concept I have frequently encountered in my own investigations of bhakti, both textually and ethnographically, is *bhāva*, best translated in this context as "love." Love is both an inner state and an external action, but most important here, love is about relationship and embodiment. This assertion has found recent support in Barbara Holdrege's book *Bhakti and Embodiment*; while presenting an understanding of bhakti in terms of embodiment she observes that bhakti is "first and foremost about relationships."[2] Indeed it is, as I learned in my early study of Rūpa Gosvāmī's *Bhaktirasāmṛtasindhu*,

Holdrege's central text.[3] There bhakti as *bhāva* (or more precisely *sthāyi-bhāva* for Rūpa) is characterized as the result of a relationship between the divine "object" of love, the *viṣaya*, and the worshipful "vessel" of love, the *āśraya*. Importantly, a vital ingredient in this ultimate relationship is embodiment or form (*rūpa*). Although the specific appearances of the divine *viṣaya* and *bhakta* or "devotee" as *āśraya* are mutually shape-shifting as the powerful connectivity of relationship develops, the essential element is embodiment. In short, bhakti is love that establishes, nurtures, participates in, and celebrates an ultimate relationship with some embodied form of divinity. But what kind of form is most conducive to relational bhakti?

That important foundational text for bhakti, the *Bhagavad Gītā*, has much to say about this—particularly in the eleventh chapter. This chapter opens with Arjuna realizing the inadequacy of his assumption that Krishna could be fully accounted for by means of the particular form through which he had appeared to encounter Arjuna—as his friend and the driver of his chariot. This way of understanding Krishna was misleadingly incomplete; he therefore requests Krishna to take off the limited mask of particularity and show his *aiśvara rūpa*—his limitless, imperishable, unmanifest majestic form. Krishna obliges him by revealing his universal form *viśva-rūpa* as the infinity of all forms situated in a single place (*eka-stha*). From the perspective of human perception there is no difference between everything and nothing—consider colorless white light (nothing) in which all colors (everything) are simultaneously present but become visible only when differentiated into singularity—and indeed this "form" of Krishna is identified as *akṣara Brahman*,[4] the all-pervasive, formless, unchanging dimension of divinity. Arjuna gains an important kind of knowledge from this revelation, but he also expresses increasing alarm that he is now disoriented and finds no peace, no means of approach, and no intimacy or loving connection with his former friend. The *viśva-rūpa* is too much! It's too vast and too amorphous. And too frightening; it is called the *ugra-rūpa*, or "terrible form."[5] Arjuna thus requests Krishna to replace his mask of particularity and resume a form that allows personal relationship—as a father to a son, a friend to a friend, or a beloved to a lover.[6] Specifically, Arjuna asks Krishna to return once again to the friendly form that had yielded their affectionate relationship, which of course will differ from *bhakta* to *bhakta*. Importantly, the form that produces the most intimate relationship is identified as a "familiar human form," the *saumya mānuṣa rūpa*. The special form that allows peaceful approach and connective relationship, moreover, is called Krishna's "own-form," *sva-rūpa*.[7]

How, we might ask, is the pursuit of an intimate relationship via a *saumya mānuṣa rūpa* put into actual practice? The worship of Mount Govardhan, the famous sacred hill located in the heart of the pilgrimage region of Braj in north-central India, provides a vivid answer. This rocky hill is regarded as a direct and visibly present (*sākṣāt*) form of Krishna; moreover, it is understood to be one of the most approachable and loving embodied forms of Krishna. Braj Vaishnavism is a religious culture that aims for an intimate relationship (*sambandha*) with Krishna through worshipful interaction with his embodied forms, and Mount Govardhan has long been considered one of the most significant and available forms of Krishna for establishing such a relationship. But how is one to establish and maintain an intimate relationship with something as large as a mountain? By global standards Mount Govardhan is not a huge mountain; nonetheless, it is difficult to have intimate interaction with the entire seven-mile long mountain. Although devotees can and do have worshipful engagements with the mountain as a whole, much more intimate connections are achieved with individual stones from the mountain typically called Girirāj *śilās*, which are all considered to be non-different from the entire mountain. Human nature is such that our most intense emotional bonds are with particular individuals. Universal love is a noble notion, but the love that seems to overwhelm and rivet us is the passionate love for a specific person. Size and particularity are significant in matters of intimacy, and a Govardhan stone is much more wieldy and human scaled than the entire mountain. The love affair with the mountainous form of Krishna, then, is typically expressed and experienced with a particular stone of a size that can easily be handled. A woman who maintains a shrine for a Girirāj *śilā* in her home near the mountain told me the stone should be about the size of your heart.

The accessibility, tangibility, and manageability of the mountain god in the form of a particular stone all lead to greater and more intimate devotional interaction, which in turn leads to closer relationships. A woman who worships a Girirāj stone in a shrine within her house informed me: "Worship of a single *śilā* is equivalent to worship of the entire mountain. There are many, many *śilās* here at Govardhan. One can worship any one of them. They are all essential forms (*svarūpas*) of Krishna."[8] Yes, but why do you worship a single stone instead of the whole mountain?

> Because I can perform loving service (*sevā*) to this one stone much more easily than to the whole mountain. I can bathe it with milk and water, I can massage its body with scented oils, I can dress it with fine clothes, I can feed it tasty sweets, and I can even put it to bed at night. I can't do that to the whole mountain. And it is by doing these acts of *sevā* to a single stone rather than worshiping the entire mountain that I experience a stronger connection (*mazbūt*

sambandha) with Govardhan as a whole. For these reasons we worship an individual Girirāj *śilā*.

Although it has decisively negative connotations in most Hindu ascetic traditions, here the concept of "myness" (*mamatā*) takes a positive turn. A man who worships a Girirāj stone in his home every day explained: "There are many Girirāj *śilās* on this mountain, but *this one is mine*. This is the one with which I have developed a close relationship (*sambandha*). For me it is very special." A woman who maintains a Girirāj stone in her home shrine confirmed this view, offering a familiar illustration: "There are many men in the world who are husbands, but the one who lives in this house is *my* husband. Likewise, there are many Girirāj *śilās*, but this one [gesturing to the Girirāj stone in her home shrine] is mine." A sense of ownership in the interaction with an individual stone is productive, for a sense of possession nurtures intimacy. The Hindi word for intimate is *ātmīya*. When one acquires an individual Girirāj stone and interacts with it in loving service (*sevā*), it becomes *ātmīya* in two senses: it becomes "intimate" as well as "one's own."[9] One of the double meanings of *svarūpa*—a term used frequently to refer to a particular Girirāj stone—is "one's *own* form [of divinity]." A priest in one of the temples located in the town of Jatipura on the edge of the mountain explained it this way: "A deep worshipful connection with Govardhan depends on a personal relationship with an individual *śilā* that is one's own. There has to be *mamatā*, a sense of 'myness.'" *Mamatā* or myness, then, is an essential element for the loving acts (*sevā*) that lead to deep connection, and is frequently—though not exclusively—associated with a motherly love. The *svarūpa* is "one's own form," just as the child or paramour we love most is considered to be "our own," as in "this is *my* beloved." The sense of ownership or myness, then, is an important ingredient in the close relationship that approaches the whole through a particular.

But perhaps most important of all ingredients in the connective relationship (*sambandha*) with a Girirāj stone is what I label "intentional anthropomorphism" (in contrast to the "unconscious anthropomorphism" articulated by Stewart Guthrie).[10] This returns us to the *mānuṣa rūpa* of the *Gītā*. A good friend and esteemed teacher Shrivatsa Goswami, a priest in the famous Rādhāramaṇa Krishna temple and knowledgeable scholar of Krishna Vaishnava philosophy and practice, told me in his Vrindavan ashram: "Our predicament is that we are in human form, so for us the most familiar form is human, and that's what we connect with most intimately." This means that the formless must be given welcoming form and familiar personality, or perhaps in other words, the aniconic must become an anthropomorphic icon. The catchphrase that I have come to rely on while thinking about the worshipful interaction

with Girirāj stones is: "The devotional tendency is to draw out form and personality from the formless." This statement was articulated by Shrivatsa in another one of our productive conversations, in which he continued as follows:

> This is the key to achieving an intimate connection with any form of God. You have to understand the way of personal adoration of the Lord within Vaishnava Hinduism. People worship in their own way, through their own relationship. They turn the aniconic into an iconic form of Krishna, they give form (*rūpa*) to the formless (*arūpa*). *Bhaktas* need something tangible. They need *saguṇa* ("with qualities") and *sākāra* ("with form"). Girirāj is not fully *saguṇa* or *sākāra*, so the devotees complete the process by making the *saguṇa* and *sākāra* aspects more fully manifest. They add eyes, ornaments, clothing, and sometimes even arms to the Girirāj stones. They bring out qualities and form more fully through this technique and draw out the full personality. This makes it easier to see the stone as Krishna and Krishna as the stone. Personal form is the source and foundation of the relationship (*sambandha*) with God. As the *Gītā* says, it is not really possible to have a relationship with the formless.

10.1 (*far left*) Decorated Girirāj stone on Mount Govardhan. Photo by David Haberman

10.2 (*center*) Girirāj stone with added eyes in a home shrine. Photo by David Haberman

10.3 (*near left*) Girirāj stone embellished with a full body. Photo by David Haberman

Key points in this statement are giving form to the formless, personality, and relationship. Giving familiar form to the formless with the aid of anthropomorphic features—or turning the aniconic into the iconic—draws out the personality of a Govardhan stone, and this in turn is the key to establishing a significant relationship.

What this means in practice is that it is commonplace to augment a Girirāj *śilā* with the addition of human-like facial features and ornate clothing, particularly in the context of home shrines (figs. 10.1–3). Again, this is all for the enhancement of the ultimate relationship. "The adornment of a Govardhan stone amplifies the divine presence (*svarūpa*) of the stone," Shrivatsa explained on another occasion; "it is always there, but the ornamentation—especially the eyes—makes it more fully manifest and perceptible, and this is the key to a close relationship with God in this form." The anthropomorphic embellishment, then, is not only a way of honoring a stone as a divine person and drawing out its personality; Govardhan stone worshipers report that the addition of the face and subsequent acts of love (*sevā*), such as personal food offerings, make stronger and more intimate relationship or connection (*sambandha*) possible with Krishna as Govardhan.

Other worshipers of Mount Govardhan affirmed these views. Standing before a decorated stone, one explained: "When people decorate a Girirāj *śilā* and worship it, the personality (*svarūpa*) comes out. Look, there are many

Girirāj *śilās* here, but the personality is really showing itself in this one because people have added eyes and decorated and worshiped it." One *bābā* residing at the sacred Rādhākuṇḍ pond had this to say: "When you put eyes and a face on a Girirāj *śilā* you feel it is a person (*vyakti*). It's easier to see the stone as a person with the face and clothing added. Dressing a Girirāj *śilā* with eyes, face, jewelry, and clothing makes the presence of the personality more evident. If a stone with no decoration is next to a fully decorated one, your eyes will immediately go to the decorated stone. Putting eyes and other ornamentations on a stone makes its personality more perceptible. This makes strong relationship (*sambandha*) with the essential form (*svarūpa*) more possible."

A woman I came to know who is very devoted to the Govardhan stone in her home shrine expressed the resulting presence of personality in a more sensorial way: "When you put eyes on a Girirāj *śilā* you can communicate with it. Since he has had eyes my stone talks to me; and because of this I have become very close to him." The connective value of the human form is confirmed in the *Bhāgavata Purāṇa*, which explains, for example: "Assuming a human body (*mānuṣa deha*) for the beneficial assistance of people, Krishna engages in various playful activities so that people become attracted to him."[11] Krishna's assumption of human form is an act of divine grace (*anugraha*) intended to enhance relational connectivity with human beings. Establishing a deep connection or relationship (*sambandha*) with Krishna is one way of expressing the goal of the Vaishnava religious culture associated with the worship of Mount Govardhan. And worshipers assert that anthropomorphic form effectively aids in establishing and nurturing this relationship. This is bhakti. It is much more than Otto's spiritualized faith; here are cultural practices involving embodied interaction with a welcoming form of divinity. And in the end, relationship—intimate interactive connection with Brahman in the form of the irresistibly attractive Supreme Personality, Pūrṇa Puruṣottama Krishna, that leads to participation in the *prema-ānanda-līlā* ("the Play of the Bliss of Love")—is what Braj bhakti is all about.

NOTES

1 Otto, *Christianity and the Indian Religion*, 8, 11.
2 Holdrege, *Bhakti and Embodiment*, 20.
3 I published a study of this text as Haberman, *Acting as a Way of Salvation*, and later a translation of the text as Haberman, *Bhaktirasāmṛtasindhu of Rūpa Gosvāmin*.
4 *Bhagavad Gītā* 11:18.
5 *Bhagavad Gītā* 11:20.
6 *Bhagavad Gītā* 11:44, a seminal expression of later *bhāva* theory.

7 *Bhagavad Gītā* 11:50.

8 All interviews with worshipers of Mount Govardhan were conducted by the author between September 2013 and April 2015 while living near the mountain with the support of a Fulbright-Nehru Senior Research Fellowship and a John Simon Guggenheim Fellowship. With the exception of Shrivasta Goswami, these interviews were conducted in Hindi and translated into English by the author.

9 These are two dictionary meanings for *ātmīya*. See McGregor, *Oxford Hindi-English Dictionary*, 84.

10 Guthrie, *Faces in the Clouds*.

11 *Bhāgavata Purāṇa* 10.33.37.

CHAPTER ELEVEN

BHAKTI THE MEDIATOR

JOHN STRATTON HAWLEY

THERE is an ongoing argument about bhakti. Some people insist that it is the sort of down-to-earth, everyday religiosity best exemplified by the unsparing "rough rhetoric" of Kabīr, as Linda Hess has put it. As if he were stopping people on the street, he shouts: "Pandit, you've got it wrong." "Monk, stop scattering your mind." "Son of a slut."[1] All this in the cause of shaking people up so they'll awake to the nature of the way the world really is. Yet on the other hand, quite by contrast, we have people who see bhakti most vividly represented in Chaitanya's ecstasies. These are his response to the call of love, enacting what the *Bhāgavata Purāṇa* had enjoined:

> If your body doesn't bristle, if your mind doesn't melt,
> If your speech doesn't stutter when you weep with ecstasy,
> If you don't have any bhakti, then how do you expect
> Your heart will stand a chance of being pure?[2]

Obviously these two moods are very different. But if we were to draw a line connecting them—connecting the fiercely confrontational and the lavishly absorptive—we could call that line bhakti. Bhakti enables us to think of these countervailing poles in the life of religion as belonging to a single field. A main purpose of the rhetoric of bhakti is to make these seemingly impossible connections possible. Despite the distance that separates these strong opposing voices, bhakti is the thread and medium that draws them together.

Bhakti plays this mediating role in many aspects of Indian religious life. Indeed, by the time this chapter concludes we will have listed fifteen of them. Yet this initial contrast between the bhakti of critical sobriety and the bhakti of encompassing emotion is regarded as being so important by Hindus that it deserves special attention, and I would like to give it that attention by zeroing in on two beautiful paintings that I happened to see in New York in the course of the same March afternoon in 2016. The first came into view at a temporary gallery established by Oliver Forge and Brendan Lynch, the London art dealers, for the duration of the annual Asian Art Week. The second turned up just a hundred yards away at the Metropolitan Museum of Art, evidently liberated from a life in storage. The last time I'd looked, it wasn't there.

The first of the pair was a page from a dispersed *Sūrsāgar* (Sūr's Ocean) that was illustrated in Udaipur around the year 1700 (fig. 11.1).[3] The lavish detail and use of gold leaf suggest almost certainly that it was painted at the court of the Mewar rulers, who had built Udaipur as their capital. As for the choice of a work to illustrate, we should understand that the *Sūrsāgar* is a collection of Brajbhāṣā or more broadly Hindi poetry attributed to the great sixteenth-century poet Sūrdās, who was reputedly blind. The oceanic metaphor suggests the size to which this collection of poems had grown by the time it was illustrated in Udaipur—about a thousand poems if you could survey collections across India. It was and is one of the most celebrated monuments of Hindi literature. The page that came into view at the Forge and Lynch gallery renders a poem that begins with the phrase "braj bhayau mahar kai pūt." Traditionally performed on the day after Krishna's birth, this poem is the longest in the *Sūrsāgar*, and that is because it has so much to celebrate. "Braj has been blessed with a headman's son," says the line that serves simultaneously as introduction and refrain, and it takes another fifty-nine verses to describe the happiness caused by the birth of that remarkable son, Krishna. That's far too many to be inscribed at the top of the page we see. The rest had to be written on the back.

This poem stands as an eloquent witness to one kind of bhakti—the colorful, narrative sort, lifting life's encompassing emotions to a divine plane. This is what critics of Hindi were to call, in a literary frame, *saguṇa bhakti*—bhakti "with qualities," that is, directed to a lord who is gloriously manifest in the world to which we have sensory access. Here the god Krishna takes on bodily form—*our* form, the form of a human body. Broadly this *Sūrsāgar* page shares its mood with Chaitanya's. It shows us a world enveloped by response to the lord. And we see the blind poet who came to be so famous for expositing this kind of bhakti in the lower lefthand corner of the painting. Armed with his hand cymbals, he joins the celebration. He is singing.

On that same March day, however, there was another painting that caught my attention, the one that made its appearance at the Met (fig. 11.2). It was displayed at the threshold of the room called Later South Asia, the last you visit if you follow the path laid out in the splendidly redesigned Islamic galleries, which opened in 2011. Wait, you may say—Islamic? This is a question that

11.1 "Braj has been blessed with a headman's son." Illustration to a *Sūrsāgar* painted in Mewar, ca. 1700. Private collection, New York. Photo courtesy of Oliver Forge and Brendan Lynch.

11.2 Kabīr and company, Mīr Kalāṅ Khāṅ, ca. 1770–75. Courtesy of Metropolitan Museum of Art

would certainly arise if you thought bhakti transpired in a strictly Hindu domain. But Navina Haider, the curator who placed this painting in the Islamic galleries, gives us reason to wonder whether the boundary represented by the term Hinduism is actually as hard and fast as we might have thought. In spring of 2016 she and her staff identified this painting as "a gathering of Hindu and Muslim saints," adding that it "is based upon a Mughal painting on the theme of a gathering of holy men of different faiths." If we may use the term broadly, this is a version of bhakti—Kabīr's type—that crosses the sorts of borders that institutional religion is so apt to want to erect.

And what about that earlier painting to which the curators refer? It turns out that it is very much worth our attention—a well-known painting (fig. 11.3) that may have been created for Prince Dārā Shikuh (circa 1650), the Mughal scion who is renowned for his fascination with crossovers between Islamic expressions of religion and Hindu ones.[4] This work, now to be found in the Victoria and Albert Museum in London, portrays at its center a Sufi *dhikr*—an ecstatic exploration of the presence of Allah that often takes the form of dance. The *dhikr* is depicted as occurring in a place where certain major figures of the Chishtīya and Qādirī Sufi orders are in attendance—perhaps the great Chishti shrine at Ajmer. These eminences stand at the top, but look at the bottom: there's Kabīr. And who are the others "supporting" these dancing Sufis? All figures in this lower register are carefully labeled so as to answer just this question, as if the painting's intended viewers—elite Muslims, probably—might need to be given signposts. We learn that it is an *aughar* ascetic who rises just behind Kabīr; then comes Kabīr's son Kamāl, in the patched garment; and further back at the left we have Sain, Nāmdev, Pīpā, and finally Ravidās, all of whom who are familiarly classed as *sants*, "the good."

Sants as a category are practitioners of a markedly different sort of bhakti from what we see in the Sūrdās painting. This is *nirguṇa bhakti*, that is, bhakti "without qualities," the sort that insists the lord is to be found in the world as it is, not as we imagine it, and that the best access to the divine is therefore provided not by images we might conjure up but by the words we speak in common. These *sants*, shown at the bottom left of figure 11.3, serve as visual counterparts to a series of Shaiva ascetics headed by Matsyendranāth and Gorakhnāth, who appear across the way at the bottom right. The group as a whole is familiarly classed Hindu, but the way the group is deployed here makes us wonder just how accurate that label might be. "Holy men of different faiths"? In some sense, perhaps. But as the painting makes clear, the dividing line between Islamic and Hindu bhakti is at best a broken one. Kabīr's own complex, border-defying identity might well have suggested just this.

There is also a more extreme possibility. Does the artist perhaps conceive of the two facing groups in the lower register as Vaishnavas and Shaivas, respectively? If so, contrary to the normal understanding, we here have Kabīr pictured as the preeminent figure among Vaishnavas, and the Vaishnavism he represents would be the big-tent version I think of as "vulgate Vaishnavism," or in Vijay Pinch's term, "catholic."[5] I am puzzled about why one of these hypothetical Vaishnavas would have been labeled *aughar*, normally a Shaiva designation, but in the eyes of this artist the stronger analogy, as suggested by the

11.3 Assembly of Sufis and *bhaktas*, attributed to Khvajā Sāhib, ca. 1650. Courtesy of Victoria and Albert Museum

11.4 Detail of figure 11.3 showing Kamāl to the left of Kabīr (*center*), Ravidās (*far left*), and musicians (*right*). Courtesy of Metropolitan Museum of Art

aughar's beard, seems to be not with the Shaivas opposite but with one of the Sufi dancers pictured just above. So on Kabīr's side of the bhakti spectrum—Vaishnava in a looser, more inclusive sense than Sūrdās's—it is possible to think of bhakti as spanning the presumed gap between different kinds of Hindus and between Hindus and Muslims altogether.

Let us remember that all this was seen from a Mughal perspective circa 1650. What happens by the time we get to the painting it so strongly influenced, the one in the Met, which was created in Lucknow in about 1770? In a way the Islamic framing persists, for the painter in this instance is Mīr Kalāṅ Khāṅ, whose name is Muslim and who trained at Delhi's Mughal court and relocated to Lucknow, where he became, as the Met's label says, "the leading court painter of Shujā' al-Daulā (r. 1754) and Asaf al-Daulā (r. 1775–98)." It's he who gives us the "gathering of Hindu and Muslim saints" that the Met's label proclaims. Interestingly, he transposes the figures of Kamāl and the *aughar*, clarifying—or perhaps establishing—the connection between Kamāl and his father (fig. 11.4). To the viewer's eye Kamāl sits directly left of Kabīr. More striking than any such inner adjustment, however, is the fact that this group remains so cohesive as it travels from the Dārā Shikuh painting to this one. In both instances Ravidās, the "untouchable" *chamār*, remains at the outer edge of the group of *sants*, while Kabīr—though he too is associated with a "low" caste, the weaver *julāhās*—is placed at the head of the group and closest to the center of the painting. In fact, he now sits absolutely at its center.

Yet a striking difference separates these two paintings. In the Lucknow painting the Muslims who clearly *were* Muslims—the dervishes once the center of our attention—have been removed, and the Shaivas and Nāthpanthīs we saw on the right side of the Mughal painting have now been replaced by musicians. This is extremely interesting, since music is deeply and intrinsically associated with bhakti. It is as if the mediations advanced for Dārā Shikuh—between Sufis and *sants* and simultaneously between Vaishnavas and Shaivas—have now been pared back so as to exemplify bhakti more specifically. But this has happened at the expense of the bhakti catholicity that earlier bound Hindus and Muslims together. So on both sides of Fifth Avenue we have evocations of bhakti—one *nirguṇa*, one *saguṇa*; one reflecting the patronage of a Muslim court, the other, of a Hindu. But music, the very essence of bhakti, plays a primary role in both.

As we think back on what we have learned from the two paintings that showed up in New York that March day, we find that we have been introduced not to a single contrast between the poles they represent but to a set of three. Each of these contrasts inhabits the shared space that bhakti provides: confrontational and absorptive, Muslim and Hindu, and *nirguṇa* and *saguṇa* (see "Bhakti as Mediator: Fifteen Opposites"). But these are only the first of a number of contrasts that bhakti can be claimed to mediate. There are also at least a dozen others, and in the space that remains we will make an attempt to thread them together on a single string. In so doing we will be weaving a garland—a

---

BHAKTI AS MEDIATOR: FIFTEEN OPPOSITES

1. Absorption and confrontation
2. Muslim/Sufi and Hindu
3. Nirguṇa and saguṇa
4. Human and divine
5. South and north (compare east and west)
6. Shaiva and Vaishnava (compare also Jain)
7. Panth and sampradāy
8. Dalit and Brahman (and in between)
9. Intellect and emotion
10. Sanskrit and vernacular
11. Regional and national
12. Conflicting emotional registers
13. Ancient and modern
14. Right and left
15. Power and protest

---

mālā or *māl*, to use the classic metaphor that Nābhādās (or Nābhā for short) adopted for his pivotal bhakti text, the *Bhaktamāl* (A Garland of Devotees), written in about 1600. At the beginning of that work, Nābhādās draws our attention to yet another bhakti dyad—number 4 on our list or garland:

bhakta bhakti bhagavanta guru / catura nāma vapu eka
inake pada bandana karata / nāse vighana aneka.

Lover of God, love of God, God, and guru—
    four names, but one single body.
Singing the praises of these—their feet—
    clears away not one block but many.

Here we find bhakti sandwiched between the devotee and the Lord, the human and the divine. Of course, Nābhā features the *bhaktas* (devotees, possessors of bhakti) in his great text—he says so in his title—but it's not accidental that after he announces his *bhakta* subject in the first word he utters, he turns immediately to bhakti to set it within the connective tissue that he weaves as he introduces us to *bhakta* after *bhakta* in the course of his enduringly influential work.[6]

Another of Nābhā's major preoccupations was the connection between South and North India, which he also saw as being mediated by bhakti, in that certain southern *ācāryas* (preceptors) came eventually to have northerners as members of the religious communities they had founded (number 5 on our growing list). Again bhakti serves as mediator, this time performing a work of simultaneously spatial and temporal integration. As such, Nābhādās's "Garland" anticipates the *Bhāgavata Māhātmya*, "The Glory of the *Bhāgavata Purāna*," a Vaishnava text produced in North India a century later, in about 1700. The framing is somewhat different between the *Māl* and the *Māhātmya*. Nābhā breaks his Vaishnavism into four constituent *sampradāys* (orders, teaching traditions), each with southern roots and northern branches. The *Bhāgavata Māhātmya*, by contrast, rallies around a single parent text, the *Bhāgavata Purāṇa*, which it sees as the spine by means of which a similar south-north, old-new integration is achieved. Drawing a line between an unnamed town on the southern Tungabhadra River and the northern city of Haridvar, situated on the banks of the Ganges, the *Bhāgavata Māhātmya* makes its south-north connection explicit. On both the Tungabhadra and the Ganges, a seven-day reading of the *Bhāgavata Purāṇa* brings the numb or dumb to life again—first the errant, evil Dhundhukari, then comatose Jñāna and Vairāgya, who are personifications of knowledge and religious discipline. In the *Māhātmya*'s most famous passage, a hypostasized bhakti makes the journey from south to north herself. Thus once again bhakti mediates; it connects.

All this elaborates a Vaishnava imaginary, yet in the south, the place from which all bhakti truth is said to flow, another story of mediation is also waiting to be told (no. 6). In South India around the end of the first millennium we see the emergence of parallel Shaiva and Vaishnava anthologies and hagiographies. They mimic one another, structurally speaking. Māṇikkavācakar and Nammāḻvār, a Shaiva and a Vaishnava, play complementary roles as the poets who completed the *nāyaṉmār* and *āḻvār* traditions respectively by adding their own bodies of poetry to what had gone before. Both do so in the course of the ninth century. Later we can also observe a parallel in the process by which these collections were effectively canonized and brought into sung temple usage. Nampi Āṇṭār Nampi accomplished that work of liturgical systematization in the Shaiva case, giving us the first full-fledged Tamil bhakti canon, the *Tēvāram*, probably in the eleventh century. Nāthamuni performed a similar task somewhat earlier, producing his *Divyaprabandham* of four thousand āḻvār poems known in Tamil as *Nālāyiratiyaprapantam*. Both these works of collation—one Shaiva, the other Vaishnava—came to be represented in somewhat later sectarian accounts as having been caused by the discovery of lost manuscripts from an earlier period. Thus the entire process of community construction along Shaiva and Vaishnava lines in Tamil south India was retroactively understood to have been driven by the force of revelation.

When we come to hagiography, similar vectors emerge. The *Periya Purāṇa*, where the lives of *nāyaṉmārs* are gathered in the comprehensive form that remains authoritative in the twenty-first century, was prepared in the mid-twelfth century by Cēkkiḻār, while its Vaishnava analog, the *Guruparamparāprabhāvam*, followed a century later. Yet here we find a difference of language: the Shaiva document was written in Tamil while the Vaishnava one adopted the mixed Tamil-Sanskrit medium known as *maṇipravāḷa*. And the number of saints involved is also different. There are only twelve *āḻvārs*, while the *nāyaṉmārs* number sixty-three—or, counting Māṇikkavācakar, sixty-four. This number probably came to serve as the official sum because it was the very number that had been chosen for a canonical collection of sixty-three exemplary Jain lives, the *Triṣaṣṭilakṣaṇa Mahāpurāṇa*. Thus Jain bhakti formation lies in the background of Shaiva, in an important act of mimesis. As in his contribution to this volume, John Cort has rightly cautioned that we must always keep Jain bhakti in mind as we think about the evolution of bhakti formulations, and several scholars—Jason Schwartz, Hamsa Stainton, Dominic Goodall, and Anand Venkatkrishnan—have recently been discovering that *śivadharma* texts share with their contemporary, the *Bhāgavata Purāṇa*, the distinctive emotional bhakti that later came to be seen as specifically Vaishnava. Thus the bhakti web is finely woven.

All this happened in the south, but in the north and west the vessels through which bhakti is channeled came to be conceived somewhat differently (opposition no. 7). In the Sikhs' *Gurū Granth*, for example, the *bhagats* (i.e., *bhaktas*, the group we have been calling *sants*) are made to constitute a specific class, and their relation to their Sikh counterparts is declared to be subsidiary. The gurus reign first and foremost; the *bhaktas* only contribute to their luster. Elsewhere, similarly, the Dādūpanthī intellectual Rāghavdās (circa 1660) made sense of the relationship between the founding guru of his sect and those Nābhādās had trumpeted by declaring that they shared a single inspiration. Here bhakti is made to span the distance between a *saguṇa* Vaishnava *sampradāy* such as Nābhādās asserts and a similarly structured set of *sant*-focused *nirguṇa panths* (paths). The names are different, Rāghavdās seems to acknowledge, but the social reality they designate is the same. Bhakti makes the connection, and we see it in the fact that Rāghavdās also calls his work a *Bhaktamāl*.

Bhakti is not always appealed to in the name of an egalitarian norm, nor is it always socially inclusive (no. 8). Yet we must not minimize the importance of the caste catholicity that in different ways animates the words of Kabīr and Ravidās. These words evidently traveled along an interurban circuit that was in some important way middle class. Can such a bhakti be fully expressive of the religiosity of Dalits? That is where Joel Lee's work, as represented in this volume, speaks loud and clear. For many of the sanitation workers of Lucknow, to embrace the sort of bhakti that is remembered as having been articulated by Ravidās is to opt for something too shallow, too Hindu, too general, a vision of religion that does not feel like their own.[7] From the point of view of others, *nirguṇa bhakti* of this sort may seem to mediate, but for some Dalits, at least, the very people it was supposed to represent and include, it alienates at the same time. "We are not Hindus!" has been a classic Dalit protest.

There are still more antipodes between which bhakti is said to mediate:

- *Intellect and emotion* (no. 9). Here is the classic duo that Friedhelm Hardy proposed—the contrast (but also the connection) between the *Bhagavad Gītā*'s bhakti on the one hand and that of the *Bhāgavata* and its Tamil interlocutors on the other.[8] Critics worried that Hardy imposed too marked a separation between these two bhakti realms, but if so, this simply underscores the fact that they do belong together within a single conceptual frame.
- *Sanskrit and vernacularity* (no. 10). This polarity calls to mind Sheldon Pollock's masterwork *The Language of the Gods in the World of Men*, with its

dismissal of the idea that bhakti serves to connect various Indian vernaculars according to the "bhakti movement" picture as suggested, for instance, by what is said about bhakti's peregrination in the *Bhāgavata Māhātmya*.[9] Pollock insists, to the contrary, that it was not a south-to-north contagion of bhakti songs that produced what he calls "the vernacular millennium" but a literarization of vernaculars that happened in a succession of regional courts and created the conditions for expressions of bhakti to flourish in the various languages involved. Other scholars, responding to Pollock's view, have come to bhakti's defense. Most striking is Christian Novetzke's effort to recover a "quotidian" register in Maharashtra and elsewhere,[10] but one could also call to witness patterns of Bengali poetry that get ventriloquized into Sanskrit in the songs that appear in each chapter of the *Gītagovinda*, as Jesse Knutson has recently shown.[11] We also have Anand Venkatkrishnan's brilliant work on how *saṃkīrtan* (the public act of communal singing) gets "overheard" in Sanskrit, as it seems to have been by the Devas of Banaras in the sixteenth and seventeenth centuries.[12]

- *Region and nation* (no. 11). As these examples from Maharashtra, Bengal, and Banaras suggest, the rubric of bhakti can both affirm regionality and simultaneously set it in a larger interregional context. We see this, for example, in the adoption and "remixing" of Nābhādās's seminal text that happens when Mahīpati writes his eighteenth-century *Bhaktavijaya* (Victory of the *Bhaktas*) in Marathi.[13] When the idea of the bhakti movement is fully articulated in the twentieth century, it performs this work on an even larger scale, drawing together regional vernacular expressions of bhakti in such a way that they seem to form a national entity.[14]
- *Conflicting emotional registers* (no. 12). A characteristic contrast said to be bridged by bhakti appears in John Carman's exposition of supremacy and accessibility in Rāmānuja's theology.[15] We see something similar in the way bhakti can designate both the violently masculine devotional fervor expressed in the *Basava Purāṇa* and the love-soaked femininity of Āṇṭāḷ.[16] These are southern instances. As for the north, the contrast between Kabīr's "rough rhetoric" and Chaitanya's absorptive but equally public passivity also comes to mind.
- *Ancient and modern* (no. 13). Additionally, we have the thousand-year bridge that the "medieval bhakti movement" is said to provide between the ancient or literarily classical period on the one hand and the modern, colonial, and postcolonial periods on the other. One finds this bridging conception in many places, but V. Raghavan's lectures for All India Radio in December 1964, entitled "The Great Integrators," provides an excellent literary example. Meanwhile, on the visual side, we have the murals that

Binodbihari Mukherji executed in 1946–47 to adorn the walls of the newly built Hindi Bhavan at Shantiniketan. These he entitled "Medieval Saints," and they articulate a clear progression from twelfth-century south India (Rāmānuja) to the beginning of the eighteenth century in the north (Gurū Gobind Singh).[17] All this is relevant to the task of situating the Hindi language, with its newly national aspirations, in the context of a pan-Indian bhakti past.[18]

- *Right and left* (no. 14). Shantiniketan's Hindi Bhavan, which opened its new building just as India and Pakistan were being born as independent nations in 1947, brings us into a deeply politicized realm, and bhakti has never been able to shed its political associations since. Once again bhakti stands in the middle, being claimed in divergent, even opposing ways by partisans of the political right and left. In contemporary India, Bharatiya Janata Party–inclined "*bhaktas*" are reviled by the Congress-leaning and Marxist people who designate themselves "secularists" by contrast. Yet these same secularists often claim that the secularism they espouse stands on good solid *nirguṇa bhakti* footing, the sort that questions any firm barrier between Sufi and Hindu modes of performing bhakti and that takes deep cognizance of social injustice.
- *Power and protest* (no. 15). This major political confrontation is not the same as the clash between power and protest per se. So much depends on who is perceived to be in power and who, therefore, is acting in protest. Yet until very recently it was safe to say that Dalits could always be situated on the protest side of this dichotomy. It was to the protest side of the bhakti legacy that they appealed in attempting to be heard by those with greater access to power.[19]

These fifteen beads or flowers, then, comprise our bhakti garland, and all that is left is to ask whether it really is a garland or just some hastily assembled laundry list. In performing the work of mediation that this garland of bhakti polarities asserts, is the concept of bhakti asked to do so much that it really accomplishes nothing? Personally, I would resist such a conclusion. I think there is meaning in the fact that the two sides of Fifth Avenue with which we began—Sūrdās's vividly social celebration of Krishna's presence in the world and Kabīr's position at the crux of a very different sort of fellowship—can be designated by a single word. And so on down the list. I would argue, in fact, that bhakti stands at the middle of much of the life of religion, not just in India but elsewhere. Bhakti may not cover the waterfront, but truly it does bridge.

NOTES

1 Hess and Singh, *Bījak of Kabir*, 10–11.

2 *Bhāgavata Purāṇa* 11.14.23, translated by Venkatkrishnan, "The *Bhāgavata Purāṇa* in History."

3 For further information, see Hawley, *Sūrdās*, 260–74.

4 Gadon, "Note on the Frontispiece."

5 Hawley, "Can There Be a Vaishnava Kabir?"; Pinch, "History, Devotion."

6 In so saying, I do not mean to minimize the importance of the *bhakta*-to-*bhakta* connection—*dāsoṅ dās* in Hindi—which can serve to accommodate, overcome, or even slightly obscure a commitment to a transhuman other. Generally on the *Bhaktamāl*, see Hawley, *Storm of Songs*, ch. 3.

7 Lee, "Recognition and Its Shadows," 184–241; lectures on Dalit religion in my Hinduism class, April 25, 2013, and April 24, 2014.

8 Hardy, *Viraha-Bhakti*, 36–38, passim.

9 Pollock, *Language of the Gods*, 423–26.

10 Novetzke, *Quotidian Revolution.*

11 Knutson, *Into the Twilight*, 72–88.

12 Venkatkrishnan, "Ritual, Reflection, and Religion."

13 Keune, "Gathering the *Bhaktas* in Marathi."

14 Hawley, *Storm of Songs*, 13–58.

15 Carman, *Theology of Rāmānuja.*

16 Rao and Roghair, *Śiva's Warriors*; Venkatesan, *Secret Garland.*

17 Raghavan, *Great Integrators*; Hawley, *Storm of Songs*, 275–84.

18 Hawley, *Storm of Songs*, 37–58, 230–55.

19 Mani, *Debrahmanising History.*

SOLIDARITIES

CHAPTER TWELVE

SINGING IN PROTEST

Early Modern Hindu-Muslim Encounters in Bengali Hagiographies of Chaitanya

KIYOKAZU OKITA

INAUGURATED by Viśvambhara, later known as Chaitanya, at the beginning of the sixteenth century, the movement we today call Bengali Vaishnavism quickly became an influential player among the devotional communities of North India, Bengal, and Orissa. Given that it was formed in the early modern period, questions about its engagement with Islam naturally arise. Two Hindu-Muslim encounters as described in two prominent Bengali hagiographies of Chaitanya, namely the *Caitanyabhāgavata* by Vrindāvandās and the *Caitanyacaritāmṛta* by Kṛṣṇadās, illuminate this subject. The first incident involves a meeting between Haridās, a Vaishnava saint who was Viśvambhara's senior contemporary, and a local Muslim governor. Haridās was born a Muslim.[1] According to the *Gauḍīyavaiṣṇavābhidāna*, he was born in the village of Buron, which is located in the Khulna division of present-day Bangladesh, in 1470 (*śaka* 1392). This made him quite unlike Viśvambhara, who was born in a Brahman family, but after the two men met, Haridās became one of Chaitanya's close companions. Together they promoted the public singing of Krishna's names (*saṅkīrtan*), and this precipitated the second incident we shall discuss. It focuses on a local Muslim judge who decided to prohibit such public chanting, which led Chaitanya to organize a massive protest.

Our sources differ markedly in the way they portray these two incidents. Kṛṣṇadās's *Caitanyacaritāmṛta*, though it was based on Vrindāvandās's *Caitanyabhāgavata*, elaborates only briefly on the first incident. As for the second incident, Kṛṣṇadās gives it a very different portrayal than Vrindāvandās does. Vrindāvandās's account is noticeably more violent. These differences apparently reflect the political environments in which our two authors operated. While Vrindāvandās wrote in Bengal in the pre-Mughal period, Kṛṣṇadās wrote in Vrindavan during the period of Mughal rule. Indeed the evolution of various forms of Mughal polity in sixteenth-century Bengal and North India—and their ultimate convergence in the Mughal state—played a decisive role in how Hindu-Muslim relations were perceived in the early modern period.

SAINTS, HAGIOGRAPHERS, AND COMMUNITIES

After the death of Chaitanya, his hagiographies proliferated. As discussed by Joseph O'Connell, S. K. De, Tony Stewart, and others, the earliest hagiographies, such as Murāri Gupta's *Kṛṣṇacaitanyacaritāmṛta* and Kavikarṇapūra's *Caitanyacaritāmṛtamahākāvya*, were composed in Sanskrit.[2] Vrindāvandās's *Caitanyabhāgavata* was the first hagiography of Chaitanya written in Bengali. Vrindāvandās was the grandson of Śrīvāsa, who was Viśvambhara's close confidant in Navadvīp. The date of his birth is not known, but he must have been born sometime in the early sixteenth century.[3] De and O'Connell suggest that Vrindāvandās composed the text in 1540s, a decade or so after Chaitanya's death.[4]

Bengal during Vrindāvandās's lifetime was marked by political instability. Shortly after Chaitanya's death, Humāyūn briefly occupied Bengal, which was under the rule of the Husain Shāhī dynasty. Then the Afghans led by Sher Khān Sūr took over Bengal from Humāyūn in 1538. This effectively ended the Husain Shāhī dynasty. Thereafter Bengal was under the control of the governors appointed by the Suri emperors in Delhi. In 1554, however, Muhammad Khan Sur, then governor of Bengal, declared independence and established the Muhammad Shāhī dynasty. As we can see, then, Vrindāvandās composed his *Caitanyabhāgavata* for a newly emerging community of Bengali Vaishnavas who were sometimes ruled by independent Muslim kings and sometimes by deputees of the Muslim rulers in distant Delhi.

Turning back to Kṛṣṇadās, roughly seventy years later we find him writing in Vrindavan in a very different social and political context. By the time he completed the *Caitanyacaritāmṛta* around 1615, Bengal had been under the Mughal rule for roughly forty years. Akbar initially struggled to keep Bengal under control, but after he appointed Rājā Mānsingh as the governor of the region, Mughal rule was firmly established there. As Akbar's most trusted Hindu general, this Kachvāhā king from Rajasthan exercised enormous political power.

Akbar's assignment of Mānsingh to Bengal was successful not only because of Mānsingh's military prowess but also due to his image as a devout devotee of Krishna. Mānsingh's Hindu identity helped Hindu subjects to accept Mughal hegemony in the region. Mānsingh had a personal connection with Bengal as well: his devotion to Krishna was deeply influenced by the followers of Chaitanya. When he defeated Pratāpsingh in 1576, Mānsingh began the construction of the second Govindadevajī temple in Vrindavan, to celebrate his victory. Govindadeva was the image initially worshiped by Rūpa, who was in many respects (especially intellectually) the principal founding father of Bengali Vaishnavism—if we except Chaitanya himself. The Mughal emperor Akbar also supported this temple construction. As a result, according to Jack Hawley, "this theatre of Hindu-Muslim collaboration at the imperial level made possible, among other things, the largest temple in all India that was ever designed as a single structure."[5] Thus by the time Kṛṣṇadās completed the *Caitanyacaritāmṛta* in the early seventeenth century, Bengali Vaishnavism was no longer an emerging religious movement. Rather, the tradition had become a part of the establishment. Moreover, the construction of the Govindadevajī temple and other similar projects amply demonstrated that Muslim sovereignty could be beneficial to the Vaishnava community.

It is important to take note of the dynamics that connected Bengal's more conservative Hindus (Śāktas, Śaivas, and Smārtas—"orthodox" Hindus for want of a better word), its Muslim authorities, and the newly emerging Bengali Vaishnavas. Although the two hagiographies portray these dynamics primarily as conflicts between the Vaishnavas and Muslim authority, the orthodox Hindu community at the time of Chaitanya was by no means supportive of the new Vaishnavas. Thus in regard to the second event both authors explain that it was the orthodox Hindus who requested the Muslim judge to ban the public singing of Krishna's name. As we consider the accounts that follow, we need to wonder how non-Vaishnava Hindus may have played a role in its unfolding.

HARIDĀS AND THE MUSLIM GOVERNOR

In the texts written in the late medieval and the early modern periods, we find many narratives in both the Hindu and Muslim contexts that feature encounters between a charismatic religious figure and the representative of power. These provide an important context for comparing in detail the narratives on Haridās and Chaitanya that we will be studying. Typically, in such stories, power makes its appearance in the form of a political authority such as a local king, a religious elite such as an *'ulamā*, or both. In the context of Sufism, the practice of *samā'*, which involved musical performance and ritual dance, often became a site of contestation.

For example, according to Isami's *Futuh al-salatin*, written in the fourteenth century, Qāzī Hamīd-ud-dīn Nāgaurī (ca. 1192–1276), a famous mystic in the

Suhrawardi order, was known for practicing *samā'*. Eminent *qāzīs* in Delhi, who considered the practice to be illegal, approached Shams-ud-dīn Iltutmish (r. 1211–36) in protest. The sultan summoned a gathering (*mahzar*) to discuss the issue. However, as he listened to the recitation of verses at this assembly, Qāzī Hamīd-ud-dīn fell into ecstasy and began dancing, disregarding fire and thorns that surrounded him. Observing this, the sultan arranged dinner and invited the mystic to attend.[6] In this narrative, the Sufi's extraordinary demonstration was taken as a proof of his spiritual advancement, which then convinced the sultan of the authenticity of the practice. Reviewing the story as a whole, we observe the following elements. Religious elites become envious of charismatic Sufis' popularity. They try to tarnish Sufis' fame by accusing them in front of political authority. However, the display of the Sufi's spiritual prowess proves his superiority over both religious and political authority—both the *qāzīs* and the sultan.

This juxtaposition of spiritual authority and secular power, and the demonstration of the former's superiority over the latter, are observed in narratives concerning Hindu saints as well. According to the *Caurāsī Vaiṣṇavan kī Vārtā*, a collection of hagiographical narratives written in the seventeenth century by Gokulnāth, one of the grandsons of Vallabha, there was once a time when Akbar listened to the recitation of one of Sūrdās's poems. That made Akbar want to meet Sūrdās in person, so he arranged a meeting with the poet. After praising Sūrdās, Akbar requested that he compose a poem in praise of Akbar himself. The poet refused, saying that his love was for Krishna only. Akbar pressed the poet further and made the same request again, but Sūrdās again declined. This time Akbar accepted his refusal and asked the poet if he wanted any reward. All Sūrdās did was request permission to leave, and he asked the emperor not to summon him again.[7]

This is a narrative of a rather happy encounter in which a benevolent secular authority appreciates a Hindu saint's firm devotion. But as Christian Novetzke points out, one can also find a very different type of encounter, one that involves the threat of death or punishment. Dattatreya's hagiography of Nāmdev, written in the eighteenth century, provides one such example. Once Nāmdev was summoned to Delhi by a person named Sultān Toblakh Pādshāh, who seems to be identical with Muhammad bin Tughluq (r. 1324–51). Once Nāmdev arrived, the sultan asked him to show him Viṭṭhal, the deity popularly worshiped in Maharashtra and neighboring regions, who is was generally considered to be a manifestation of Krishna. Nāmdev replied by stating that God is present in the heart of everyone, including that of the sultan: no need for a special showing. Unimpressed with this answer, the sultan demanded that Nāmdev resurrect a slaughtered calf, allow himself to be trampled by an elephant, or convert to

Islam. Finding himself in this precarious situation, Nāmdev began remembering Viṭṭhal, and sure enough Viṭṭhal came to his rescue. The elephant suddenly died after touching Nāmdev's feet, and a slaughtered calf was resurrected. Dattatreya praises Nāmdev, comparing him with Prahlād, the ideal devotee of Vishnu who endured torture from his own father Hiraṇyakaśipu.[8]

The story of Haridās's confronting the local Muslim governor belongs to this second type of encounter, as the saint was threatened with death. The association with Prahlād is also made in relation to Haridās. In the sixteenth chapter of the first book (*ādikhaṇḍa*) of the *Caitanyabhāgavata*, Vrindāvandās describes Haridās's encounter as follows. Once Haridās was staying at Phuliyā, a village in present-day West Bengal. (The village is next to Śāntipur and is located roughly fifty miles north of Kolkata.) There he spread among village people the practice of *saṅkīrtan*, that is, group singing of Krishna's names in public. As it spread and as Haridās's popularity increased, a local *qāzī* (Bengali: *kājī*) became alarmed. In premodern times a *qāzī* was a Muslim judge who was appointed by the state to issue binding rules.[9] The *qāzī* went to the local governor and recommended that he question Haridās. According to the *Caitanyabhāgavata*, the *qāzī*'s charge was that Haridās was a Muslim but behaved as a Hindu. In other words, the *qāzī* considered Muslim and Hindu identities to be mutually exclusive, regarding it an act of apostasy that they should be mixed. As we will see, Haridās challenged precisely this presupposition.

As Joseph O'Connell points out, *yavana* is a common term used by the Bengali Vaishnava hagiographers to refer to a Muslim. After surveying several hagiographies of Chaitanya, O'Connell notes that the Bengali Vaishnava texts often refer to Muslims as *yavana* or *mleccha*, and sometimes as *turka* or *turuka*, or *paṭhān*. The term *yavana* was used already in the fifth to the fourth century BCE to refer to Bactrian Ionians and Greeks. The term later came to mean "foreigners," especially those coming from the northwest. O'Connell also suggests that the term carried the connotations of vigor and violence as observed in the character of Kālayavana, whose story is narrated in the *Mahābhārata* and the *Bhāgavata Purāṇa*.[10] As we will see, once again, Vrindāvandās explicitly connects this figure of Kālayavana with Muslims.

Thus we resume our story. Following the *qāzī*'s advice the local governor brought Haridās to the court, when the governor himself questioned him. The text portrays the governor as a rather friendly figure who approaches Haridās calling him "brother" (*bhāi*):

> Look how fortunate you were to be a Muslim [*jaban*]. Then why do you give your mind to the practice of Hindus? After seeing [how] Hindus [behave], we do not eat rice. Besides, you were born in a

> great family. Transgressing the religion of your birth, you perform another practice. How on earth will you achieve salvation after death? Whatever improper behavior you performed without knowing better—remove that sin by uttering *kalmā* [i.e., the basic article of faith in Islam].[11]

In a certain way this point of view parallels Muhammad bin Tughluq's suggestion that Nāmdev convert to Islam. Yet the governor's inquiry also reiterates the *qāzī*'s assumption that religious identity is exclusive, and the governor further emphasizes the privilege of being born Muslim, as against the lower status of Hindus.

Haridās begins his reply by stating that the governor has been deluded by Vishnu's illusory power (*māyā*). Then he offers a theological argument reminiscent of *nirguṇa* saints such as Kabīr and Nānak. Haridās challenges the inquisitors' presupposition that religious identities are mutually exclusive:

> Listen my son. The lord is only one for everyone. Name alone creates a difference between Hindus and *yavanas*. Ultimately according to the Qur'ān and the Purāṇas, it is said, "There is one (*ek*)." This one Being—pure, eternal, indivisible, undecaying, and complete—resides in the heart of everyone. The entire world acts according to the way in which he causes people to assume [certain] mindsets. In the entire world everyone speaks the name and qualities of that same lord, but according to their own scriptures. . . . Hence, as that lord prompts me in [my] mind, so indeed do I act.[12]

To put the matter strongly, then, Haridās argues that it is Allāḥ who causes him to chant Krishna's names. An important implication of this argument is that Haridās does not believe that he is transgressing the religion of his birth. Tony Stewart in fact argues that Haridās was never a convert to Vaishnavism in the first place.[13] He describes him instead as a Sufi who practiced chanting (*dhikr*) with Krishna's name.

According to Vrindāvandās's narrative, nearly everyone was satisfied with Haridās's reply. However, the *qāzī* insisted that he be punished. As a result Haridās was hit with a chain in twenty-two markets. While he was being tortured, he kept chanting Krishna's name. When Haridās did not die after being punished so severely, the Muslim guards who were torturing him became perplexed and thought he might be a saint (*pīr*).[14] Thus they eventually released him.

The encounter between Haridās and local Muslim authorities as described in the *Caitanyabhāgavata* belongs to the second group of encounter narratives as categorized by Novetzke, which involve the threat of death or punishment. It also offers an example of passive resistance. On the one hand, Haridās persisted in his chanting of Krishna's names even when his life was threatened. On the other hand, he neither protested against nor rebuked the Muslim judge. Haridās's persistence in chanting also reminds us of the narratives of Qāzī Hamīd-ud-dīn Nāgaurī who continued in his practice of *samā'* despite the *'ulamā'*s opposition.

In contrast to the elaborate description we find in the *Caitanyabhāgavata*, we hardly find any reference to this incident in Kṛṣṇadās's *Caitanyacaritāmṛta*. The only explicit reference is found in the tenth chapter of the first book, where Kṛṣṇadās praises prominent co-religionists of Chaitanya. After praising Haridās for chanting Krishna's names three hundred thousand times every day, the *Caitanyacaritāmṛta* refers to Haridās's dealings with Muslim authorities: "The waves of his qualities were equal to those of Prahlād. When he was beaten by the Muslims (*jaban*) he did not so much as contract his eyebrows."[15] The contraction of eyebrows indicates an experience of pain. That Haridās does not flinch in even this minor way shows the magnitude of his devotion.

After praising Haridās in a few verses, Kṛṣṇadās explicitly states that Vrindāvandās had already described Haridās's exploits; as a result he would write only those stories of Haridās that had not been mentioned by Vrindāvandās. Clearly Kṛṣṇadās saw no problem in accepting the way Vrindāvandās describes the incident with the *qāzī*. He is more than happy to direct his readers to Vrindāvandās's account. But when it comes to a similar confrontation that concerns Viśvambhara, Kṛṣṇadās takes quite a different approach.

VIŚVAMBHARA AND THE QĀZĪ

As Viśvambhara—that is, Chaitanya—popularizes the practice of *saṅkīrtan*, Muslim and non-Vaishnava Hindu communities complain to the local Muslim judge that he should stop this new religious practice. Both Vrindāvandās and Kṛṣṇadās describe this encounter but in quite divergent ways. Vrindāvandās's portrayal of Chaitanya in this moment is extremely violent and triumphalist, while in Kṛṣṇadās's description violence is toned down and Chaitanya appears much more inclined to act within the bounds of reason. I would suggest that this difference is at least partly due to the two authors' divergent understandings of the position of Bengali Vaishnavas in relation to their Muslim rulers.

Vrindāvandās describes this incident in the twenty-third chapter of the second book of the *Caitanyabhāgavata*. One day, as he tells the story, the local *qāzī* notices the loud chanting of Hari's name at Vaishnavas' residences, the practice young Viśvambhara was promoting. To stop it, the *qāzī* "attacked whomever he could reach. He broke *mṛdaṅgas* and behaved badly."[16] Every day the *qāzī* roams through the town, taking wicked people with him and looking for the *kīrtan*.[17] In Vrindāvandās's portrayal, non-Vaishnava Hindus also complain about the practice of loud *kīrtan*, but it is clearly the *qāzī* who is blamed for obstructing it. Kṛṣṇadās's account is quite different. There the *qāzī* obstructs *kīrtan* not out of his own volition but because non-Vaishnava Hindus ask him to do so. Kṛṣṇadās shifts the blame clearly from the *qāzī* to the Hindus.

Vrindāvandās says that when *kīrtan* was prohibited by the *qāzī*, Viśvambhara storms the judge's house with his followers and angrily shouts: "O Kājī [i.e., *qāzī*], where are you, bugger! Bring him quickly and cut off his head. Today make the entire world devoid of *yavanas*, just as I killed Kālayavana previously. How did the Kājī manage to escape with his life? Destroy his house! Destroy it!"[18] Viśvambhara's violent words are shocking. Moreover, the wordplay between *yavana* and Kālayavana suggests a general vilification of Muslims. Vrindāvandās's readers would have known the story well. As reported in *Bhāgavata Purāṇa* 10.51, Kālayavana was an *asura* who tried to kill Krishna and take over Mathura. As a result of his penance he secured a boon from Śiva to the effect that no Yādava could kill him. But when Kālayavana, so armed, attacks Krishna, Krishna manages to lead him into the cave where Mucukunda—a king who had previously defended gods from *asuras*—sleeps. Mistaking Mucukunda for Krishna, Kālayavana kicks him and wakes him up. Enraged, the king burns Kālayavana to ash. Kālayavana was immune to attack from all Yādavas, including Krishna, but Krishna managed to find someone else to kill him. In the story we have heard, Vrindāvandās compares Viśvambhara with Krishna—indeed, for him, Chaitanya *is* Krishna—and his followers with Mucukunda. The *yavanas*, that is, Muslims, he compares with Kālayavana. Just as Krishna had Mucukunda kill Kālayavana, so Viśvambhara wishes to destroy Muslims through the agency of his followers.

Following Viśvambhara's order, his followers destroy the *qāzī*'s house, his flower garden, and the surrounding plantain forest. Vrindāvandās writes that they shout Krishna's names while performing these acts of violence. Then Viśvambhara orders his followers to set fire to the *qāzī*'s house. In the midst of this, he also spreads his gospel of *kīrtan*:

> Set fire inside the house. Let him be burnt to death with everyone. Encircling the whole house, set fire in four directions. You see what their king can do to me. . . . Yama, time, death—they are the servants of my devotees. Everything is revealed according to my gaze. . . . I will kill the sinner who goes against *kīrtan*. I will certainly remember even a completely sinful person, if he performs *kīrtan*. Ascetic,

> renunciant, those who follow the path of knowledge, those who follow the path of *yoga*, or whoever, I will kill all of them if they don't perform *kīrtan*. Set fire to the house. You all, do not fear. Today I will destroy all the Yavanas.[19]

In this passage Vrindāvandās identifies Viśvambhara with the ultimate controller who determines everyone's fate. Even Yama, the god of death and time, is at his disposal, and *kīrtan* is the only means of attaining liberation. In the end the followers pacify Viśvambhara and the *qāzī*'s life is spared, but along the way this iconic Muslim authority figure has been cast in a very negative light—demonic and violent.

In his *Caitanyacaritāmṛta*, Kṛṣṇadās describes the same incident, but the contrast could scarcely be more complete. Kṛṣṇadās barely mentions the violence that Vrindāvandās highlights. According to Kṛṣṇadās, rather than storming into the *qāzī*'s house and destroying it, Viśvambhara has what we might call an interreligious dialogue with the *qāzī*. In the end, Viśvambhara obtains permission to perform *kīrtan* through negotiation rather than through violence.

In Kṛṣṇadās's narrative too, Viśvambhara approaches the *qāzī*'s house to protest against the ban on *kīrtan*. Kṛṣṇadās does acknowledge that some of Viśvambhara's followers act in the violent manner that Vrindāvandās had described.[20] After reporting these acts of violence in one verse, however, Kṛṣṇadās swiftly moves to the conversation between Viśvambhara and the *qāzī*. The *qāzī* welcomes Viśvambhara as a guest of honor. He starts their conversation by clarifying his relation to Viśvambhara, saying that Viśvambhara's maternal grandfather (*nānā*) is like a paternal uncle (*cācā*) to him, and therefore he considers Viśvambhara to be his nephew (*bhāginā*). The *qāzī* is aware that this relationship is not based on blood. Thus he also argues that a relationship based on community ties (*grāma-sambandha*) is stronger than a biological relationship (*deha-sambandha*) and goes on to say that "an uncle tolerates his nephew's anger, and a nephew is not offended by his uncle." By emphasizing their community ties, the *qāzī* tries to appease Viśvambhara's anger. Then Viśvambhara asks why the *qāzī* does not prohibit the performance of *kīrtan* now, even though he had banned it previously. At this, the *qāzī* reveals a dream he has had in which Narasiṃha, the man-lion *avatāra* of Viṣṇu, appeared and punished him for prohibiting *kīrtan*. Narasiṃha pardoned the *qāzī* but warned that he would kill all the Muslims should the *qāzī* behave inimically against *kīrtan* again. Then the *qāzī* explains that he banned *kīrtan* because certain impious Hindus (*pāṣaṇḍī hindū*) had complained to him about this new religious practice, arguing that while the name of God is a great mantra, it loses its power if everyone hears it. Clearly Kṛṣṇadās makes non-Vaishnava Hindus the real culprit in this affair—the *qāzī*, their mere instrument.

In the end the *qāzī* accepts Viśvambhara as none other than Nārāyaṇa. Hearing this Viśvambhara asks the *qāzī* not to disturb the practice of *kīrtan* any further, and the *qāzī* pledges that no one born in his family will ever do so. After receiving this assurance Viśvambhara bids farewell to the *qāzī* and, performing *kīrtan*, returns to his home.

CONCLUSION

How do we explain the fact that Kṛṣṇadās is happy to accept Vrindāvandās's treatment of a violent threat to the new vocabulary of religious practice that Chaitanya espouses when the narrative involves Haridās and the *qāzī* but not when it involves Chaitanya himself? In the latter case Kṛṣṇadās's portrayal of violence is decidedly muted—the relationship between Chaitanya and the *qāzī* is quite cordial. The key to the difference is the change in historical context.

Vrindāvandās composed his *Caitanyabhāgavata* for the newly emerging community of Bengali Vaishnavas, and he wrote it in politically unstable Bengal that was sometimes ruled by independent Muslim kings and sometimes controlled from distant Delhi. In contrast, Kṛṣṇadās composed his *Caitanyacaritāmṛta* in Vrindavan, close to the heart of the Mughal rule. By then the Mughal hegemony in North India and Bengal had been firmly established, and he wrote for the Bengali Vaishnava community that had become a part of that establishment. By the time Kṛṣṇadās composed his text, in about 1615, the construction of the Govindadevajī temple and other similar projects had amply demonstrated that Vaishnava communities could prosper under the Muslim rule. With that information, Kṛṣṇadās could write a radically different account of Muslim authority, at least where Chaitanya himself was concerned. The radical voice of protest against the possible excesses of Muslim state power decreased as the Bengali Vaishnavas' relationship with Muslim rulers changed from the fifteenth century to the seventeenth century. And who emerged as the real enemy? Other Hindus.

NOTES

I am grateful to Shimanta Roy for reading with me in February 2016 Bangla materials used in this paper. Earlier versions of this paper were presented at the following conferences and workshop: *Exploring Bhakti: Is Bhakti a Language of Power or of Protest?* (Yale University, May 14, 2016); *The 29th Annual Session of the Japanese Association for South Asian Studies*, (Kobe City University of Foreign Studies, September 25, 2016); *Culture and Society in Early Modern South Asia: Cross-Linguistic Comparative Studies of Literary and Religious Texts* (Tokyo University of Foreign Studies, December 11, 2016). I am grateful for the comments from the following colleagues who helped me improve this paper: Bergljot Chiarucci, Jack Hawley, Rembert Lutjeharms, Ayako Ninomiya, Christian Novetzke, and Lucian Wong. My research was supported by a JSPS Grant-in-Aid for Young Scientists (B)(15K16726) and by the Hakubi Centre for Advanced Research, Kyoto University.

1 Haridās, *Śrī-Śrī-Gauḍīya-Vaiṣṇava-Abhidhāna*, 1408–9.

2 O'Connell, "Vaiṣṇava Perceptions of Muslims"; De, *Early History*; Stewart, "Jaban Haridās."

3 De, *Early History*, 48–49.

4 De, *Early History*, 47–48; O'Connell, "Vaiṣṇava Perceptions," 204.

5 Hawley, "Seeing the Bhakti Movement," 236–37.

6 Nizami, *Religion and Politics in India*, 318–19.

7 Hawley, *Three Bhakti Voices*, 182.

8 Novetzke, *Religion and Public Memory*, 187–88.

9 Ali and Leaman, *Islam*, 106.

10 O'Connell, "Vaishnava Perceptions," 3–4, 199–200.

11 Vrindāvandās Ṭhākura, *Śrī-Śrī-Caitanyabhāgavata Ādikhaṇḍa*, 343–44: *Caitanyabhāgavata*, Ādi 16: 71–74:

71. kata bhāgye dekha tumi haijācha jaban / tabe kene hindura deha' man //
72. āmrā hindure dekhi' nāhi khāi bhāt / tāhā chāḍ' hai tumi mahāvaṃś-jāt //
73. jāti-dharm laṅghi' kara anya-byabahār / paraloke kemane bā pāibā nistār //
74. nā jāniyā je kichu karilā anacār / se pāp ghucāha kari' kalmā uccār //

12 Vrindāvandās Ṭhākura, *Śrī-Śrī-Caitanyabhāgavata Ādikhaṇḍa*, 344–45: *Caitanyabhāgavata*, *Ādi* 16: 76–80, 82:

76. . . . śuna bāp, sabārai ek-i īśvar //
77. nām-mātra bhed kare hindūye jabane / paramārthe 'ek' kahe korāṇe purāṇe //
78. ek śuddh nityavastu akhaṇḍa abyay / paripūrṇa haiyā baise sabār hṛday //
79. sei prabhu jāre jena lauyāyen man / seimat karma kare sakal bhuvan //
80. se prabhur nām śuṇa sakal jagate / balen sakale mātra nija-śāstra-mate //
82. eteke āmāre se īśvar jehen / laujāichen cite, kari āmi tena //

13 Stewart, "Jaban Haridas."

14 Vrindāvandās Ṭhākura, *Śrī-Śrī-Caitanyabhāgavata Ādikhaṇḍa*, 350: *Caitanyabhāgavata*, Ādi 16.118: mareo nā āro dekhi, hāse kṣaṇe kṣaṇe / "e puruṣa pīr vā?" sabei bhāve' mane //

15 Kṛṣṇadās, *Śrī-Śrī-Caitanyacaritāmṛta Ādilīlā*, 276: *Caitanyacaritāmṛta*, Ādi 10.45: prahlād samān tāṃra guṇer taraṅga / jaban tāḍane yāṃra nahila bhrūbhaṅga //

16 Vrindāvandās, *Śrī-Śrī-Caitanyabhāgavata Madhyakhaṇḍa*, 789: *Caitanya-bhāgavata*, Madhya 23.105: yāhāre pāila kāji mārila tāhāre / bhāṅgila mṛdaṅga anācār kaila dvāre //

17 Vrindāvandās, *Śrī-Śrī-Caitanyabhāgavata Madhyakhaṇḍa*, 789: *Caitanya-bhāgavata*, Madhya 23.108: eimata pratidin duṣṭagaṇ laiyā / nagar bhra-maye kāji kīrtan cāhiyā //

18 Vrindāvandās, *Śrī-Śrī-Caitanyabhāgavata Madhyakhaṇḍa*, 803: *Caitanya-bhāgavata*, Madhya 23.388–90:

388. . . . āre kāji veṭā kothā / jhāṭ ān' dhariyā kāṭiyā phela māthā //
389. nirjaban karoṃ āji sakal bhuvan / pūrve jena badh kailūṃ se kāljaban //
390. prāṇo lañā kothā kāji gela diyā dvār / ghar bhāṅga bhāṅga prabhū bale bār bār //

19 Vrindāvandās, *Śrī-Śrī-Caitanyabhāgavata Madhyakhaṇḍa*, 804: *Caitanya-bhāgavata*, Madhya 23.398–405:

398. . . . agni deha bāḍir bhitar //
399. pūḍiyā maruk sabgaṇer sahite / sarba bāḍī beḍi' agni deh' cāri bhite //
400. dekhoṃ more ki kare uhār nara-pati / dekhoṃ āji kon jane kare avyāhati //
401. jam kāl mṛtyu mor sevaker dās / mor dṛṣṭipāte hay sabār prakāś //
402. saṃkīrtan ārambhe mohor avatār / kīrtan-virodhī pāpī karimū saṃhār //
403. sarba pātakī o jadi karaye kīrtan / avaśya tāhāre mūñi karimū smaraṇ //
404. tapasvī sannyāsī jñānī yogī je je jan / saṃhārimū jodi sab nā kare kīrtan //
405. agni deh' ghare sab nā kāriha bhay / āji sab jabaner karimū pralay //

20 Kṛṣṇadās, *Śrī-Śrī-Caitanyacaritāmṛta Ādilīlā*, 248: *Caitanyabhāgavata*, Ādi 17.142:

uddhata lok bhāṅge kājīr gharpuṣpavan /
vistāri varṇilā iha das vṛndāvan //

CHAPTER THIRTEEN

BHAKTI AND POWER FROM THE INSIDE

A Devotee's Reading of What Chaitanya Achieved

SHRIVATSA GOSWAMI

THE question of bhakti's relationship to power inevitably takes us outside the boundaries of the fledgling Gauḍīya community to the historical forces that made its foundation possible. Yet these connections to the outside world would have been insipid and powerless had it not been for a certain sense of power that was deeply encoded within the new bhakti community itself. Being a member of that community, inspired and founded by Chaitanya Mahaprabhu (1486–1533), I would affirm that this internally generated power was not just something felt five hundred years ago; it persists today. Both then and now, it is not just a matter of bhakti and power that ought to draw our attention but the power of bhakti as well.

The information recorded about the life of Chaitanya Mahaprabhu in the canonical *Caitanyacaritāmṛta* seems to indicate that he decided to journey to Vrindavan, in north-central India, in 1515, though the text itself gives no dates. His purpose was to explore and experience the theater of bhakti. This had become his life's dream—to live in the land that had been sanctified by the presence of Krishna and Radha—for by then he had unmistakably discovered how bhakti was being empowered by his own religious instincts. His devotion to a life in which bhakti would be experienced and performed in public acts of singing and remembering the divine name—*saṅkīrtan*—developed as a consequence of his own ecstatic realizations. *Saṅkīrtan* was intended to cultivate and sustain those moments of realization for his own sake, as a personal project, and at the same time for the benefit of everyone he met. As we learned in chapter 12, however, these strikingly new religious modalities were hardly acclaimed by everyone on the scene, but that did nothing to take away from

Chaitanya's conviction. He fairly overflowed with his own understanding of how bhakti should be cultivated, and he seems to have taken very seriously the task of giving it an intellectual formulation.

THE TENETS OF AN INTEGRATED BHAKTI PHILOSOPHY

For all his gifts as a political actor—we sense this especially in his later interactions with the royal court at Puri—Chaitanya was also in a deep way a philosopher. To bring bhakti within the realm of philosophical discourse, Chaitanya started a bhakti school of thought at Vrindavan. With the exception of the youngest among them, Jīva, all members of the faculty of this "school"—the six Gosvāmīs[1]—were personally educated by Chaitanya himself. So the biographical sources assure us. To develop his bhakti rhetoric in the Vedantic domain, Chaitanya entrusted the main work to Gopāl Bhaṭṭ.[2] Coming as he did from the lineage of ritual actors and theoreticians that had grown up in the southern Vaishnava stronghold of Srirangam, Gopāl Bhaṭṭ had the strongest possible grounding in the bhakti tradition of Vedanta that had been formulated by Ramanuja in the eleventh and twelfth centuries. Gopāl Bhaṭṭ was ably assisted by Rūpa Gosvāmī's nephew Jīva, who had been properly trained in Vedantic concepts and Navya Nyāya linguistic philosophy at—where else?—Kashi. The result of their collaboration was the voluminous six-part philosophical treatise called the *Bhāgavata Sandarbha* or alternatively, because of its six parts, the *Ṣaṭ Sandarbha*.[3]

Under the clear influence of Chaitanya, whose inspiration Gopāl Bhaṭṭ and Jīva directly acknowledge, we see in this massive work a number of fundamental propositions. These emerge first and foremost from the text itself, of course, but we also see them in the great work of Kṛṣṇadās Kavirāj, who composed his *Caitanyacaritāmṛta* under the watchful eye of Raghunātha, Jīva, and other Gosvāmīs and devotees at whose behest he wrote.

First, as the *Sandarbha* itself says, "*Vṛhat-vastu* Brahman is Bhagavān": the absolute truth is God, the Lord. All the Vedas, in turn, relate to Bhagavān as *sambandhi tattva*, the reality to which all *śāstra* and all deliberations relate. And the various forms of bhakti—*śravana* (listening), *kīrtana* (singing praises), and so forth—are all means of gaining Bhagavān-Krishna. These forms are therefore called *abhidheya*, means of realization. First we have *sādhana bhakti*, bhakti as a means. Out of this, in turn, sprouts *premā bhakti*, the devotion of love, which transpires at the feet of Krishna. By this means the spiritual aspirant, who is simultaneously the lover, comes to taste and enjoy the *rasa*—the relishable flavor—of the happiness found in Krishna's service. Loving service of this sort is identified by the Vrindavan theologians as being the fifth goal of life (*pañcama puruṣārtha*) because it follows upon and integrates the more traditional four that are widely accepted in Indian systems of thought, namely, eros (*kāma*), effectiveness (*artha*), ethics (*dharma*), and release from the entanglements of this world (*mokṣa*). *Seī prema-mahādhana*, it is said, is the *prayojana tattva*; that is, the love of Krishna is the greatest wealth one can obtain, the *summum bonum*. Kṛṣṇadās Kavirāj lays this all out in a systematic fashion and concludes his account by saying that in so doing he has been charting the three elements of life. These are *sambandha*, *abhidheya*, and *prayojana*: relationship with reality, the means of its realization, and the goal of the spiritual journey. These, he says, "fully cover the realm of philosophical discourse."[4]

A second matter is suffering. The object of all this effort of thought is to chart the road to happiness—a road that is at the same time a process of integration. We must acknowledge that suffering is a fundamental aspect of our condition and attempt, if not to explain it, at least to indicate how it can be overcome. To move beyond suffering (the technical term is *abhyudaya*), the primary question becomes "kasmai devāya haviṣā vidhema," that is, "With what and how shall we relate to the whole in which we have our being?"[5] In this regard the *Sandarbha* specifies two alternative yet interrelated paths—intellectual and experiential. Here too the life of the mind is not understood as operating apart from the rest of our being any more than the subtler parts of what we call nature are actually separable from its more manifest aspects. As to the two aspects we have just been considering, the realm of pure intellect and the realm of experience—the latter being touched by suffering—which is which? The *Sandarbha* characteristically refuses to make a judgment. They both swim within the bhakti whole.

Consider how this operates with regard to suffering. If one's point of departure is intellectual or philosophical, then one tries to disperse suffering by means of the *via negativa*. This is the realm so memorably designated in the Upanishads as *neti neti* ("Not this, not that") or in the *Tattva Sandarbha* as "māyā mayatva anusandhānena eva," that is, "seeing through that which is illusory in nature." Here we explore the unreality of the phenomenal world around us, and of ourselves. In the path of philosophical analysis, the realization of our limitations is the threshold of our awareness of the unlimited. Reason and logic do not create this reality; rather, they respond to it, and in its own terms. They uncover it by removing the doubts (*asambhāvanā*) and conflicting views (*viparīta bhāvanā*) that persist in thinking about what it is. Thus philosophy helps reveal the ultimate reality, which can also be realized as a fact of intuitive experience through, as Jīva says, yoga or the spiritual path (*anuṣṭhiten yogen vā*).[6]

Yet as we follow the path of philosophical analysis, in our reflective awareness, we naturally come to understand that our psychological makeup defines not only the preferred nature of our quest—the pristine terrain of the intellect—but the path we follow through it, as well.[7] For this reason, we find that the authors of the *Ṣaṭ Sandarbha* are careful to demarcate a tripartite domain that expands outward from the intrinsic realm of knowledge as such. It has the following aspects:

Aspect	Status	Path	Goal
Cognitive	Object	*Jñāna* (knowledge)	*Sat* (truth, existence)
Conative	Subject	*Karma* (will)	*Cit* (consciousness)
Emotive	Both	*Bhakti* (feeling)	*Ānanda* (happiness)

Any spiritual discipline is basically a path or means of empowerment that we mobilize against pain and suffering. Happiness, in any of the three realms charted above, comes from our relating to the source of happiness. In the paths of knowledge and will, either the subject or the object of the relationship being explored or pursued is in the end negated. T. R. V. Murti puts it succinctly:

> Knowing involves the distinction of the object from consciousness; the object is something accomplished and independent. In willing, consciousness is distinguished from the content, which is immediately felt as having a being only through the former. In both of these, a distinction between content and consciousness seems necessary and can be validated by experience. Now if we can prove that there is a mode of consciousness in which the distinction between consciousness and content is either not made or only very imperfectly made, we could have evidenced feeling. Feeling is the contact or identification of consciousness with object. It is the nature of feeling that it is a unity which militates against any aloofness or emphasis of one side against the other.[8]

As we see from this analysis, in the realms of knowing and willing there is actually no occasion for relation to survive. With this the Gosvāmīs concurred. Yet there was something about relation, they argued, that meant it could not ultimately be discarded as a fact of experience, hence they dignified it as an independent concept implying something fundamentally real: *sambandhi tattva*, "the reality of connection." After all, in the cause of happiness—and happiness is the "object" of everything—we seek precisely that: relationship. Yet it is only in the path of feeling or bhakti alone, the third of those charted above, that we are able to make our peace with the fact that relation is indeed reality. It is not *māyā*, some illusory thing. Relation and bhakti presuppose each other.

The nature and function of relation is to bring together two beings or aspects or dimensions—the subject and the object, as they are most often called.

Relationship, then, is a fundamental aspect of being—perhaps it *is* being—but we need not conclude from this that all relationships are alike or that they have an equivalent ontological status. A look at our human condition reveals, rather, that there are a variety of fundamental relationships. Famously the Gosvāmīs, beginning with Rūpa, classified these as *dāsya*, *vātsalya*, *sakhya*, and *mādhurya*—master/servant, parent/child, friend/friend, and lover/beloved[9]—and we see that classification also reflected in the *Caitanyacaritāmṛta*.[10] These four are perceived as being arranged in a certain hierarchy, from bottom to top in the order we have listed them, but ironically the ultimate criterion of this so-called hierarchy is intimacy or immediacy. This means that as we climb the ladder from master/servant to lover/beloved, then, we are not actually climbing but going deeper or moving closer. A second irony in the system is that intimacy at the climax of this progression does not necessarily emerge as being simpler than what one experiences at the point of departure, despite the fact that the notion of lovers' intimacy would seem to imply this. Rather, the amorous love relationship, *mādhurya*, is more complex and comprehensive than anything that precedes it: the lover/beloved relationship has room for all the others within itself and must necessarily comprise them. Thus perceived, the most complete form of relationship is to be found in the *mādhurya* or *kānta-kāntā bhāva*, the mood that envelops lovers in an amorous space. This includes and transcends all the others.[11]

These necessary ironies help us see that a deep encounter with bhakti has a driving force and a culminating logic that lies behind the generation of any system. Bhakti is what it is in some truly inconceivable (*acintya*) way. On this point Rūpa quotes the *Mahābhārata*: "The *bhāvas* are inscrutable. Logic cannot touch them. Thus to all these, logic cannot be applied, for what is beyond material nature is defined as incomprehensible"[12]

Once relation has been established—both in ordinary human life and in the working out of this philosophical system—the concern shifts to the question of how it can be sustained. This too is an essential concern: we do not want suffering to return. In the view of the Gosvāmīs—again, I believe, replicating the view of Chaitanya himself—bhakti interpreted as service (*sevā*) provides the way forward. Bhakti that is true bhakti cannot be engaged at any level for the purpose of mere show or as a response to any kind of duress. True and effective relationship is instead manifested out of love—*premā bhakti*—and in that mode the focus is upon the welfare of the other to whom we are connected in love.[13]

Fortunately, seekers on the path of *premā bhakti*, as illuminated by philosophical analysis, can also benefit from the experience of those who have trod the path before them. Once again the analysis provided by Professor Murti is helpful in getting a sense of what is involved. He writes about feeling in general, but what he says is applicable to the felt phenomenon of *premā bhakti:*

> Is feeling known? . . . Feeling is not known, and this for two reasons. Feeling is not an object existing by itself, an accomplished fact, which we only view calmly and dispassionately. There cannot be feeling, if such a detachment or distinction is made between consciousness and content. Secondly, the difference between feeling, if it were objectified, and knowledge would not be a functional or co-ordinate difference, for feeling would be a species of object as red or the table and not a mode of relation between consciousness and content. The difference between feeling and the table would be sought to be made on the ground that the latter is an outer object while the former is an inner one. But this very distinction of the "inner" and the "outer" would involve feeling; we call that "inner" with which we are identified intimately and perhaps inseparably. . . . The essence of feeling is not its unreflective character which may be its limiting case, but the comparative non-distinction between consciousness and content. This is available in a reflective state too. A reflective feeling can be defined as that state in which to feel and at once to be aware of it as feeling are not distinct, distinguishable. . . . It might be seen that feeling is more primitive and basic than the other two [i.e., knowing and willing]; it is "thicker."[14]

This line of thinking opens the way toward a second and alternative way of spiritual seeking, whereby one digs deeper into investigating what is given in human life. This too is an experiential journey, though it may not initially seem as full of loving relationship as "love itself." Both are embraced in bhakti. This time, rather than raw emotion and its fruits, we have the path of religion, the journey within. For progress to be made along this spiritual path we require *sākṣāt-kṛta dharmāṇa ṛṣayaḥ*, that is, accomplished persons who have actually seen firsthand (*ṛṣir-darśanāt*) the reality we seek.[15] Seen from a distance this may seem not an alternate path to the goal but a detour from it, a wholesale abandoning of the immediacy of love. Why do we need the institution of a guru as a way of opening up the fullness of the bond between the seeker and the sought?

Once again the answer comes from taking into account the nature of the subject—who we actually are. Learning is a fundamental constituent in the life of any human being. To live is to learn—this the human way. As a species, we gestate long, and our gestation largely happens outside the womb, in the realm we can call broadly education. Truly, humans do not accomplish anything they have not learned. As the *Bhāgavata Purāṇa* says, "guror-anugrahena-eva pumān pūrṇa praśāntaye" (it is only by the grace of a preceptor that one attains complete tranquility).[16] Learning the grammars of life is a basic need in all spheres, from the mundane to the spiritual and back. The focal point of Hindu spirituality in this regard is the guru, literally a "heavy," but in practice more likely a person who switches us on. Then, under a guru's guidance we are required to learn to do *premamayī sevā*, service that consists of love.

This discipline is called *vaidhi bhakti*, devotion that is enjoined. It is widely described as having nine steps.[17] The first five are as follows:

1. *Śravaṇa*: listening to the names, qualities and pastimes of the Lord
2. *Kīrtana*: repeating what is heard, allowing it to sprout and unfold
3. *Smaraṇa*: remembering it, that is, nourishing it by means of any kind of mental connection with the Lord
4. *Pādasevana*: serving the Lord's feet, i.e., exhibiting adoration for what one has been taught
5. *Arcana*: celebration through acts of offering.

This leads us to second stage in the discipline of bhakti, where love is released from the regimen of enacting what has been taught and comes to take its own course. Here injunctions and grammar mature into spontaneity, the poetry of love:

6. *Vandana*: general veneration and praise of the beloved
7. *Dāsya*, including *vātsalya*: a mind-set in which all actions are offered to the Lord
8. *Sakhya*: trust and friendship
9. *Ātma-nivedana*: the total merger that is attained by offering one's soul and body to the Lord ("sarva dharmān parityajya mām ekam *śaraṇam* vraja").[18] In this education-driven parallel economy of bhakti, *ātma-nivedana* stands in for the intense amorous relationship typically described by the Gosvāmīs as *mādhurya*.

There is much more to be said, but I hope this discussion begins to clarify what a carefully and multiply integrated intellectual system this is and how it attends to the actual facts of human life insofar as one sees these facts from the point of view of relationality. Relationality is a distinctive feature of bhakti ways of thinking, as has been signaled in chapters 10 and 11 of this book. Here we see how these relations, under the guiding influence of Chaitanya, were understood to form a common, integrated system. Not that it solves all mysteries: the whole enterprise is *acintya-bheda-abheda*, the inconceivable co-presence of difference and nondifference at all levels. Seen most deeply, this is what relationality always means; the bhakti dimension is its greatest depth.

And there is one special mystery: bhakti, to be useful to humankind, must have a body. It cannot just be a philosophical idea or doctrine. Bhakti can only happen fully when it is practiced not just as a means of realization (*abhidheya*) but also as its own goal (*prayojana*), and that brings us back to the person for the forming of the historical and theoretical enterprises that opened up in the course of the sixteenth century: Sri Chaitanya himself. Those who looked upon him in his own lifetime and those who looked back upon him in later generations regarded Chaitanya as a joint incarnation of Radha and Krishna—male and female, divine and human, goal and means, opposites united in a single body.[19] Chaitanya is *acintya-bheda-abheda* in bodily form.

PROTEST AND EMPOWERMENT

The history of Indian culture—perhaps like any culture—is a history of protesting, rebelling against, rejecting, and correcting the given at any given point of time. To be able to take such a stance is to feel a sense of empowerment and to see the whole historical process that results from it as testimony to that fact. Certain British writers alleged that a sort of stultification broadly characterized Indian history. Undoubtedly there have been moments of encrustation—one thinks inevitably of caste—but on the whole, I would see a much more dynamic and self-correcting pattern of gradual change. In such a history Chaitanya played a remarkable role. Empowered by the bhakti logic of *acintya-bheda-abheda* and persuaded of its metaphysics, Chaitanya manifested a continuous dynamic of protesting and empowering. Deeply grounded in tradition, he nonetheless injected quite new dimensions into the philosophic discourse of his time, and into its spiritual discipline. Not only did he liberate logical minds from the shackles of binary opposites—*bheda* and *abheda*—he also dared to bring under review the postulates of the four-*varṇa* system, the debilitating logic of caste.

One of the most dramatic of Chaitanya's acts of empowerment, as registered in the acts of his followers, concerned language itself. A. K. Ramanujan is famous for having insisted that Indian culture maintains a broad contrast between Sanskrit and the vernacular mother tongues, with the mother tongues—inherently vivid—capable of rebelling against the ritually oriented, typically Brahmanical learning that Sanskrit represents. In many regards Ramanujan was right, but under the framework of *acintya-bheda-abheda*, both those streams flowed freely in Vrindavan. Sanskrit and vernacular, the classical and folk, *śāstra* and *loka*, *vaidhi bhakti* and *rāgānugā bhakti*—all these were encouraged to flourish, with the one empowering the other in a single, complex field.[20] Here we have the integral power *of* bhakti. It generated a dynamic new reality that touched seemingly every aspect of life.

But at the same time there was also the reality of power *and* bhakti, the dialogical alliance that the Gosvāmīs forged with the Mughal court—or was it they who forged it with them? In either case, as we know, the Kacchvāhā kings played an important mediating role, and in 1598 Vrindavan was concretized as a separate revenue entity.[21] This was, for its time, an unparalleled example of interfaith engagement, whereby the holiest of Hindu *dhāms* was blessed by and administratively constituted as a gift of a Muslim emperor. Things were not always so rosy. As we saw in chapter 12 there was a famous confrontation with a Muslim *qāzī* in Bengal, and as we also saw, that encounter is reported in two quite different ways in the Chaitanyite biographies. My favorite of these two is Kṛṣṇadās Kavirāj's, of course, not Vrindāvandās's; there Chaitanya leads his interreligious protest by means of peaceful noncooperation. But the empowering energy of bhakti is felt in both, for as long as Chaitanya was involved, no one was going to shut down the public act of *saṅkīrtana*. This was an activity Chaitanya saw as spanning all boundaries of religion and class; in that way it achieved a broadening of perspective that was interestingly parallel to what the philosophy of *acintya-bheda-abheda* achieved in a more rarefied domain. Chaitanya's close companions had names like Yavan Haridās, Sākar Mallik, Dabīr Khās, and Anupam Mallik, all indicating a Muslim background of some kind.[22] Two of these men, Sākar Mallik and Dabīr Khās, emerged as among the greatest theologians of *acintya-bheda-abheda*. We know them more familiarly by the names they adopted when they traveled to Vrindavan, as Sanātana and Rūpa Gosvāmī. And a host of Hindus not adjudged by Brahmans to be high-caste were the backbone of his movement—Rāya Rāmānand, Raghunāth Dās Gosvāmī, and many others.

All these are externally ascertainable facts to the extent that we can retrieve them from the historical record, and Chaitanyites left behind quite a remarkable trove of such records. But there is also an inner dimension without which this external history of seemingly inconceivable bhakti consolidation cannot be understood. This internal dimension has the name of Chaitanya Mahaprabhu written all over it. Without him one can scarcely imagine how such events—intellectual, diplomatic, expressive—could ever have taken place.

NOTES

1 De, *Early History*, 11–165; Rosen, *Six Goswamis of Vrindavan*; Jana, *Vṛndāvaner Chaya Gosvāmī.*

2 Shrivatsa Goswami, "Gopal Bhatt," 335–53.

3 Jīva Gosvāmī, *Bhāgavata Sandarbha.*

4 *Caitanyacaritāmṛta, ādi līlā* 7.132–39, 246–47.

5 *Ṛg Veda* 10.121.1.

6 "svayam vāmadevāderiva māyāmayatvānusandhānen devahūtyāderivānuṣṭhiten yogen vā" (Jīva Gosvāmī, *Tattva Sandarbha, anuccheda* 38, 22).

7 "atha-ivam-advaya-jñāna-lakṣaṇam tat tattvam sāmānyato lakṣayitvā punar-upāsaka-yogyatā-vaiśiṣṭyena prakaṭita nijasattāviśeṣam" (Jīva Gosvāmī, *Bhāgavata Sandarbha, anu*, 1, 1).

8 Coward, *Studies in Indian Thought*, 23.

9 Rūpa Gosvāmī, *Bhaktirasāmṛtasindhu, dakṣiṇa vibhāga, pañcama laharī* 6–7, 354.

10 "cāri bhāva-bhakti diyā nācāmu bhuvana" (*Caitanyacaritāmṛta, ādi līlā* 3.17, 178). "dāsya, sakhya, vātsalya āra je sṛṅgāra, cāri prema caturvidha bhaktaī ādhāra" (*Caitanyacaritāmṛta, ādi līlā* 4.38, 190).

11 "nija nija bhāva sabe śreṣṭha kare māne, nijabhāve kare kṛṣṇa āsvādane. taṭastha haiyā hṛdi bicāra jadi kari, sab rasa haite sṛngāre mādhurī" (*Caitanyacaritāmṛta, ādi līlā* 4.39–40, 190).

12 *Bhaktirasāmṛtasindhu, dakṣiṇa vibhāga, pañcama laharī* 93, 376.

13 "ātma sukh-duhkhe gopir nāhika bichār, kṛṣṇa-sukha hetu kare sab byabahār" (*Caitanyacaritāmṛta, ādi līlā* 4.149, 202).

14 Coward, *Studies in Indian Thought*, 24–25, 27.

15 Etymology of *ṛṣi* as per Yāska Muni.

16 *Bhāgavata Purāṇa* 10.80.43.

17 *Bhāgavata Purāṇa* 7.5.23.

18 *Bhagavad Gītā* 18.66.

19 *Bhāgavata Purāṇa* 11.5.32; *Tattva Sandarbha* 2.1; *Caitanya Caritāmṛta, ādi līlā* 1, *śloka* 5, 151.

20 "Likhyate ṣāstra-lokābhyāṃ kṛṣṇa-janma-tither-vidhiḥ"; also "lokavad gokulasyāpi vyavahārādi darśanāt, ityādi-dṛṣṭyā daṣamāt brajabhāvena sevinā" (Rūpa Gosvāmī, *Kṛṣṇajanmatithividhiḥ* 1.74, 1.21).

21 Nath, "Srī Govindadeva's Itinerary from Vṛndāvana to Jayapura, ca. 1534–1727," and Horstmann, "Śrī Govindadeva and His Custodians from 1643 through the Time of Jaya Siṃha II (1700–1743)," as cited in Case, ed., *Govindadeva*, 162 and 193n12.

22 "Haridāsa Ṭhākur and Rūpa and Sanātana—these three did not go to the temple of Jagannātha" (*Caitanyacaritāmṛta, madhya mīlā* 1.57, 339). I would correct the past-tense translation "did" to the present-tense "do" in this instance.

CHAPTER FOURTEEN

FALL FROM GRACE?

Caste, Bhakti, and Politics in Late Eighteenth-Century Marwar

DIVYA CHERIAN

TEMPLES were for praying, not playing—so the Rathor state, with Maharaja Vijai Singh (r. 1752–93) at its apex, made clear. It taught this lesson the hard way to a handful of young boys, all from *mahājan* (merchant and moneylender) families in 1770.[1] Those boys had made the mistake of accidentally knocking over a Krishna idol (*kanhaīyyā jī rī mūrat*) while playing inside a temple in the *mahājan* quarter of Jalor.[2] The idol broke, and news of the accident reached Jodhpur, from where central administrators at the Shrī Hajūr rā Daftar (henceforth, the crown[3]) demanded a list of all the boys' names, along with their ages and their fathers' names.[4] Similarly, in 1793 the crown ordered an inquiry into reports of a treasury officer in Phalodhi flinging *prasād* into the air in the melee following Kārtik Pūrṇimā prayers.[5] And in 1786 it ordered punishment of a temple worker (*sevag*) who was accused of molesting a *mahājan* woman inside the Gangshyamji Temple in Jodhpur, noting "īṇ tarai mandir maiṃ beadbī karai," or "he misbehaves in this way inside a temple."[6] These episodes tell us that the late eighteenth-century Rathor state took upon itself the responsibility to ensure that temples, especially Vaishnava temples, were sites of respect, dignity, and prestige.

A great number of other incidents pertaining to temples also attracted the crown's attention. Scholarship on Maharaja Vijai Singh's reign has explained his adoption of the role of Krishna devotee and his enthusiasm at being a patron and protector of Vaishnava worship in Marwar as being driven by a desire to win the support of the nonelite classes, such as artisans and service groups, within his domain. This conclusion rests on the widespread assumption that bhakti in general and Krishna bhakti as practiced by the Vallabh Sampradāy in particular were informed by a spirit of egalitarianism and inclusivity.[7] But in Vijai Singh's Marwar, was bhakti such a religion of antihierarchical protest, or did the Vallabhites' "Way of Grace"—*puṣṭimārg*, its central article of self-definition—lead bhakti in a different direction altogether?

The Rathor historical record reflects the political struggles that unfolded around Vaishnava temples in the last few decades of the eighteenth century in Marwar. It reveals efforts to marginalize "lowly" artisanal communities and eject Muslims from Vaishnava ritual and spaces and demonstrates the erosion of Islamic sites in the face of an expanding and ever more visible Vaishnava public. The Rathor crown and its provincial officers played central roles in each of these struggles, as did merchants and brahmans who had become by this period leaders of local bhakti communities. Proximity to power transformed Vaishnava bhakti and the communities that had formed around it.

The Rathor state under Vijai Singh and his successor Bhim Singh (r. 1793–1803) made arrangements to ensure that Vaishnava temples and the service (*sevā*) of the Krishna idol within them were not neglected. In 1793 Purohit Mishra Hariram abandoned his duties as *kathā vāchak*, that is, a reciter of tales from Krishna's life, for a few months in order to earn some extra money by joining a local militia.[8] Possessive of his *kathā vāchak* appointment, Hariram refused even to let his brother recite *kathā* while he was away. When news of this dereliction of duty reached the Rathor state in Jodhpur, it ordered the local *kachedī* to fine him and to confiscate his land and wells. It took several fervent appeals by Hariram for Rathor administrators in the capital to rescind the order of confiscation.[9] The Rathor state's concern for temples was extensive. It wanted to ensure that every temple in its domain was actively in worship. In 1797, thus, it dispatched an order to four of its populous *parganās*—Jodhpur, Nagaur, Sojhat, and Didwana—commanding that every single temple within its jurisdiction should receive active worship ("koī devsthān apūj raiṇ nā pāvai"). If any temple lay abandoned, provincial officers were to direct a brahman priest from a nearby temple to revive worship in it.[10]

It was not just the prestige of existing Krishna temples that occupied the Rathors. Instead, from the mid-1750s onward, the Rathor state supported the construction of new Krishna temples by allocating land, wells, and other sources of income tax-free toward this end, such as a temple in Parbatsar *parganā* that it built in 1789 and to which it assigned two hundred *bīghās*[11] of rain-fed land.[12] Earlier, in 1782, the crown ordered the replacement of the tiara and loincloth, both made of gold-embroidered cloth (*tās*), that adorned the Krishna idol in a local temple in Merta.[13] In these decades, the Rathor state allocated funds, tax-free lands, and other resources for the construction, maintenance, and repair of Vaishnava temples, and for worship within them.[14]

The Rathor state also generously supported the temple construction initiatives of its subjects. While *mahājans* were able quite often to finance their own temple construction, the Rathor state also bolstered their efforts when needed. So, when a Bajaj moneylender's efforts to build a Ram temple stalled in 1787, the Rathor crown ordered its officers in Merta to help him in collecting debts due to him.[15] When devotees ran up against obstacles to their temple-building plans, they were frequently able to draw the crown's coercive might to their side.[16]

There is much indication from the Rathor archival record of the initiative taken not just by the state but also by its subjects in the construction and upkeep of Vaishnava temples. While a *jāṭ* (landholding peasant) or a Brahman occasionally shows up as attempting to build a new temple, it is the more prosperous *mahājan* community that appears to have taken the lead in initiating and supporting temple construction. In these very decades, the *mahājans* of Marwar were in the process of consolidating their position as holders and movers of capital across the Indian subcontinent, and as creditors within Marwar. Groups of *mahājans* in Parbatsar, Koliya, and Nagaur and a *mahājan* moneylender in Merta appear in the historical record as playing an active role in the construction, upkeep, and renovation of Krishna temples.[17] Their significance as wealthy patrons of these localized, temple-based bhakti congregations likely allowed *mahājans* to take a position of dominance within local bhakti communities.

Another group that enjoyed much prominence within temple-centric devotional communities were brahmans. By the late eighteenth century, the responsibility to recite *kathā* and the steady salary accompanying the office[18] appear to have been placed solely in brahman hands across the full range of Krishna temples in Marwar.[19] The Rathor state recognized the position as hereditary, thus helping to retain both the power and the material gain associated with it in the hands of brahman families.[20] The eighteenth-century Rathor confirmation of *kathā* recitation in temples as a solely brahman privilege is noteworthy when read against evidence pointing to the role of non-brahman groups such as *kāyasths*, Muslims, and *ahīrs* in sixteenth-century Avadh in the composition and performance of Krishna *kathās*.[21]

Vaishnavism, albeit in a "vulgate" form, had made its way into Rajasthan in the sixteenth century, entering a diverse religious landscape clustered around such loci as Sunni Islam, the Nizarpanth, local *pirs*, Devi worship, Shaivism, and Nath Yogis.[22] By the eighteenth century, peasant communities such as the *jāṭs* as well as a large number of artisanal groups had joined local, temple-based bhakti communities in Marwar. As more organized forms of Vaishnava practice and proselytization developed with the rise of the Braj-centered Vallabh and Chaitanya Sampradāyas from the late sixteenth century onward, some segments among the Rajputs of Marwar, especially the more elite ones exposed to the cosmopolitan Mughal milieu, took initiation into these sects. The Vallabh Sampradāy in particular also drew a large following among the mercantile communities of Marwar, who maintained close ties with the vibrant port cities and merchant groups of neighboring Gujarat.[23] Gujarat had been a magnet for the proselytizing activities of the leaders of the Vallabh Sampradāy who succeeded in attracting a large following among merchants there.[24] The spread of the type of Krishna bhakti preached by the Vallabhites and Chaitanyites received a further boost when the centers of gravity of both communities shifted from Braj to the Rajput kingdoms of Rajasthan in the late seventeenth century.[25]

The initiation of Maharaja Vijai Singh, the ruler of Marwar, into the Vallabh Sampradāy in 1766 therefore must be understood as part of a much larger shift in which sectarian Vaishnavaism reshaped the religious commitments of a significant segment of the population of Marwar.[26] Since the seventeenth century, Rajput ruling elites beyond Marwar had also been moving toward an embrace of newer forms of sectarian Vaishnavaism.[27] By the eighteenth century, Vaishnava bhakti had cemented its place as a "public, cosmopolitan Mughal religion," and a kingly embrace of it brought benefits both political and material.[28]

In eighteenth-century Marwar this fusion of sectarian Vaishnavism and temporal authority—both in the form of royal allegiance as well as in the growing power of merchant members—resulted in an effort to mark off Vaishnava sacred spaces as being accessible only to the ritually "pure." For local elites—especially for *mahājans* and brahmans in urban areas—Vaishnava bhakti now offered a path not only to divine grace but also to worldly status. As a result, these groups, along with *jāṭs* in rural areas, led efforts to expel from their midst those they saw as too lowly. At the receiving end of these efforts were members of artisanal and service castes, loosely categorized at the time as *pūṇ jāts*.[29] Another result of this process was that Muslims, whose membership in the Vaishnava bhakti community was already tenuous if at all possible, were now unambiguously pushed beyond its pale. As far as groups such as leatherworkers (*chamārs*, *bhāmbhīs*, *meghvāls*) and sweepers (*bhangīs*) were concerned, their inclusion in Vaishnava bhakti communities, it appears, was already out of the question.

Artisanal communities such as shoemakers (*mochīs*), oil-pressers (*ghānchīs*), and tailors (*darjīs*) had to contend with localized efforts to eject them from the devotional communities they had become part of over prior centuries. Between 1786 and 1788, for instance, the *mochīs* of Merta fought to fend off efforts by fellow, likely more elite, Vaishnava devotees to push them to the spatial and ritual margins of their local community of *bhaktas*. The Rathor state appears to have been pulled in different directions when it came to adjudicating the matter. In 1786 the crown received news that the *mochīs* of Merta were dipping their hands in the local Chaturbhujji Temple's saffron bowl and receiving the deity's *darśan* from behind the wooden fence demarcating a more sacred area within the temple; thus—at this distance—they participated in his royal audience. The crown reprimanded its officers in Merta for allowing these "transgressions" and ordered them to ensure that the *mochīs* should not touch the saffron bowl and that they should offer prayers in a half-standing position that would presumably cause them to keep away from the wooden fence.[30]

When disciplined for their alleged misbehavior in Merta, the *mochīs* banded together into a delegation and petitioned the crown at Jodhpur. They refuted the allegations, accepting that such behavior should rightly attract punishment. The *mochīs* of Merta asserted that they had only adhered to their customary place in temple devotion, that is, they had received the deity's audience from an appropriate distance behind the wooden fence, anointed their foreheads with the sacred *tilak* at a prescribed distance (*uparāṁ su*), and also received blessed saffron-water (*charaṇāmrit*). Pressured by the *mochīs* and confronted with the primacy of past practice, the crown commanded its officers in Merta to permit the *mochīs* to offer their prayers and receive blessings as they "always had."[31]

Despite being armed with this royal missive, however, the *mochīs* found upon their return to Merta that their adversaries now refused to even let them enter the temple, claiming to be armed with a rival royal *sanad* (state order) authorizing this action. Only ten days after their first appeal, therefore, the *mochīs* were back before the crown with the same petition. Once again, they returned to Merta armed with a supportive ruling that stated that not just the *mochīs* but all artisanal and service castes (*pūṇ jāt*) be allowed to receive the deity's *darśan* inside the temple, as well as maintaining access to all the other symbols of being an integral (if specifically marked) part of the temple community.[32]

Despite this, two years later, in 1788, they were back before the crown a third time, complaining that some other members of the local Vaishnava community continued to debar them from entering the temple. Once again the *mochīs* were being forced to receive the deity's *darśan* from outside Merta's Chaturbhujji temple. Yet again the crown backed the *mochīs*. Recognizing implicitly that its authority as earlier expressed had been insufficient in this matter, the crown buttressed this final order by also citing the authority of three Vaishnava *gosvāmīs* ("gusāīṁjī shrī lachhmaṇjī shrī mhārā nadlāljī shri dvārkānāthjī rī āgyā su").[33]

In this protracted episode, different functionaries of the Rathor government appear to have been at odds with one another. The *mochīs*' complaints mention that their adversaries also kept marshaling legal documents called *sanads* to bolster their own efforts to eject the *mochīs* from their community.

It seems likely that the Rathors' provincial administrators in Merta were sympathetic to the *mochīs'* adversaries. This may indeed have been why the *mochīs* were pushed to take their appeal to the crown in the first place—and repeatedly. This tension within different organs and levels of Rathor government also played out in other conflicts over the place of "low" castes in Vaishnava sectarian life.

The same pattern repeated itself when the *mochīs* of Sojhat reported being prevented from holding a public performance of Krishna devotion. On the occasion of Jhūlnā Igyāras in 1787, the local *chauntrā* (literally, "platform" and shorthand for *koṭwālī chauntarā*, or the provincial magistrate) prevented these *mochīs* from conducting a processional march carrying the Krishna idol from their own temple (one they had built). The *mochīs* secured an order from the crown that commanded local officers in the *chauntrā* to stop obstructing the *mochīs'* effort to express their Krishna bhakti publicly.[34] Yet the next year saw the same tussle play out again, with the *chauntrā* disallowing the *mochīs'* Jhūlnā Igyāras procession and the *mochīs* winning the crown's support for their customary claim to it.[35]

This tension—between the crown and its provincial officers—reflects a state caught between the rival pressures exerted by the structural dominance of its elites on the one hand and the ideological basis of its own rule on the other. The Rathor crown rested its claims to legitimacy upon the rhetoric of upholding justice.[36] Custom was a powerful plank upon which the discourse of justice in early modern Marwar stood. At the same time, when its more locally influential subjects tried to reorder local hierarchies and practices, the crown found itself in a spot, caught between appeals to custom and the political resources of its more powerful subjects. Further, these subjects—especially brahmans and *mahājans*—manned the highest echelons of Rathor government, both in Jodhpur and the provinces.[37] When confronted by a delegation of its less fortunate subjects who were able to make a case that their claims rested squarely on custom, crown officers in Jodhpur might have felt compelled to uphold their claim, as we have seen. Yet in a range of other instances the Rathor crown came down heavily in favor of protecting a sanctified Vaishnava domain from being "defiled" by "low" castes.

An episode of this sort occurred in 1786, when news reached the crown that an officiant in Jodhpur's Gangshyamji Temple, Sevak Jivraj, had made the "mistake" of placing the offerings brought by a *darjī* (tailor) and a *ghānchī* (oil-presser) before the Krishna idol in the two artisans' own vessels. For this lapse in judgment the crown ordered that Jivraj—and anyone else who committed the same "crime" (*taksīr*)—lose two months' salary.[38]

It was not just "low" castes but also Muslims who were driven out from the expanding public of Vaishnava devotion. The association of Vaishnava temples and public rituals with temporal authority, through the patronage and public participation of the king and local elites, imbued these spaces with prestige and power. The simultaneous fencing out—both real and metaphorical—of both "low" castes and Muslims then marked them as ineligible to participate in new arenas of elite public life.

A member of the local community of devotees in Merta, the *bairāgaṇ* (renunciant) Tulchhi, was discovered in 1786 to be Muslim ("jāt rī turakaṇī huī nīsrī") and so was expelled from the community with the support of the crown.[39] "Why does a Muslim have to come to a Krishna temple?" ("musalmān nu ṭhākurdvārai kyuṁ āvaṇo paḍai?"), the crown asked the *chauntrā* of Nagaur in response to a report of two Muslims sitting on the parapet of the Murlidharji Temple in Nagaur. It ordered the *chauntrā* to fine the two Muslims.[40] Similarly, in 1787, a *jāṭ* from a village in Parbatsar *parganā* complained to the crown that Muslims—"Sipāhīs and so forth" ("musalmān sīpāī vagairai")—were coming to the Krishna temple (*thākurdvāro*) he had built. This was not correct ("su ṭhīk nahī"), said the *jāṭ*. Agreeing with this view, the crown ordered that the village's *jāgīrdārs* and peasant leadership (*chaudharīs*) should keep Muslims out of the Krishna temple.[41] Despite ongoing efforts to reshape its practice, however, a more open Vaishnava bhakti continued to exercise a powerful pull upon those seeking modes of religious practice that did not turn the accident of birth into a barrier for entry.

Simultaneously, however, efforts to limit the sites of Muslim communal life so as to accommodate an expanding Vaishnava public also unfolded. In 1789 the *qāzīs* (*kājī*) of Rohal village in Nagaur *pargana* were forced to petition the crown when a local revenue officer (*havāldār*) sided with a group of *bhagats* (i.e., *bhaktas*) who were intent on turning a Sufi *fakīr*'s hospice into a temple. These *bhagats* had secured pre-emptive permission for their plans from the *kachedī* in Nagaur. While it remains unclear if the *bhagats* succeeded in building the temple, the dispute triggered a longer conflict in which a *bhagat* accused boys of these *qāzī* families of stealing, thus giving an opportunity to local officers to harass the *qāzīs*.[42] Such *qāzīs* could, however, protest, taking advantage of the crown's professed allegiance to equanimity and the protection of customary rights.

Despite the still compelling claims of custom and impartiality, the crown's inclination to favor efforts on the part of Vaishnavas—especially well-financed, "high"-born Vaishnavas—to expand their sway in Marwar's cultural and religious economy is discernible. Thus, in the same year, 1789, the crown granted permission to a Srimali Brahman to build a Vaishnava temple near the Jodhpuria Gate in Sojhat, on the site of what used to be a "Muslim hospice" (*turak ro takīyā*) but was now just an empty plot because its bricks had been used to build the town's fortifications.[43]

Marwar in the late eighteenth century witnessed the elevation of Vaishnava bhakti to a position of preeminence and prestige due to the affiliation and patronage not just of the Maharaja himself but also of the increasingly wealthy and influential *mahājans* of the region. Initiatives to push "low" castes and Muslims to the spatial and ritual margins of bhakti communities arose in local contexts, centered on individual temples. I would suggest that Vijai Singh's embrace of bhakti was not intended to win artisanal and other nonelite groups' assent to his reign. To the contrary, his and other regional elites' embrace of bhakti coincided with and abetted the transformation of localized Krishna bhakti communities into more rarefied realms than before, increasingly inaccessible to the nonelite.

In some cases, the crown in Jodhpur felt obliged to support resistance to these efforts in the name of custom. On other occasions, however—the majority of instances—provincial and local functionaries of the Rathor state under Vijai Singh and Bhim Singh, many of them *mahājans* themselves, fueled exclusionary efforts by enlisting the state's coercive and legal authority in their cause. The resulting marginalization and exclusion of "low"-caste *bhaktas* and Muslims from Vaishnava ritual and spaces was part of wider shift underway in Marwar in these decades, one that pushed for the construction of an elite, caste-constituted Hindu identity in opposition to an "Achhep" ("Untouchable") one.[44] Vaishnava bhakti was a locus around which this eighteenth-century, precolonial Hindu identity gathered strength, its more powerful patrons pushing "lowly" *bhaktas* such as shoemakers, tailors, and oil-pressers together with Muslims to the periphery of the new public spaces that heralded its ascendance. As we have seen, newer forms of bhakti public-making and the state's claim that it dispensed impartial justice often encouraged protest on the part of excluded, but at least as often the crown acceded to the exclusivist demands of this newly instated bhakti public. The picture is certainly complex, but it supports the conclusion that new forms of bhakti in late eighteenth-century Marwar tilted more toward power than protest.

NOTES

This essay relies on an examination of the Jodhpur Sanad Parwana Bahi record series, abbreviated in the notes below to JSPB, which is housed in the Rajasthan State Archives, Bikaner, Rajasthan. The series consists of annual compilations of the rulings and decrees sent by the Rathor ruler and his office in Jodhpur to the kingdom's provincial headquarters. In the notes below, references to these records list the *bahī* or register number (as assigned by the Rajasthan State Archives and written on each *bahī*), the Vikram Samvat (VS) year and the year in CE of its inscription, and the folio number (f) and side (a or b) within the *bahī* on which the information being cited is written.

1 *Mahājan* (literally, "great man"), in eighteenth-century Rajasthan, designated a person engaged in trade and usury. Despite the diversity of castes encompassed in this social category, by the eighteenth century in Marwar, it was a cohesive category that enjoyed currency in state records. Elsewhere, the term held different meanings, such as an urban association of elite merchant-moneylenders, as in seventeenth-century Gujarat (Pearson, *Merchants and Rulers in Gujarat*, 123–26) and a brahman recipient of an *agrahāra* grant, as in the medieval western Deccan (Novetzke, *Quotidian Revolution*, 62).

2 JSPB 10, VS 1827/1770 CE, f144b.

3 I use the term "crown" as a metonym for the office of the mahārājā and not to denote the mahārājā himself. The decrees and judgments that I draw upon for this essay were largely issued, I contend, on behalf of the mahārājā, by high-ranking bureaucrats generally led by brahmans (Bhati, *Rājasthān kī Praśāsanik Vyavasthā*, 101–2).

4 Bhati, *Rājasthān kī Praśāsanik Vyavasthā*, 101–2. I could not locate any further information on how the case was resolved. In the rest of this essay as well, where I leave unsaid how an episode finally played out, it is because I do not have any additional information about it.

5 JSPB 45, VS 1850/1793 CE, f413b.

6 JSPB 35, VS 1843/1786 CE, f61b–62a.

7 Sahai, "Artisans, the State, and the Politics," 702.

8 JSPB 45, VS 1850/1793 CE, f389b.

9 JSPB 45, VS 1850/1793 CE, f396b and 400b.

10 JSPB 49, VS 1854/1797 CE, f248a.

11 A unit of land measurement that has varied over time and place. Under Akbar, one *bīghā*, which was 60 *gaz* by 60 *gaz*, with each *gaz* equal to 33 inches, came to 27,255 square feet or 0.6256 acres. While the *bīghā* measure in eighteenth-century Marwar may have varied, working with the Akbar-period standard, 200 *bīghās* of land will come to about 125.12 acres or half a square kilometer (Chandra, *Medieval India*, vol. 2, 156).

12 JSPB 41, VS 1846/1789 CE, f148b.

13 JSPB 28, VS 1839/1782 CE, f86b.

14 JSPB 11, VS 1828/1771 CE, f85b; JSPB 18, VS 1834/1777 CE, f123b; JSPB 35, VS 1843/1786 CE, f214a; JSPB 38, VS 1845/1788 CE, f83b–84a; and JSPB 61, VS 1866/1809 CE, f26b–27a.

15 JSPB 36, VS 1844/1787 CE, f89b.

16 JSPB 8, VS 1825/1768 CE, f63b; JSPB 14, VS 1831/1774 CE, f247b; and JSPB 36, VS 1844/1787 CE, f90b.

17 JSPB 14, VS 1831/1774 CE, f247b; JSPB 18, VS 1834/1777 CE, f123b; JSPB 36, VS 1844/1787 CE, f89b; JSPB 38, VS 1845/1788 CE, f83b–84a; and JSPB 61, VS 1866/1809 CE, f26b–27a.

18 JSPB 38, VS 1845/1788 CE, f83b–84a; JSPB 44, VS 1849/1792 CE, f110+14b (several folios between those numbered 110 and 111 in this Bahi are unnumbered).

19 JSPB 15, VS 1832/1775 CE, f160a; JSPB 38, VS 1845/1788 CE, f83b–84a and 210b; JSPB 40, VS 1846/1789 CE, f172b and 174b; JSPB 44, VS 1849/1792 CE, f110+14b; JSPB 45, VS 1850/1793 CE, f225a.

20 JSPB 38, VS 1845/1788 CE, f210b.

21 Orsini, "Inflected *Kathas*," 196, 201, 228.

22 Hawley, *Storm of Songs*, 97, 286; Sreenivasan, "Marriage of 'Hindu' and 'Turak'"; Talbot, "Becoming Turk the Rajput Way"; Daftary, *Short History of the Ismailis*; Khan, *Crossing the Threshold.*

23 Hawley, *Storm of Songs*, 179; Saha, "Movement of Bhakti."

24 Saha, "Creating a Community."

25 Horstmann, Introduction, 3–4; Saha, "Creating a Community," 89.

26 Reu, *Marvāḍ kā Itihās*, 381.

27 Chatterjee, "Cultural Flows and Cosmopolitanism"; Ghosh, *Temple to Love*; Kolff, *Naukar, Rajput and Sepoy.*

28 Hawley, *Storm of Songs*, 124; Chatterjee "Cultural Flows and Cosmopolitanism."

29 In eighteenth-century western Rajasthan, *pūṇ jāt* designated an imprecisely defined set of castes (*jāt* or *jāti*), notionally thirty-six in number, that were engaged in artisanal and service occupations. Sitaram Lalas suggests that *pūn* is derived from *pavan* (literally "wind," "Vishnu") but does not offer an explanation for why the term may have been applied to these castes. Elsewhere, Lalas translates "*pūṇ*" into "three-quarters" (Lalas, *Rājasthānī-Hindī Śabdakoś*, 47, 93). This suggests that members of these castes may have been considered incomplete persons, in line with the relatively lower and dependent status they held. Sahai also reports the attribution in Marwar of such a meaning to the term *pūṇ* when applied to caste groups (Sahai, "Artisans, the State, and the Politics," 688).

30 JSPB 35, VS 1843/1786 CE, f149b–150b.

31 JSPB 34, VS 1843/1786 CE, f138b.

32 JSPB 34, VS 1843/1786 CE, f140b.

33 JSPB 39, VS 1845/1788 CE, f169b–170a.

34 JSPB 36, VS 1844/1787 CE, f168a.

35 JSPB 38, VS 1845/1788 CE, f179b.

36 Sahai, "Artisans, the State, and the Politics"; Cherian, "Ordering Subjects."

37 Bhati *Rājasthān kī Praśāsanik Vyavasthā*, 101–2, 134–48.

38 JSPB 35, VS 1843/1786 CE, f21b.
39 JSPB 34, VS 1843/1786 CE, f135b.
40 JSPB 30, VS 1841/1784 CE, f59b.
41 JSPB 36, VS 1844/1787 CE, f213b.
42 JSPB 41, VS 1846/1789 CE, f82b–83a.
43 JSPB 41, VS 1846/1789 CE, f82b–83a.
44 Cherian, "Ordering Subjects."

CHAPTER FIFTEEN

THE TIES THAT BIND

Individual, Family, and Community in Northwestern Bhakti

TYLER WILLIAMS

In the region now known as Rajasthan, the case of the so-called *nirguṇ sant bhakti* traditions—whose followers orient their religious practices toward a vision of the divine that is purely transcendent or "without qualities" (*nirguṇ*)—and the role of merchant communities in shaping these traditions reveal that among the many other things that bhakti is and does, bhakti works as a mode of structuring and understanding relationships of sovereignty and subjection between the individual, the family, the religious community, and society at large. For the individual, the ideology of bhakti affords a degree of independence and mobility on the spiritual plane while reaffirming the subjection of the individual to the material demands of the family (thus distinguishing bhakti from asceticism).[1] The idea that the individual can move spiritually between stations and identities while remaining within the structure of the family parallels the growing occupational mobility of merchants in the seventeenth and eighteenth centuries, when the changing political economy of Rajasthan allowed merchants to move into positions of power at royal courts and in local administrations while maintaining their roles in familial business networks. As for those familial networks, the idiom of bhakti imagines the family as a unit not just of economic production but of the production of spiritual merit as well. The religious community, headed by the guru and administered by his initiated disciples, is then the arena in which these families convert material wealth into spiritual wealth through offerings and service. Finally, bhakti imagines the religious community—the *panth* or *sampradāy*—in the form of a polity having its own laws and structures of authority and administration.

A number of these features will be familiar from a reading of the preceding chapter, also based in Rajasthan, where the focus is on the Vallabh Sampraday, a *saguṇ* ("with qualities," i.e., immanental) Vaishnava tradition. Bhakti also functions as a mode of imagining and governing the behavior and relations of individuals, families, and religious communities that inhabit two *nirguṇ sant* traditions of Rajasthan: the Dadu Panth and the Niranjani Sampraday. Both groups coalesced in the late sixteenth and early seventeenth centuries, expanding their numbers and geographic reach during the second half of the seventeenth century and maintaining their influence in the region throughout the eighteenth century.[2] Both counted merchants among their monastic leaders and lay followers, and the influence of mercantile sensibilities is evident in the traditions' theology and poetic texts, which borrow from idioms of the market, exchange, and accumulation. Until now, the majority of scholarship on *nirguṇ sant bhakti* has emphasized its function as a technique of ideological resistance employed by subaltern groups against caste and class repression, and it no doubt performed this role at various places and times, including in the Dadu Panth and Niranjani Sampraday.[3] Yet it was and did much more than that, and studying how *nirguṇ sant* bhakti meshed with the mercantilism and evolving political forms of the period can help us to understand how new notions of the individual, society, and governmentality were taking root on the eve of the European colonial encounter.[4]

THE INDIVIDUAL

The hymns, epigrams, and hagiographies of the Dadu Panth and Niranjani Sampraday address the existential conundrum of the householder: how is one to attain liberation from the cycle of birth and death (imagined as *karm ke bandhan*, the bonds of karma), and from the suffering of the phenomenal world (Hindi *saṁsār*, Sanskrit *saṁsāra*), when one is thoroughly enmeshed in familial, social, and economic webs (the *saṁsār kā jāl*, or web of *saṁsāra*)? This was a particularly vexing problem for the merchants who made up a significant portion of the Dadu Panth and Niranjani Sampraday's lay membership, since the individual merchant was a member of an extended family that functioned not only as a kinship network but also as a business network. Saints of these religious orders, through their poetry and through the examples of their own lives, offered such devotees practical strategies for liberation that allowed individuals to remain within the bonds of worldly life while divesting themselves of the karmic debt accrued from worldly transactions.

The founding saints of the Dadu Panth and Niranjani Sampraday, Dadu Dayal (1544–1603) and Haridas Niranjani (d. 1601?) respectively, are themselves exemplary in this respect. Dadu became a renowned regional saint, even being worshiped as an incarnation of the divine by many of his followers, while maintaining his identity as a householder. The *Dādū Janm Līlā* (The Divine Play of the Life of Dadu, 1620) of Jangopal, himself a merchant devotee of the Dadu Panth, reports that Dadu was born into a family of cotton carders near Ahmedabad. (Variants of the text dating to the mid-seventeenth-century claim that he was born into a merchant family near Ahmedabad.)[5] Jangopal mentions that Dadu never abandoned cotton carding, continuing his vocation as he composed hymns and taught devotees.[6] Jangopal also relates that Dadu was married and had two sons and two daughters, all of whom joined the "family business" of religious ministration, the sons serving as heads of the community after their father's death and the daughters becoming nuns in the *panth*'s main monastery at Naraina.[7] Dadu did not exhort his followers to give up familial and other worldly ties; his poetry, in the form of *sākhīs* (couplets) and *pads* (hymns), instead urges the listener to worship God precisely in order to give those worldly acts and relationships meaning:

> māta pitā kula jātī dhaṁna jobaṁna sajaṁna saṁgātī
> graha dārā suta bhāī hari bina saba jhūṭhā hai jāī
>
> Mother, father, clan, caste,
> wealth, youth, kinfolk and friends,
> House, wife, children, brothers—
> Without Hari, all are false, and pass.[8]

Dadu's verses advocate not the renunciation of action or ties but rather the severing of emotional attachment to the fruits of those acts and ties, namely kin relations, spousal relations, and material wealth. The emotional capital formerly directed toward these objects is to be redirected toward God, and the literal, material capital directed toward these objects is also to be redirected toward religious activity through redistribution within the monastic community: the young Dadu again sets an example by giving away his family's wealth to *sādhus*, much to the chagrin of his family.[9] Later, as a married man with his own family, he travels constantly for work while his family stays at home (much like a merchant), but he never keeps any of the wealth he is given for his ministrations.

In contrast with Dadu, Haridas Niranjani reportedly gave up life as a householder and became a renunciate, but his message to devotees was largely the same as that of Dadu: the devotee should give up attachment to family and wealth but not his responsibility to *produce* family and wealth. According to the two earliest written hagiographies of the Niranjani Sampraday, the *Dayāl Jī kī Pañc Paracai* of Hariramdas (composed between 1738 and 1779) and the *Paracaī* of Raghunathdas (ca. 1800), as well as oral traditions, Haridas was originally a highway robber in the hills near Didwana until, much in the manner of the famous "first poet" Valmiki, author of the *Rāmāyaṇa*, he attempted to rob a holy man, only to be converted by the *sādhu* into a devotee of *nirguṇ* Ram.[10] Importantly, it is the realization that his family will not share the responsibility for his sins—that the matter of sin and merit, spiritual profit and loss, is strictly an individual affair, the burden his own—that convinces Haridas to give up violence and take up the worship of God.[11]

The conundrum of the individual householder is again addressed in the story of Haridas's first devotee, a prominent merchant of Didwana named Dwarkadas Bihani. Instructed by his own clan goddess to give up worship of her and instead serve Haridas, the newly converted *sādhu* absorbed in meditation on a nearby hill, Dwarkadas brings his new guru water and food and asks how a householder like himself might be saved. Haridas answers that no path to liberation exists for a householder, but when Dwarkadas breaks down in tears, the saint adds that:

> phir dayāla bole upagarī,
>   serī eka gṛsata kuṁ bhārī
> santajanāṁ kī saṁgati karai,
>   mana maiṁ hari ko sumarana karai
> kathā kīratana hari jasa gāvai,
>   prema prīti pravāha baḍhāvai
>
> Then Dayāl [the merciful one: Haridas] spoke a blessing—
>   "There is one path, [though] difficult, for the householder:
> Keep the company of good people.
>   Remember Hari in your heart.
> Sing Hari's fame in stories and hymns.
>   Increase the flow of love and devotion."[12]

The upshot of this prescription, elaborated elsewhere in Raghunathdas's *Paracaī* and in the poetry of Haridas (which is, like Dadu's oeuvre, primarily composed in the form of *sākhīs* and *pads*), is that while extricating oneself from the ties of the biological family and of economic production may not be possible, it is indeed possible for an individual to give up emotional attachment to those ties. The emotional energy that is conserved thereby, in the form of *prem* or love, can be redirected toward God and the religious community (the *santajan* or "good people").

The theology of the Dadu Panth and Niranjani Sampraday thus accords the individual subject a degree of spiritual mobility and agency, even while acknowledging that such a person is implicated in the inescapable webs of kinship and economic production. It is tempting to draw a parallel between this ideology and the increasing occupational mobility of individuals from merchant backgrounds in seventeenth- and eighteenth-century Rajasthan and in North India more generally. During this period we see individuals from a variety of merchant communities—Maheshwaris, Marwaris, Oswals, and Khandelwals—taking up positions of service in the Kacchwaha, Marwar, and Shekhawati kingdoms, with a number of prominent merchants becoming ministers and military generals (in addition to being *bhaṇḍārīs* or treasurers to royal courts).[13] This mobility is perhaps best epitomized by the Jagat Seth family of Murshidabad, Oswal Jains who became financiers and power brokers to the Mughal Empire.[14] Merchants could occupy postions of power within monarchies while maintaining and profiting from their family networks and businesses. We see a direct homology between this situation and the logic proffered by the poetry of *sants* like Dadu and Haridas: just as one could ascend political and social hierarchies while remaining engaged in the family business, so could one attain spiritual heights despite remaining within the structures of family and trade. One might even ask whether these two were necessarily intertwined: how could one appreciate spiritual release (*chuṭkārā*) if one did not in some way remain connected to the webs of associations that showed how important such a transvaluation of one's experience in life really was?

THE FAMILY

If the individual remains a productive member of the family—both biologically, by producing children, and economically, by contributing capital and labor for the family's business ventures—then the family works as a unit for the production of both material and spiritual wealth. Individual striving for salvation thus becomes reintegrated into the family unit through its contribution to the family's production and its accumulation of spiritual capital in the form of spiritual merit. The spiritual community, overseen by the guru and his monastic representatives, is then the market in which material wealth is converted into spiritual currency.

Hagiographical narratives of the Dadu Panth and Niranjani Sampraday are populated with families: the guru's family (as discussed above) as well as the families of devotees. The majority of the *Dādū Janm Līlā* is devoted to describing Dadu's travels, in which he moves from town to town, ministering to local populations. Most often a devotee calls Dadu to his town, where the devotee, his family members, and others in the community provide food and hospitality to Dadu and his retinue.[15] Devotees frequently finance religious celebrations (*melās*) in which hymns are sung, sermons are given, and food is distributed to the public. The terms used to describe many of these devotees—*mahājan*, *seṭh*, and *kāyasth*—suggest that they were merchants of some sort or another. Jangopal assiduously records the spiritual merit these devotees accrue through their service to the guru; indeed, much of the *Dādū Janm Līlā* reads like a spiritual account book or ledger.[16] It also records how devotees got their entire kin networks in on the deal by introducing Dadu to their extended family across the region.[17]

The hagiographies of the Dadu Panth and Niranjani Sampraday also dramatize the guru's bio-power—his power over life and death—in regard to the family. Oral tradition recounts how Haridas Niranjani's first devotee, Dwarkadas Bihani, was childless until his devout service to the saint moved Haridas to reward the merchant with a son. This is a stock trope in South Asian hagiography, but the import is nonetheless clear: the guru has the ability to extend one's biological family (the economic unit) through the conception of progeny. The guru can also end biological (and with it, economic) reproduction: Raghunathdas's *Paracaī* tells of how a *mahājan* patriarch in Didwana insisted on cutting a sacred pipal tree that was threatening the foundation of his house. Upon hearing of the matter, Haridas sprinkled water on the tree, saying, "Neither shall this tree grow, nor shall your lineage," effectively chopping off the *mahājan*'s family tree at its roots.[18]

THE COMMUNITY

The authority of the guru extended to the bodies and material wealth of his devotees, as well as to the spiritual dimension of their persons, which was alternately imagined as the subtle body (*sūkṣma śarīr*) or the soul/spirit (*ātmā*). The guru thus stood at the head of a community that was more than simply religious in the post-Enlightenment sense. Rather, the guru's community had its own law and modes of governmentality that made it function as a type of polity.[19] As we trace the history of the Dadu Panth and Niranjani Sampraday from the late seventeenth century through the eighteenth, we see a gradual transformation of the figure of the guru from a mobile merchant into a geographically grounded monarch as well as an increasing characterization of his community as a form of territorialized polity.

Upon the deaths of their founders, the Dadu Panth and Niranjani Sampraday faced a question of authority: to whom, or what, would the guru's authority and power over the production of life, wealth, and spiritual merit be transferred? In the case of the Dadu Panth, authority came to be vested in a corpus of scripture, the human guru, and the guru's monastic administration; in the case of the Niranjani Sampraday, authority devolved to local monastic centers that remained connected in a loose federal structure. The foundations for a territorialized notion of community governance were laid soon after the passing of these saints—or perhaps even in their lifetimes—in the hagiographical traditions that grew around their personas. The hagiographies of Dadu and Haridas both emphasize the geographical extent of the Guru's influence: the *Dādū Janm Līlā* meticulously records every location and community that Dadu visited while Hariramdas's *Dayāl Jī kī Pañc Paracai* and Raghunathdas's *Paracaī* recount how Haridas cleared the region's trade routes of evil spirits, animals, and malevolent ascetics, making them safe for passage—a feat that the region's Rajput rulers were often unable to accomplish.

After Dadu died in 1604, his songs and sayings were compiled into the *Dādū Vāṇī* (Words of Dadu). According to seventeenth-century Dadu Panthi monk Madhavdas, a copy of the *Dādū Vāṇī* was installed, much as would be done for a monarch, in the temple at the Panth's central monastery in Naraina.[20] This closely paralleled developments in that same year at Ramdaspur (present-day Amritsar), where Guru Arjan had the Sikh gurus' compositions compiled into the *Ādi Granth* and ritually installed in the temple there.[21] An elaborate courtly ritual idiom developed around this scripture, and through the seventeenth century Sikh religious leadership itself developed a structure of governance resembling a royal court, complete with forms of revenue (*mansad*), an organized military, and a capital, centered around the dual authorities of the scripture and the human guru.

Developments in the Dadu Panth during the first half of the seventeenth century provide interesting parallels: the *Dādū Vāṇī* attained the status of a central scriptural authority in the Panth, being worshiped in a temple setting not unlike a *divān-i ām* or hall of royal audience, while the human guru occupied the *gaddī* (seat) representing worldly human authority in the community. A large monastic complex was constructed at Naraina in the architectural idiom of a palace, complete with a *naubat khānā* (a tower for musicians to herald a monarch's approach and departure), grand gateways, and the aforementioned hall of audience for the *Vāṇī*.[22] The guru of the Panth continued to travel often to minister to local devotee populations, but he now had a center, a capital connected to a network of other monastic centers across Rajasthan.[23]

In contrast, the Niranjani Sampraday appears to have developed a decentralized structure of governance during the seventeenth century. After Haridas's passing, several of his initiates established their own lineages and monasteries in different parts of the region, but all remained part of the *sampradāy*. The community's textual sources and contemporary oral tradition insist that none of these branches was greater or lesser than any other in stature or authority.[24] Not even the monastery at Didwana, where Haridas had preached and where his *samādhi* (monument) was built, seems to have been given special prominence. Instead, this monastery is remarkable for another reason: the sprawling complex on the edge of Didwana has the form of a settlement, a small city unto itself with roads, wells, residential areas, and an administrative center—a group of monastic buildings arranged around the *samādhi* of Haridas—where residents of the settlement would gather once a day to discuss community matters. It is also where the entire Niranjani community continues to gather once a year in the spring, on the occasion of Haridas's death anniversary, to make decisions for the *sampradāy* as a whole.[25]

In the uncertain and constantly changing political scene of Rajasthan in the seventeenth and eighteenth centuries, religious communities like the Dadu Panth and Niranjani Sampraday offered a type of stability that local rulers could not. Both sects maintained standing armies of warrior ascetics to protect their monastic centers and ensure the safe movement of monks between them.[26] (In contrast, Rajput rulers often raised revenue by looting travelers on roads within their or others' domains.) Monastic centers served as educational institutions, providing training in reading and writing, as well as skills like *jyotiṣ śāstra* (astrology) and *oṣadhi* (compounding medicine). It is therefore unsurprising that the merchants of the region allied themselves with these religious orders and that we find monasteries of the Dadu Panth and Niranjani Sampraday at most major trade centers of the period. This monastic govermentality coexisted with royal authority in a relationship that was usually amicable but sometimes marked by conflict, as dramatized in hagiographical narratives that pit the military power of Mughal emperors and *subahdārs* (provincial governors) against the spiritual (and ultimately superior) power of the Guru.[27]

EMERGING "PUBLICS"

Although there are antecedents for this manner of imagining sovereignty in the religious traditions of the region (e.g., *vilāyat*, a territorialized sphere of spiritual power within Sufism) there is something novel in this formulation, which consists of multiple elements but is not reducible to any single one: an often written scriptural law that governs the community, a system of governance consisting of monastic institutions, a courtly idiom, and a system of revenue.[28] Although we should be careful in how we characterize such sociopolitical formations in this period of emergent modernity, there are clear signs that these communities are imagining themselves as something like polities. This lends further weight to assertions that bhakti is a way of making publics and that bhakti represented a fundamental rethinking of what religion is in a way that jibed with the political dispensation of the Mughal era.[29] The example of *nirguṇ sant* communities in Rajasthan suggests that bhakti was, in fact, a way of thinking through questions of the self, the family, the community, and governance, and a framework in which experiments in self-governance were carried out. The power of bhakti, then, lies not in its ability to produce liberation or submission but in its ability to restructure relationships of liberty and submission.

NOTES

I thank Swapna Sharma and the South Asian Studies Council for the opportunity to present these ideas at Yale in 2016, and Elizabeth Chatterjee, John Cort, Jack Hawley, Manpreet Kaur, Francesca Orsini, Heidi Pauwels, Ramya Sreenivasan, and Faridah Zaman for contributing valuable feedback on aspects of the project.

1 There is, of course, a robust tradition of monastic asceticism in bhakti communities, including those profiled in this chapter. Yet what was new about the type of bhakti discussed here was its extension of liberation not only to renunciates—as was the case with certain Nath and tantric traditions of the region—but to householders as well. On this contrast, see Pauwels, "Who Are the Enemies of the Bhaktas?" and Burchett, "Bitten by the Snake."

2 The Niranjani Sampraday has received little attention from scholars despite its important role in the development of *nirguṇ* bhakti in North India. The primary source for Niranjani history is Mangaldas, *Śrī Mahārāj Haridās Jī kī Vāṇī*; with the exception of Neha Baid's recent work, *Santakavi Harirāmadās Nirañjanī Kṛt Chandaratnāvalī* and *Santakavi Harirāmadās Nirañjanī Praṇit Nāmaprakāś*, most subsequent studies reproduce Mangaldas's research. The Dadu Panth has received more attention (though far less than contemporary Vaishnava sects); see for example Horstmann, "Dadupanthi Anthologies" and "Symbiotic Antinomy"; and Callewaert, *Hindī Biography of Dādū Dayāl*.

3 See, for example, Lorenzen, *Bhakti Religion in North India*.

4 One central question that has emerged from this study is whether a type of bio-power was evolving during this period, not necessarily *within* the realm of a state per se but perhaps *between* the realm of the religious

community or polity and that of the administrations of monarchic power. As the following discussion will highlight, monastic institutions of governance in early modern Rajasthan were particularly concerned with the sexual and reproductive behaviors of devotee populations and with the family unit as the site of economic and biological production.

5 Jangopal, *Dādū Janm Līlā*, in Callewaert, *Hindī Biography of Dādū Dayāl.* The interpolated sections of the text can be found in verses 1.6.1–9.

6 Jangopal, *Dādū Janm Līlā*, 4.5–6.

7 Jangopal, *Dādū Janm Līlā*, 9.1–6.

8 Callewaert and Op de Beeck, *Nirguṇ Bhakti Sāgar*, 12.44, 282.1.

9 Jangopal, *Dādū Janm Līlā*, 1.12.

10 Hariramdas, *Dayāl Jī kī Pañc Paracai*, Manuscript 24778, 1817 CE, Rajasthan Oriental Research Institute, Jodhpur; Raghunathdas, *Paracaī*, 2.1–2, in Mangaldas, *Śrī Mahārāj Haridāsjī kī Vāṇī*, 216–42. On this trope, see chapter 5 herein.

11 Raghunathdas, *Paracaī*, 2.7.

12 Raghunathdas, *Paracaī*, 3.17–18.

13 See, for example, Bajekal, "State and the Rural Grain Market." Despite the frequent mention of merchants at Rajput courts in contemporary sources, little scholarship has addressed their presence. Some light has been thrown on this by Lawrence Babb, in "Violence and Construction of Trading-Caste Identity," in *Multiple Histories*, ed. Babb, Joshi, and Meister.

14 On the Jagatseth family, see Little, *House of Jagatseth*; Leonard, "The 'Great Firm' Theory"; and Richards, "Mughal State Finance."

15 See, for example, Jangopal, *Dādū Janm Līlā*, 9.9–22, 11.13–21, 12.19–29, 13.1–5, 13.9–23, 14.1–34, 15.1–6.

16 I thank Monika Horstmann for sharing this observation.

17 A pertinent example is the case of the Bihani clan of merchants, who arranged for Dadu to minister to branches of their clan in multiple cities (Jangopal, *Dādū Janm Līlā*, 12.22, 28; 13.1). In highlighting the process through which kinship and business networks were transformed into networks for the circulation of bhakti-influenced ideas and texts, I attempt to add an additional layer of depth to Jack Hawley's notion of bhakti as a *network* of texts, poets, and beliefs (as opposed to a more unitary or homogenous movement). See Hawley, *Storm of Songs*, 295–97.

18 Raghunathdas, *Parcaī*, 6.11.

19 My analysis in this section is highly influenced by Indrani Chatterjee's concept of monastic governmentality; see Chatterjee, "Monastic 'Governmentality.'"

20 There is some reason to doubt the early date of 1604 CE for Madhavdas's *Sant Guṇ Sāgar* (Ocean of the Virtues of the Saints); I nevertheless include his account here because it is indicative of how the Dadu Panth *remembered* the importance of the creation and installation of the *Dādū Vāṇī* as scripture in

the seventeenth century. On the *Sant Guṇ Sāgar* and its authenticity, see Horstmann, "Dādūpanthī Anthologies."

21 Mann, *Making of Sikh Scripture*, 13–14, 60–68.

22 The early career of Garibdas is related in the closing chapter of Jangopal's *Dādū Janm Līlā*; details about his later tenure as well as the tenure of Maskindas can be found in Raghavdas's *Bhaktamāl* and in Narayandas, Śrī *Dādū Panth Paricay*.

23 It should be noted that this was not always the case. In the years immediately following Dadu's passing, there appears to have been a bit of contestation between Naraina and the monastery at Fatehpur, where the influential poet Sundardas was the *mahant* (religious authority).

24 The earliest source on the Niranjani Sampraday, the *Bhaktamāl* (1660) of Raghavdas, lists twelve *mahants* for the community including Haridas, giving all equal prominence (v. 429). In the early eighteenth century, the Niranjani poet Hariramdas wrote that "None is greater or lesser among the heads of each *dhām* [center] / The twelve *mahants* always dwell in Hariram's heart" (Mangaldas, *Śrī Haridās Jī kī Vāṇī*, 179).

25 On the early history of the Niranjani Sampraday at Didvana, see Swami Mangaldas's introduction in *Śrī Haridās Jī kī Vāṇī*; and Williams, *Sacred Sounds and Sacred Books*, 337–38.

26 See, for example, Hastings, "Poets, Sants, and Warriors."

27 Raghavdas, *Bhaktamāl*, v. 504. See also Narayandas, *Śrī Dādū Panth Paricay*, 32–34. Narayandas gives a different verse number (621) but the same reading for the verse as in the Nahata edition.

28 On Sufi antecedents, see Digby, "Sufi Shaykh"; and Digby, "To Ride a Tiger."

29 Novetzke, "Bhakti and Its Public"; Pinch, *Warrior Ascetics*, 17–20, 211–25.

CHAPTER SIXTEEN

WATERSCAPE AND MEMORY

The Āīna-i-Tirhut *of Bihārī Lāl "Fitrat" and the Politics of a Bhakti Past*

ADITI NATASHA KINI AND WILLIAM R. PINCH

> People say that as he was nearing death a Maithil Brahman named Vidyāpati Ṭhākur, who lived in the time of Maharaja Shiv Singh and was a well-known pandit and Siva-devotee, left his home to go immerse himself in the Ganga. With the riverbank still six miles off he decided to rest, his mind fixed upon the Ganga. On the morning of the next day the Ganga had begun flowing past that very spot, so Vidyāpati Ṭhākur immersed himself in it and breathed his last. His last rites were performed right there. On the site of his funeral pyre is the mahādev pragaṭling.
>
> BIHĀRĪ LĀL "FITRAT," *MITHILA IN THE NINETEENTH-CENTURY*

BIHĀRĪ Lāl "Fitrat" recorded this story in his *Āīna-i-Tirhut* (Reflections on Tirhut) in the late nineteenth century. It is one of many stories involving water that percolate through Fitrat's account of north Bihar, a region that he referred to as Tirhut or Mithila—many of these are origin stories of Tirhut's numerous tanks and ponds, of which he singled out forty-nine for special mention. Narratives of tanks and ponds in Mithila's waterscape evolved and endured over time. Inter alia, this topic concerns Vidyāpati, Raja Shiv Singh, and Bihārī Lāl Fitrat, and through Vidyāpati how bhakti informs the politics of memory.

Fitrat begins with the problem of naming. The terms *Mithila* and *Tirhut*, he explained, are intertwined in the deep past and reflect a connection to water.

> The reason for the origin of the name Tīrbhukt is that in Sanskrit *tīr* is the word for "river" and the meaning of *bhukt* is "splendid." Because there is a profusion of small and big rivers in this district, the name Tīrbhukt arose. This, in fact, is the very reason given for the origin of the name in the second section of the *Mithilā Māhātmya*. And the reason for the origin of the name Tirhut is that the brahmans of this district were expert in the Rg Ved, Yajur Ved, and Sām Ved, and they made *āhūti* [burnt offerings] in the fire rite according to those three Vedas—due to this the name Tiriyāhut arose (*tiri* [three] + *āhūt*); slowly "Tirhut" evolved and became commonplace.[1]

The size of the region varies by source and era. It is usually remembered as a wide agricultural plain straddling what is now the state of Bihar north of the Ganges and the Nepal terai south of Kathmandu, between the southeast-flowing Gandak River in the west and the Mahananda in the east. Generally referred to as Tirhut in Persian records, the region has increasingly been remembered (especially since the eighteenth century) as Mithila, the homeland of Sita. The countryside abounds with references to the *Rāmāyaṇa*, particularly the districts of Sitamarhi and Janakpur on the Nepal-India border.[2] Interestingly, when Biharis speak of Mithila today they usually mean the districts of Madhubani and Darbhanga, an area of about 1,500 square miles closely associated with the Darbhanga Raj.

Tirhut's relationship to water is fraught: seven rivers drain south into the region from the Himalayas, some with legendary violence, causing annual flooding. Thousands of tanks and ponds were excavated over the past millennium to manage this flooding, thus creating a distinct man-made, nature-necessitated waterscape. Around 70 percent of Darbhanga was irrigated by tanks and ponds during Fitrat's time, according to sociologist Hetukar Jha's recent village-level survey.[3] The British official L. S. S. O'Malley similarly noted in 1907 that tanks are "used all over the [Madhubani] subdivision for the irrigation of the fields in their neighborhood."[4]

More recently, anthropologists and folklorists have noted the importance of the waterscape for understandings of gender, fertility, and folklore in Mithila.[5] Certain tanks are accorded special significance. These tanks, referred to as *pokhar* (Maithili *pokhir*), are reserved for domestic rituals and village festivals, and secondarily for aquaculture (especially *makhāna*—*Euryale ferox* or fox nut) and pisciculture. They inevitably irrigate the historical imagination—as Hetukar Jha puts it, "a powerful bond was forged between *pokhar* and society" through centuries, maybe millennia.[6] Jha observes that the preoccupation

16.1 Rājokhar Pokhar, near Bithuar village, east-southeast of Madhubani, said to have been built by Shiv Singh. One of several tanks known as Rājokhar Pokhar in Tirhut. Photo by William Pinch

with tank construction is as old as Indian history itself, finding expression in the Veda-inspired *Dharmasūtra* and *Grihyasūtra* texts (ca. 800–300 BCE), and in later *purānic* treatises (ca. 300–600 CE) that classify tanks by size. By the twelfth and thirteenth centuries we see the production of *pokhar*-related ritual texts, or *paddhati*, specific to the Tirhut-Mithila region. Jha points to three such works: the *Taṛāgāmritlatā* and *Jalāśayādivāstu*, written by Vardhmān Upādhyāya during the period of Karnāṭ rule (1097–1325), and an early fifteenth-century text, the *Jalāśayotsarga*, inspiring Budhakar's commentary.[7] Jha attributes the spread of pokhar excavation to a combination of a desire for merit, the importance of water, and the requirements of agriculture.

What historical significances did *pokhars* possess for Bihārī Lāl Fitrat? Fitrat was born in 1829 into a prominent Kayastha family of Darbhanga that, seven generations earlier, had migrated into Bihar from a village near Ayodhya.[8] He was fluent in Maithili, Urdu, Hindi, Sanskrit, Bengali, Persian, and Arabic—a fairly typical array for educated Kayasthas, a community that had long served in the clerical ranks of the Mughal Empire and subordinate provincial regimes. When he wrote *Āīna-i-Tirhut*, Fitrat was already a respected member of the official elite as a lawyer and administrator in the Darbhanga Raj, the largest landed estate of Bengal Province (of which Bihar was still a part). In his own terse account, he became a lawyer in 1856, an honorary magistrate in 1876 (for famine relief work in 1874), a government lawyer at the *munsif* court of Darbhanga in 1877, a member of the district school committee in 1878, and a municipal commissioner in 1879. He was also something of a poet. Fitrat, meaning "nature" or "temperament," was his Persianate nom de plume. He is mentioned in an earlier historical work, the 1867 *Riāz-i-Tirhut* by Ayodyhā Prasād, as a fixture of local *mushā'iras*, or Persian-Urdu literary gatherings and impromptu recitals held by the literati.[9]

Fitrat wrote the *Āīna-i-Tirhut* not simply because he loved history but because of self-confessed chagrin at the low level of historical understanding in his circles. To Fitrat, history was "the highest form of knowledge" and crucial for educating rulers. He observed that while history could make "a fool cunning," it could also make the "cunning sensitive."[10] History, for Fitrat, fostered good governance.

Āīna-i-Tirhut is split into four parts: Part 1, a discussion of the origins of Tirhut and Mithila, the question that sparked the book. This part also discusses Darbhanga of yore—the condition of people in ancient Mithila, especially Maithil Brahman traditions. Part 2 is a list of prominent scholars and religious men from among the Hindu and Muslim communities, as well as Kayasthas, whom he marks as a third, separate class. Part 3 lists notable features of the region—temples, mosques, forts, and tanks—and describes famine relief, the administration of the region, and the building of the railway. Part 4 describes the gentry of Darbhanga. One could read *Āīna-i-Tirhut* as a who's who and what's what of Fitrat's Darbhanga, which in those days included the present-day Madhubani and Samastipur districts. Interestingly, Fitrat draws religious distinctions in his list-making (Hindu and Muslim, temple and mosque) and positions Kayasthas outside of these lists, indicating perhaps that he felt they belonged to neither community—or both.

Fitrat listed forty-nine tanks in Part 3, noting that "in addition to the aforementioned tanks, there are extant thousands of small and large tanks in this district. Were a separate account of all these tanks to be written, it would require another book."[11] Given that there were thousands to choose from, why did he mention the tanks he did? He seems to have been drawn to well-known tanks. "This is a famous and beautiful tank" is a common refrain. While some listed tanks are in or close to Darbhanga town, the average geographical range suggests that his selections were not governed by proximity to the administrative center. In fact, two were quite distant: one just over the northern border with Nepal, and one just across the western border with Muzaffarpur.

Another selection factor was historicity. Fitrat commented frequently about the believed historical provenance of a given tank. Thus he described two tanks called Rājokhar—one in Lehrā village, *pargana* Parihārpur Rādho, and one in Kevaṭī village, *pargana* Pinḍarūchh. For the former, he wrote, in this village "is a grand and very beautiful tank. Its name is Rājokhar; it must be about sixty or seventy *bīghās*. People say that this is Raja Shiv Singh's excavation." For the latter, he wrote, there is "a second tank named Rājokhar. In village Kevaṭī, pargana Pinḍarūchh, is a twenty-*bīghā* tank. People say that this is also Maharaja Shiv Singh's excavation."[12]

For thirty-two of the forty-nine tanks, Fitrat was able to provide some historical information—not always confident, he was careful to note that he was simply relating what others said, noting "people say that this tank was built by" so-and-so. Otherwise, Fitrat often wrote something along the lines of "it is not known who built it." Once, about a tank in Sāgarpur village, *pargana* Hāṭī, he wrote, "despite much effort, information was not forthcoming about who commissioned it."[13] This phrasing suggests that he may have visited the tanks in person or at the very least made pointed inquiries. His sources seem to be living—he mentions no texts or records. He thus relies on oral tradition, one resembling more fable than textbook, more bhakti than bureaucracy.

The person responsible for the greatest number of tanks (sixteen of the forty-nine) is evidently Shiv Singh—the same Shiv Singh mentioned in the tale about Vidyāpati's death recorded by Fitrat.[14] Shiv Singh, a member of the Oinwār dynasty, ruled in the early fifteenth century. His association with *pokhars* was reflected in a popular couplet that the administrator-linguist George Grierson recorded at nearly the same moment that Fitrat was compiling his work: "Pokhari rājokhari, aur sabh pokharā. / Rājā Sib Siṃh, aur sabh chhokarā" (the tank at Rājokhari is indeed a tank; all the rest are puddles. / Raja Shiv Singh was a king; all others were princelets).[15] The couplet still resonates: Pinch heard it repeated without prompting during a visit in June 2016, including at a tank named Rājokhar (near Nehra village, about forty kilometers east of Darbhanga town).[16]

Fitrat voiced skepticism about the ascription of so many tanks to one ruler. In describing the first four tanks listed for Darbhanga town, which locals attributed to Shiv Singh, Fitrat wrote,

> It is said that all these tanks were commissioned by Maharaj Shiv Singh. But this seems doubtful to the author because Maharaj Shiv Singh ruled for three years and nine months before passing away. Digging so many tanks in such a short period of time is a tall order.

> It is possible that among these tanks, some were commissioned by Shiv Singh during the reign of his father, Dev Singh. Or, some tanks were built before Dev Singh's time, and some during Shiv Singh's time, and some after Shiv Singh's reign by different kings, and the commencement of the digging could have begun in Shiv Singh's reign. In fact, upon reflection this seems more believable. Some people say that the Gangā Sāgar tank was commissioned by Maharaj Gangā Dev, son of Maharaj Nānya Dev. All these tanks are about 500 years old.[17]

Fitrat had cause for concern: a full twenty-five of the thirty-two tanks (78 percent) for which he provided some kind of dating, either by indicating the name of the person who built the tank or by describing their age, would have been built in the fifteenth century.[18] Other authorities on the history of Tirhut's waterscape, by contrast, do not see the fifteenth century as an unusually active time of tank construction in the region, though they don't preclude the possibility. These sources indicate Tirhut's tanks were built over the course of a millennium—starting in the eleventh century with the rise of the Karnāṭ Dynasty (1097–1326) and continuing under the Oinwārs (1326–1526) and Khandavāls (1577–1947).[19] This timeline is also supported by Hetukar Jha's account of the production of *paddhati* texts from the twelfth to the fifteenth centuries that describe the proper ritual observances to be followed in the dedication of tanks.

Why the emphasis on the fifteenth century in collective memory? And why Shiv Singh? We suggest two possible explanations. First, the early fifteenth century corresponds with the shift from Tughlak to Sharqi (i.e., Jaunpuri) dominance over Tirhut.[20] It was popularly understood that Shiv Singh was himself imprisoned and possibly even killed in an unsuccessful attempt to establish political independence from the overlordship of the Delhi Sultanate. Ironically, this seems to have ushered in a long period of Sharqi influence in the region. It is possible that Shiv Singh's rebellion, ill-fated though it was, resonated with emerging Hindu political sensibilities in the late nineteenth century. His failed rebellion may compare to the lauded (and also failed) *sanyasi* and *faqīr* insurgency against company power in the late eighteenth century, which was later fictionalized in the celebrated nationalist novel *Ānandamaṭh* by Bankimchandra Chattopadhyay—in the same years Fitrat was composing his *Āīna-i-Tirhut.*

For the second explanation we look to Vidyāpati, the Maithil Brahman pandit whose story was told in our opening vignette. Vidyāpati is today remembered as the greatest poet of Mithila-Tirhut and a major influence on the development of Maithili as well as Bengali and Hindi. While his impact on literature and language is now widely accepted, it was only coming into focus in the 1870s and 1880s alongside a greater appreciation for the distinctive significance of Maithili language, culture, and history.[21] The heightened scholarly sensitivity to and awareness of Vidyāpati in this period, we believe, contributed to a local tendency to perceive in the historical waterscape of Tirhut a reflection of Vidyāpati's era. Of course, determining this in terms of knowledge and information flow, and how it informed collective memory, is fraught with methodological difficulty.

Vidyāpati, whose dates are disputed but who certainly lived in the late fourteenth and early fifteenth centuries, is well known in Mithila as the author of plays, geographic works, rhetoric, aesthetics, and ritual texts in Sanskrit and Avahaṭṭa, as well as popular bhakti verse in early Maithili describing the love of Krishna and Radha.[22] We know about this latter body of verse thanks in part to George Grierson, who in the early 1880s collected eighty-two songs by Vidyāpati to supplement a grammatical and linguistic study of the Maithili language, observing the poet's name was a "household word throughout the whole of Bihar and Bangal."[23] Twelve of the eighty-two songs collected by Grierson invoke Shiv Singh.[24] The only other historic figures identified in these verses are the wives of Shiv Singh, and they are always mentioned alongside the ruler; the remaining seventy songs do not mention historic persons at all. While Fitrat was exploring Mithila's past and collecting oral histories, his neighbors and community were reciting bhakti poetry from the early fifteenth century, when Shiv Singh reigned in spoken word and spirit.

Vidyāpati employed two kinds of phrasing when invoking his patron: either "I say this in the presence of Rājā Śiv Siṃh Rūp Nārāyaṇ, and Lakhimā Dai," or "Vidyāpati the poet sings a song of love, and Rājā Śiv Siṃh understands it."[25] A heightened awareness of Vidyāpati in the latter half of the nineteenth century would translate into a higher historical profile for Shiv Singh as well. In fact, one legend that was reported in the 1870s described how Shiv Singh was freed in Delhi by Vidyāpati's miraculous intervention—the Tughlak sultan, duly impressed, granted the poet the village of Bīpasī in Mithila.[26]

Vidyāpati's fame increased in the following decades, his renown underscoring his centrality to the historical and cultural identity of the region. Grierson published his chrestomathy in 1882, speculating that the eighty-two songs constituted "very nearly all that are known by Bidyápati in Tirhut." In 1904 Nagendranath Gupta gently corrected this, pointing out that Grierson was relying solely on poems circulating by word of mouth. Gupta declared that "a great number of poems and songs, some of great poetic power and beauty, are to be found in Mithila in old palm-leaf and other manuscripts, scattered about in different households and villages."[27] He even located one manuscript "said to be in the handwriting of Vidyāpati's great grandson and believed to be genuine, containing no less than 400 poems." Gupta later lowered his estimate of the poems this manuscript contained to 350, nevertheless claiming to have amassed between 600 and 700 poems overall.

The increased knowledge about Vidyāpati would have further highlighted his importance to the region. Gupta cites a poem concerning Shiv Singh's resistance to Sultanate rule, in which Vidyāpati identifies himself as "the new Jayadeva" and celebrates Shiv Singh as "the son King of Deva Siṁha, the uprooter of the dynasties of hostile kings, the essence of all virtues, the lion-like Rāja Śiva Siṁha defended and preserved his own faith like Rāma, and in charity rivaled Dadhīci."[28]

Fitrat attributes several tanks to the women of Shiv Singh's family who reigned after him. Thus Lakhima Devi, Shiv Singh's wife, is credited with building an unnamed tank just east of Madhubani town, in Rānṭī village, Hāṭī *pargana*, and another named Lakhansār (presumably short for Lakhima-sāgar) near Darbhanga town, in Tārālāhī village, Pharakpur *pargana*. According to legend, Lakhima fled Tughlak aggression along with Vidyāpati to the Nepal court, eventually becoming a *satī* after receiving no news of Shiv Singh. Vishvas Mahadevi, Shiv Singh's sister-in-law, who is said to have reigned for a dozen or so years after Lakhima Devi, is credited with commissioning two tanks, both named Mahādai (a shortening of Mahādēvi, or "great goddess," a term of respect also occasionally used for Lakhima Devi). One is listed in Shri Singhpur village, Sihorā *pargana*, the other in Chandaur village, Lavānvān *pargana*. Perhaps, like Shiv Singh, they benefited in historical memory from their continued patronage of Vidyāpati after Shiv Singh's demise. Both Lakhima Devi and Vishvas Mahadevi are invoked in Grierson's collection of Vidyāpati songs.

Fitrat would have had numerous official and literary sources at his disposal, especially given his administrative role. The scholarly works of Grierson, Beames, and later Gupta were ostensibly not consulted in pursuing his investigations. Instead, Fitrat's sources were closer to the ground: the locals, the people living *in* Mithila's waterscape. His refrains were "people say that . . ." and "according to knowledgeable people. . . ." Sadly, he does not give us much more about his informants. Of course, Beames, Grierson, and Gupta also consulted locals, and it is possible that their interlocutors—or Grierson's at any rate—overlapped in type if not in fact with Fitrat's. Beames's essay cites a piece published in the Bengali literary and cultural magazine *Bangadarsan*; he does not identify the author, but it was none other than Bankim himself.[29] Grierson informed readers that the majority of songs were collected from "blind singers, and others whose profession it is to sing these Vaishṇava songs," but he was "also indebted to the Maharaja of Darbhanga for many of them." Grierson added that he "searched everywhere for them that I could consistently with my official duties, and I regret that these prevented my directly having much communication with Bidyápati's present descendants."[30] Gupta worked on Vidyāpati a generation later, but he reports having visited many families who possessed manuscripts—who were tenaciously reluctant to part with them—and that he received the help of one "Pundit Chunda Jha, 'the best authority living on Vidyāpati.'"

Fitrat's discussion of Mithila's topography suggests that origin stories attach themselves to the waterscape, handed down from generation to generation. Similarly a sense of the past is stitched into the fabric of poetry—of time, memory, and legend. When listening to the "blind singers," Maithili speakers must have remembered Shiv Singh and his consorts as not simply aesthetes who understood the mysterious tendrils of love and longing but sovereigns who presided over the poet's realm. Embedded in any people's history is an emotional understanding of culture; Vidyapati and bhakti cannot be divorced from records and remains.

Historiographical issues persist. It is now well known that Vidyāpati's Radha-Krishna songs inspired Chaitanya, whose Bengali followers were dispatched to Mathura-Vrindavan in search of the homeland of Radha and Krishna. Thus, in Gauḍīya Vaishnavism, Vidyāpati's art begets life—and that life, in turn, more art. This brand of ecstatic, erotic bhakti became a constitutive force across the western Doab and into Rajasthan, shaping the emerging Ram-Sita *rasika* bhakti that developed in sixteenth- and seventeenth-century Amer and Galta (and later Jaipur), and in Orchhā in western Bundelkhand. It prompted a search for the ancient homelands of Ram and Sita, encouraging travel to Ayodhya and Janakpur in the eighteenth century—an eastward flow that was the mirror image of Chaitanya's westward search for religious origins in Braj two centuries earlier. Vidyāpati had come full circle, geographically, by the end of the eighteenth century, only to be "discovered" by moderns—people like Fitrat, Jha, Grierson, and Gupta—in the nineteenth. It is striking that during this "discovery," Bihar's very waterscape had become an expression of political, religious, and aesthetic commitments dating back four centuries. Here is a frontier of bhakti sensibility that needs more attention. We hope this is a first step in charting a course through that unfamiliar realm.

NOTES

1 Fitrat, *Mithila in the Nineteenth-Century*, 8–9 (Urdu), 12 (Hindi).

2 Burghart, "Disappearance and Reappearance."

3 Jha, "Prāchīn Mithilā," 329.

4 O'Malley, *Bengal District Gazetteers*, 52.

5 Brown, "Contested Meanings," 728–29; Davis, *Maithil Women's Tales*, 136.

6 Jha, "Prāchīn Mithilā," 331.

7 Jha, "Prāchīn Mithilā," 326. Jha adds: "Pokhars were only considered proper pokhars once a sacrifice [*yagya*] was performed. Consequently the rules concerning sacrifice and dedication [*utsarga*] became a profoundly important element of pokhar excavation" (326).

8 Fitrat, *Mithila in the Nineteenth-Century*, 204–5 (Urdu), 193–94 (Hindi); see also Jha's introduction, "Prāchīn Mithilā," 49–53.

9 Prasad, *Glimpse of Tirhut*, 63.

10 Fitrat, *Mithila in the Nineteenth-Century*, 6 (Urdu), 8–9 (Hindi).

11 The list is on 148–55 (Urdu), 141–49 (Hindi). In the original Urdu, Fitrat used *pokhar* and *tālāb* interchangeably; in the Hindi translation, *pokhar* is generally used.

12 Fitrat, *Mithila in the Nineteenth-Century*, 150 (Urdu), 143 (Hindi).

13 Fitrat, *Mithila in the Nineteenth-Century*, 149 (Urdu), 142 (Hindi).

14 There are seventeen if we count Nizam Shah ki Dighghi, "built during the reign of Shiv Singh."

15 Grierson, *Bihar Peasant Life*, 202. Several tanks in the region claim the name Rājokhar or Rājokhari.

16 Pinch is grateful to Dr. Shrutidhari Singh and Kailash Jha for facilitating his June 2016 visit to Mithila, and to the former in particular for sharing his wide knowledge of the cultural geography of the region.

17 Fitrat, *Mithila in the Nineteenth-Century*, 148 (Urdu), 141 (Hindi). Nānya Dev and Gangā Dev ruled in the twelfth century. See Choudhary [Chaudhuri], "Karnats of Mithila," 92–93.

18 In addition, two were dated by Fitrat's informants to the nineteenth century, and one each to the eighteenth, seventeenth, sixteenth, fourteenth, and eleventh centuries.

19 See for example, Dās, *Tirhut in the Early Twentieth Century*, 59–104; Choudhary [Chaudhuri], "Political History of North Bihar," 282, 319; and Jha, *Civilizational Regions*, 62–72.

20 See, e.g., Ahmad, "Aspects of the Historical Geography," 7.

21 For example, Gupta, "Vidyāpati Ṭhākur," 20–24.

22 For an introduction to Vidyāpati and the historiographical blind spot that he occupies despite his rise to literary prominence in the twentieth century, see Jha, "Beyond the Local," 1–10; and Diamond, "City of the Turks," 11–25.

23 Grierson, *Introduction to the Maithili Language*, part II, 34. Vidyapati's poems are given on 42–78, Grierson's translations on 79–112.

24 See Grierson, *Introduction to the Maithili Language*, part II, verses 6, 13, 14, 24, 30, 32, 37, 41, 73, 75, 76, for invocations of Shiv Singh; in five of these, he adds the term *Rūp Nārāyaṇ*, a dynastic title adopted by many of the Oinwār

kings. In verse 61 Vidyāpati invokes Raghab Singh, which Grierson argues is another name for Shiv Singh. Other persons mentioned are Lakhima Thakurani (five times), Modabati Dei (twice), and Pranbati Dei (once). The first is known to have been Shiv Singh's wife; Grierson argues that the other two were as well.

25 See e.g., v. 14, line 12, and v. 24, line 6 in Grierson, *Introduction to the Maithili Language*, part II, 48 and 53 for the Maithili, and 84 and 89 for Grierson's translations (which have been updated slightly here). Lakhima Dai (or Devi) was Shiv Singh's senior wife.

26 Beames, "On the Age and Country of Bidyâpati," 300. Beames paraphrased here the contents of an article on the poet and the question of his linguistic status (as a Maithili as opposed to Bengali writer) in *Bangadarśan* 2, part 4 (Jyoishtho 1262 or June 1875).

27 Gupta, "Vidyāpati Ṭhākur," 20–24.

28 Gupta, "Vidyāpati Ṭhākur," 22. Gupta noted that this and the extracts of other verses were from unpublished poems. Vidyāpati would become increasingly central to Mithila historiography in the coming decades. For example, Singh, *History of Tirhut*, cited Vidyāpati no fewer than ninety-one times.

29 See discussion of Bankim in Ratte, *Un-Colonized Heart*, 94–112.

30 Grierson, *Introduction to the Maithili Language*, 36.

CHAPTER SEVENTEEN

BHAKTI IN THE CLASSROOM

What Do American Students Hear?

RICHARD H. DAVIS

For my first year of teaching, in 1987–88, I was asked to develop five new undergraduate courses covering various aspects of Hinduism and South Asian studies. For one of those courses, I decided to have my American students read Hindu devotional poetry in translation. The title I came up with, Devotion and Poetry in Medieval Hinduism, was not exactly designed to attract the masses, and, as a new and naïve assistant professor, I did not realize that faculty could choose the class meeting times. The registrar assigned me an 8:30 a.m. slot. Sure enough, the turnout was small. Although only seven hardy students (out of six thousand undergrads) found their way to my classroom on cold January New England mornings to learn about Indian bhakti poetry, it was my most enjoyable course that first year. After thirty years of teaching, I can still vividly recall that particular basement classroom. (Yes, the registrar stuck us in a basement at 8:30 a.m.)

GOALS AND QUESTIONS

After that first incarnation I have taught Devotion and Poetry in India eight more times, at Yale University and Bard College, most recently in spring 2016. The central focus of the course is simple and consistent: to read and discuss together in a seminar format some of the best available English-language translations of Indian devotional literature. My primary pedagogic goal is likewise simple and consistent. I want students to get into the poetry. The primary aim of bhakti poetry, Kenneth Bryant observes, is to enable the audience to participate directly in the reality that the poet seeks to convey.[1] It is, as Norman Cutler emphasizes, a "poetry of connections."[2] In a secular American liberal arts college, I do not aim for my students to become Krishna *bhaktas*, of course. But I do want to use Indian religious poetry to enable students to enter into a subjectivity that is different but human, challenging to their own values and assumptions but also sympathetic. My hope is that students will learn to accept the coherence and pertinence of another way not just of viewing the world but of constructing and living within it that differs greatly from their own way. In my experience, bhakti poetry can do this powerfully and accessibly without requiring undue professorial explication. The course also serves a valuable purpose in my own education. By teaching it every two or three years, I am able to keep up with new scholarship and new publications in the lively field of bhakti studies.

In this final chapter of the book I wish to reflect on the study of Indian bhakti from the perspective of this often reincarnated course. Aside from my personal memories, the sources that enable me to launch into this subject are a sequence of the nine course syllabi from my computer and paper files. They register archeological strata in my computational resources over time: from WordStar word processing software (with files stored on floppy disks) to WordPerfect to Microsoft Word, and from an ugly eight-dpi dot-matrix printer to a twenty-four-dpi one, then to my first prized HP LaserJet printer. The syllabi also illustrate a history of reading choices over three decades, based on student responses and my own sense of classroom effectiveness. From these syllabi I prepared a tabulation of readings and the number of times I have used each. Other written sources include the processing notes I occasionally compiled at semester's end, the notes I've taken at course review sessions, and student comments on evaluation forms. I also consulted a published interview that Steven Rosen conducted with me after I had taught the course twice.[3] Since this chapter is so firmly based in my own experience, it will inevitably be self-referential, but I trust some of these experiences can be instructive and helpful to others.

The classroom is one place where scholars of South Asia construct bhakti. It is a site of transmission: we convey and disseminate scholarly research and translations to audiences beyond our scholarly cohort. What is it we transmit? This is the fundamental question I am posing, in this essay, to myself. In Devotion and Poetry, what representation of Indian bhakti do I transmit? What aspects of bhakti do I highlight, and what do I occlude? What are the consequences of my choices of readings and sequence? I do not have complete control of this. In a seminar format I am not sovereign lord of the classroom lecturing to a passive audience. Students respond to the readings, to me, and to each other with enthusiasm or disinterest. That becomes part of the classroom dynamic. Their responses also provide feedback that affects future incarnations of the syllabus. In this undergraduate course on bhakti, what do students hear?

COURSE NARRATIVE

Courses unfold in time, just as poems do. Choices of readings and their order form a sequence. Later readings may support, expand, modify, challenge, or subvert earlier ones. Over a semester they create a narrative and frame an experience for students. Like managers of a baseball team, teachers set a lineup and make substitutions. But we do not control all of what happens on the field of play.

A teacher's first opportunity to set forth that narrative is in the description in the course catalog and on the syllabus. Here is how I oriented the students the first time I taught "Devotion and Poetry" in 1988: "*Bhakti* means 'participation in' or 'devotion to' God. From roughly 800 A.D. to 1600 A.D., in every region of India, *bhakti* poet-saints sang songs and lived lives of intense, emotional devotion to their chosen gods. The songs, legends, and theologies of these saints and the communities they established permeate contemporary Hinduism. In this course we explore the poetry and the history of this medieval Hindu religious movement (or movements)." And so on. The ninth time around, in 2016, I still used nearly the same orienting paragraph, with slight changes of dates.

This is the most stable course I teach. In other recurrent courses, the syllabi change more abruptly and dramatically, either because I am dissatisfied with the narrative I am creating or because I fear becoming bored myself with the same old readings. With Devotion and Poetry I found the first time around an outline of topics and an orientation that was pleasing to me and, I felt and still feel, that was pedagogically effective. Some core readings I use over and over. Four readings have appeared in all nine lineups. Others have joined the order and stayed five or six times. The course also offers me an opportunity to keep up with and try out new work. I can insert new readings into the lineup, like pinch-hitters. Some strike out; others get a clutch hit.

I always use, as lead-off reading, A. K. Ramanujan's *Speaking of Śiva* (1973). I believe it offers the best, most succinct, and most accessible initiation into bhakti poetry for American neophytes. This work and Dimock and Levertov's 1967 *In Praise of Krishna* are the two foundational works for modern American bhakti studies. Beginning a course on bhakti with *Speaking of Śiva* has two major consequences. First, by starting with Virashaiva poetry of the eleventh and twelfth centuries, I choose not to follow strict historical chronology. I do not wish to represent Hindu devotionalism as a single unfolding bhakti movement. Second, as Ramanujan presents them, the Virashaivas fit into the revolutionary side of bhakti. Ramanujan was actively engaged with the ideas of anthropologist Victor Turner, his Chicago colleague. Turner's processual model of structure, antistructure, and counterstructure and his comparative descriptions of liminality and *communitas* orient Ramanujan's treatment of the Virashaivas. Turner in turn cited the Virashaivas to exemplify his theoretical model. (See Gil Ben-Herut's critique in chapter 2.)

Throughout the course I focus primarily on a direct reading of poetry, but I also use secondary readings along the way. My goal is to provide select terms and analytic tools that will aid in reading and discussing the poetry, and my hope is that students will internalize and apply them throughout the course and beyond. When I first prepared the course in 1988, three secondary treatments of bhakti poetry made a deep impact on me: Kenneth Bryant's 1978 analysis of Sūrdās poetry, *Poems to the Child-God*, Norman Cutler's 1987 treatment of early Tamil devotional poetry in *Songs of Experience*, and Linda Hess's 1983 introduction to *The Bījak of Kabīr*. All three continue to inform my reading of bhakti literature.

For introductory purposes I most often use three secondary readings. I ask students to read Eleanor Zelliot's 1976 essay "The Medieval Bhakti Movement in History," though I do not discuss it directly in class. While it is a useful survey that covers the whole subcontinent and arranges things chronologically, it is surely out of date. (Philip Lutgendorf's 2003 survey is more recent and suitable.) I always assign some brief reading of Victor Turner, so students can see where Ramanujan gets his antistructure idea.[4] This is sometimes a problem. Teaming up Ramanujan's sympathetic Virashaivas with Turner's attractive exemplars of liminality and *communitas* (Saint Francis of Assisi, Chaitanya, Bob Dylan, and the Bauls of Bengal) can throw off the balance of the course, pushing the students—especially at an alt-institution like Bard College—to embrace too closely the antistructural side of bhakti.

My favorite among the secondary readings is the first chapter of Cutler's book, "Poet, God, and Audience in the Poetry of the Tamil Saints." Cutler adapts Roman Jakobson's model of a verbal event to the rhetorical analysis of bhakti poetry. He provides convenient diagrams for envisioning who is speaking to whom. I find myself often drawing communication triangles on the board in class and more complex diagrams of internal and external addressers and addressees throughout the semester. Students sometimes become exasperated with me: "You mean the triangle again?"

From the twelfth-century Virashaivas, we go back in time. Where does bhakti begin? What origin story do we choose to tell? In this course I bypass the commonly cited point of philosophical origin, the *Bhagavad Gītā*. I avoid explicit theology in favor of more direct religious expression. But I do want to introduce Krishna early on. Krishna is the most important deity in this course. Other deities also have their moments in the bhakti spotlight: Shiva, the Goddess, and the formless Nam or Ram. However, Krishna will provide the connecting thread, and I want students to know his story. So we begin with *Harivamsa*, the narrative origin point of bhakti. There is no good scholarly translation of the Krishna portion of the *Harivamsa*, but I find Francis Hutchins's 1980 *Young Krishna* a charming almost-translation that gets the flavor and much of the narrative detail right. Although out of print, *Young Krishna* stays in the batting order.

I like to juxtapose two versions of the Krishna story, separated by several centuries, to illustrate how a devotional narrative can change and develop in the retelling. Indian stories are not told once and for all. Students often find it a challenge to accept the non-finality of Indic religious narratives; perhaps they are too familiar with the apparent canonical fixity of the Judeo-Christian Bible. The *Bhagavata Purāṇa* is central to the Krishna devotional tradition, but it is long and theologically complex. We read portions of Edwin Bryant's 2003 translation, *Krishna: The Beautiful Legend of God*. One invariable portion is the five-chapter section in the *Bhāgavata* dealing with the *Rāsa* dance. Here students meet the Gopis for the first time and must address the tension between bhakti and dharma. I often use an excerpt from Manu's *Dharmashastra* to highlight the female roles the Gopis were leaving when they followed Krishna on those lush spring escapades. Manu sets out the subordinate status of women starkly, but in class it can be a mixed blessing. I must caution students not to over-apply Manu. Important but not hegemonic, Manu articulates a conservative Brahmanical vision of an ideal society, the Indian equivalent to some of the Dead White Males of the West that Bard students must read in their first-year seminar. Over the years I have followed student interest by increasing attention to gender issues in this course and cross-listing it with the Gender and Sexuality Studies Program.

From the Sanskritic narratives of the Krishna story, we move on to the vernacular bhakti poetry of the Tamil saints, the Shaiva Nayanmars and the Vaishnava Alvars. We go "from classicism to bhakti," as Ramanujan and Cutler put it, and from "intellectual bhakti" to the "emotional bhakti" of the Tamil movements, in Friedhelm Hardy's useful distinction.[5] This is a less settled part of the syllabus, with no standard translation. My favorite is still Ramanujan's 1981 translation of Nammāḻvār selections, *Hymns for the Drowning*, but I found that difficult for students without background in Indian religious culture. Too much professorial explication was required, and as a pedagogical preference I want students to generate much of the interpretive discussion themselves. I've been happy recently with two new translations, both of female saints: Archana Venkatesan's 2010 work on Āṇṭāḷ and Karen Pechilis's 2012 study and translation of Kāraikkāl Ammaiyār.[6] Both the poetry and the biographical accounts are valuable. I often use Ramanujan's short 1982 article "On Women Saints" to sketch out the life trajectories of bhakti women, as set out in hagiographic narratives. I appreciate Pechilis's direct translation of Cēkkiḻār's telling of Kāraikkāl Ammaiyār's story. I would love to see many more translations (rather than summaries) of lives of the bhakti saints.

One observation on female saints: I thought I'd taught a really good class on Āṇṭāḷ's *Tiruppavai*, a poem-cycle I love. But at the end of the semester, students couldn't remember Antal at all. By contrast, they totally remembered Kāraikkāl Ammaiyār, particularly Cēkkiḻār's dramatic account of her life. Perhaps this shouldn't be a surprise. When it comes to bhakti poets (like celebrities), students are going to remember the drama-queen over the nice village girl every time.

I often introduce, at this point in the semester, some parallel non-bhakti poetry. I've tried out Tamil, Sanskrit, and Prakrit comparisons. I want students to see both connections and differences. Bhakti poetry in India is not *sui generis*, but neither is it simply continuous with other bodies of sophisticated poetry in classical or medieval India. Here we face a question of representation. By organizing a course around bhakti poetry, I am setting up bhakti as a distinctive object of knowledge, and I want students to struggle, as the semester goes on, with the definition of this complex, changing phenomenon. But I also want them to see bhakti as an integral part of Indian religious and literary history, in dialogic relation with other parts of the tradition. As Ramanujan put it, early bhakti movements "used whatever they found at hand, and changed whatever they used."[7]

Krishna Devotionalism in Bengal is the next section of the course. Here we have an invariable key reading in Dimock and Levertov's *In Praise of Krishna*. Sometimes I use the *Gitagovinda* in Barbara Stoler Miller's 1977 translation, *Love Song of the Dark Lord*. Introducing this section, I cite the Krishna tree metaphor from Daniel Ingalls's 1968 article on the *Harivamsa*.[8] The *Gitagovinda* and the Bengali poems represent a major branch off the *Bhāgavata* trunk. Perhaps the tree should be envisioned as a banyan, though, and the Radha branch an aerial prop root giving rise to a whole new trunk and more branches.

Gender is again a key concern. In the Bengali *In Praise* poems, as in many bhakti genres, we encounter male poets writing in female voices, taking on the roles of Radha, her female attendant, or an old messenger woman. Why do they do this? The theological answer has to do with the essential femaleness of the soul in its relation to a male deity. But it also has intriguing poetic possibilities, thanks to the convention of the *bhaṇitā*, the poet's self-identification incorporated into the poem. The poet is present within each brief lyric in two registers, as an actor or actress within the Vrindavan drama, and as the male poet assuming different positions in the *bhaṇitā* in relation to the action of the drama. Cutler's diagrams spring onto the board here, to unpack the often intricate verbal relations within these deceptively simple verses.

In Praise of Krishna deals with sexuality too. Here, students have helped me see some of these poems in a new and more troubling light. The sequence of poems starts off with a seduction scene, in which Krishna forcefully embraces a violently trembling Radha.[9] When I first read this poem as a male undergraduate in the early 1970s, I enjoyed it simply as a sexy vignette. But as postfeminist college students have become increasingly conscious of the threats of sexual abuse, Krishna's conduct has begun to take on a creepy quality. I'm reminded that I am also a situated reader, within my own changing cultural and personal attitudes. Now, therefore, if students don't raise the question, I do: is this date rape? How do we deal with such a provocative and questionable act of God? Of course, gods behaving badly is a regular feature of Hindu religious literature. For students in their first encounter with Hinduism through bhakti, it can be a challenging notion. Isn't God supposed to be moral and good?

Bengali Krishnaite devotionalism is also the place to introduce the aesthetics of *rasa* and Rupa Gosvami's model of bhakti *rasa*. The premise that human relationships serve as models for devotional relationships to God, and Rupa's articulation of specific relational categories prove useful through the remainder of the course. This also helps clarify for students the dual-level discourse found in much Indian devotional poetry. How is the Radha-Krishna story a human one, and how is it a religious metaphor or metonym? How do poets shift our attention back and forth between human and divine levels of reference?

The next big section is Varieties of North Indian Bhakti. Here the almost-canonical text is Jack Hawley and Mark Juergensmeyer's *Songs of the Saints of India*, which appeared in 1988, in time for the second incarnation of my course. This collection juxtaposes three *saguṇa* poets with three *nirguṇa* ones, with clear introductory notes to each and brief, well-chosen selections of poetry. I usually follow those briefer treatments with a more detailed examination of several—Kabīr and Mīrābāī almost always, Sūrdās and Nānak less often.

I like the juxtaposition of Kabīr and Sūrdās, exemplary figures of *nirguṇa* and *saguṇa* approaches respectively. But for students it is an unequal contest. They accept readily the bracing critical edge, the "rough rhetoric," of Kabīr. Sometimes they praise it as more "modern." This allows me to ask: what do they mean by this term? But the more intricate poetic strategies of Sūrdās—the unfolding epiphanies and the self-absorbing artifacts—prove difficult for students to appreciate. So too the *vātsalya* mood in many of Sūrdās's poems seems saccharine to college students, especially after the erotic charge of the Bengali Radha-Krishna poems.

Mīrābāī is a special case. Here is an Indian devotional poet whose name students already know. Mira even has a bookstore named after her not far from Bard's campus. She is important for the ongoing gender thematics of the course, but I am dissatisfied with all the available translations. Some are egregious, while others are simply partial, reflecting too heavily the sensibilities and choices of the translators. I have experimented with translation comparisons, juxtaposing three or four translations of the same poem, but I fear the experiment may have the subversive effect of casting doubt on all translations of bhakti poetry. On the positive side, ethnographic literature on Mīrābāī in contemporary North India—such as the work of Lindsey Harlan and Nancy Martin—brings bhakti into the modern world for students.[10] What model does Mira provide nowadays for women in Rajasthan, and what challenges do her radical life choices pose?

In the fourth incarnation of the course I added a section on Devotion to the Goddess, and it has been part of the regular lineup ever since. Students welcome the shift in divine gender, and they always find the complex, multifarious character of the goddess Kali intriguing and challenging. Personally, I find Ramprasad Sen's depiction of the world as a difficult and chaotic place and of his divinity as fickle and undependable to be provocative and somehow "modern." (I hope students will ask me what I mean by this.) Here again there are strong translations. Leonard Nathan and Clinton Seely's 1982 *Grace and Mercy in Her Wild Hair* contains an excellent selection of verses from Ramprasad, while Rachel McDermott's 2001 *Singing to the Goddess* provides a larger thematically organized corpus of Shakta devotional poetry from Ramprasad and other Bengali Goddess devotees from the eighteenth through twentieth centuries.

I have space for one more unit in the course. My indecision here reflects my awareness of just how much bhakti this course leaves out. Which omission should I address? Should I try to wedge in one more female vernacular poet, such as the Kashmiri Shaiva poet Lalded? Should I expand the boundaries of bhakti beyond the denominational borders of Hinduism by including Sufi poetry? Should I try for a more recent mode of devotion, like the Bauls of Bengal? Or going outside the written word, is there a way to introduce bhakti performance? In the era of YouTube, videos of various Indian devotional performances are increasingly accessible. Perhaps the most successful final reading, first adopted in 2016, has been David Haberman's 1994 *Journey through the Twelve Forests*. Centered around a contemporary Krishnaite pilgrimage in Vrindavan, this participant-observation narrative successfully draws together multiple themes from earlier in the course and combines them with local history, rituals of devotional pilgrimage, and the friendly personal voice of the author. This may become a regular part of the course lineup.

LADY BHAKTI ABROAD

Those of us who are historians of Indian religions study the circulation and dissemination of bhakti as a religious sensibility, literary mode, and social movement of profound importance. Yet we recognize that, like other great terms of Indic discourse—*dharma*, Veda, Brahman, and the like—bhakti has been a word too important to be left undebated. As a contested term in India, bhakti resists our scholarly attempts to give it a stable definition. Consequently we find ourselves examining a plurality of bhaktis: the varied theologies, poetic expressions, ritual practices, performative traditions, and devotional communities in different regions throughout the subcontinent that have taken shape within the great banyan tree of bhakti. As scholars, translators, and teachers of Indian religions, we also participate in the circulation and dissemination of bhakti beyond the geographical boundaries of South Asia.

From medieval times onward, Indian observers have also sought to comprehend this complex term and the varied religious phenomena it encompasses. Often they wish to portray bhakti as a unified religious movement spreading from region to region over time. The late seventeenth- or early eighteenth-century *Bhāgavata Māhātmya* depicts bhakti as a divine person, Lady Bhakti, who describes her own life of growth and travels. "I was born in Dravida," she announces, and goes on to relate her coming of age, maturity, hard times, and final recovery in Vrindavana as once again "a young woman of superb appearance."[11] Is it Lady Bhakti herself who has been appearing in my classes? Are we enabling her to thrive in another new region? Or perhaps providing her with comfortable assisted living in secular modernity? If this is Lady Bhakti in my Devotion and Poetry course, how does she appear to my students?

Foregrounding poetry, this course allows Lady Bhakti to speak through her poet-saints. Hindu devotional poetry constitutes a remarkably large, varied, and rich corpus of religious literature. Much of it speaks from its own time and place of composition, across cultures, with a directness and spiritual force that twenty-first-century American students can readily comprehend. Despite its apparent simplicity, bhakti poetry utilizes sophisticated rhetorical strategies, refracts mythical narratives in clever and surprising ways, and conveys subtle theological arguments. And from the 1960s on, the shelf of excellent English translations of bhakti poetry has grown wide. Words on the printed page may lose the musical dimension of poems that were meant to be sung, but good translations can go quite a ways in enabling Lady Bhakti to travel and speak abroad. Retaining her superb appearance through translated poetry she charms and challenges undergraduate students.

Yet it is important to recall that Lady Bhakti has other sides to her. Focusing on the poetry and lives of individual poet-saints, my course Devotion and Poetry presents a dematerialized version of bhakti. Bhakti also involves the construction and growth of shrines and pilgrimage sites, built places where devotees can seek a direct encounter with their lord.[12] My course leaves aside the ritual practices that have developed within bhakti communities in favor of the seemingly inspired, seemingly spontaneous outpourings of the poet-saints. Students recall the critiques of orthodox ritualism sprinkled throughout Indian devotional poetry, but the course neglects the new or modified ritual practices that make up another aspect of Lady Bhakti. Bhakti poet-saints and Indian devotional movements act as political agents within their social and cultural circumstances, but I choose to deemphasize this. I supply modest historical background along the way as necessary, but my intention is to keep class attention on literary primary sources.

Finally, is bhakti one or many? The *Bhāgavata Māhātmya* provides Lady Bhakti with an organic identity and a unified life story. My own view as a historian of religion is that bhakti is diffuse and pervasive within Indian religious history. Bhakti is a contested term and a religious modality with porous and changing dimensions. In my syllabus I changed long ago from the singular to the plural, *religious movements*. Yet students may well come to their own conclusions.

For an essay on what students hear, it is fitting to allow them the final word. While writing this, I contacted the seven students from my 1988 class. They are now in their late forties, far from their experiences as Yale undergraduates, and memories are selective. One recalled the earliness of the class: "walking across the old campus before anyone else was up made it seem like a special experience." More special were the course readings. Bhakti's unfamiliarity to these American students was itself an attraction, like "an invitation to a different weather system." One student spoke of the "clarity and immediacy of the poetry" and "the depth and range of emotion." That student continued: "I've really never experienced anything quite like it since. Perhaps the Psalms come closest, when translated well." Equally important was the demonstration—modeled by the professor and joined by the students—of passionate excitement directed toward a seemingly obscure subject that "is not a direct, personal inheritance from their own cultural context." Here is the pedagogic value of respectful alterity. That student observed, "The something itself is not important, but rather the being carried away." I believe Lady Bhakti would approve.

NOTES

1 Bryant, *Poems to the Child-God*, 21.
2 Cutler, *Songs of Experience*, 19.
3 Davis, "Bhakti Poetry."
4 Turner, *Ritual Process*, 94–203; Turner, "Metaphors," 272–99.
5 Ramanujan and Cutler, "From Classicism to Bhakti," 232–59; Hardy, *Viraha-Bhakti*.
6 Venkatesan, *Secret Garland*; Pechilis, *Interpreting Devotion*.
7 Ramanujan, *Hymns for the Drowning*, 104.
8 Ingalls, "Harivaṃśa as a Mahākāvya," 381–94.
9 Dimock and Levertov, *In Praise of Krishna*, 11.
10 Harlan, *Religion and Rajput Women*, 205–22; Martin, "Mirabai," 7–46.
11 Hawley, *Storm of Songs*, 59.
12 Francis and Schmid, "Introduction," 7.

BIBLIOGRAPHY

Abbas, Ali Akbar, trans. *Bullhe Shāh Kā Kālām*. Lahore: Panjab Council of the Arts, 1989.

Ahmad, Qeyamuddin. "Aspects of the Historical Geography of Bihar." In *The Comprehensive History of Bihar*, vol. 2, edited by Bhindeshari Prasad Sinha. Patna: Kashi Prasad Jayaswal Research Institute, 1983.

Ahmed, Sara. "Feminist Killjoys (and Other Willful Subjects)." *The Scholar and Feminist Online* 8, no. 3 (Summer 2010). http://sfonline.barnard.edu.

Akkamahādēvi, and L. Basavarāju. *Akkana Vacanagaḷu*. Mysore: Geetha Book House, 1966.

Ali, Kecia, and Oliver Leaman. *Islam: The Key Concepts*. London and New York: Routledge, 2008.

Anderson, Benedict. *Reflections on the Origin and Spread of Nationalism*. New York: Verso, 2006.

Anjum, Tanvir. *Chishti Sufis in the Sultanate of Delhi, 1190–1400*. Karachi: Oxford University Press, 2011.

Apte, V. G., ed. *Brahmavaivartapurāṇa*. Pune: Ānanda Āśrama Sanskrit Series, vol. 102, 1935.

Babb, Lawrence, Varsha Joshi, and Michael W. Meister, eds. *Multiple Histories: Culture and Society in the Study of Rajasthan*. Jaipur: Rawat Publications, 2002.

Bagchi, Jasodhara. "Representing Nationalism: Ideology of Motherhood in Colonial Bengal." *Economic and Political Weekly* 25, no. 42/43 (1990): WS65–WS71.

Baid, Neha, ed. *Harirāmadās Kṛt Chandaratnāvalī*. Jodhpur: Rajasthani Granthagar, 2010.

———, ed. *Nāmaprakāśa (Sampādana evaṃ Samīkṣā)*. Jodhpur: Royal Publications, 2015.

Bajekal, Madhavi. "The State and the Rural Grain Market in Eighteenth Century Eastern Rajasthan." *Indian Economic and Social History Review* 25, no. 4 (1988): 443–73.

Bakhle, Janaki. *Two Men and Music: Nationalism in the Making of an Indian Classical Tradition*. New York: Oxford University Press, 2005.

Barnett, L. D. "Two Illustrated Assamese Manuscripts." *British Museum Quarterly* 8, no. 1 (1933): 1–12.

Beames, John. "On the Age and Country of Bidyâpati." *Indian Antiquary*, October 1875: 299–301.

Behl, Aditya. *Love's Subtle Magic: An Indian Islamic Literary Tradition, 1379–1545*. New York: Oxford University Press, 2012.

Bellamy, Carla. *The Powerful Ephemeral: Everyday Healing in an Ambiguously Islamic Place*. Berkeley: University of California Press, 2011.

Ben-Herut, Gil. "Arguing with Vaiṣṇavas, Annihilating Jains: Two Religious Others in Early Kannada Śivabhakti Hagiographies." In *Regional Communities of Devotion in South Asia: Insiders, Outsiders, and Interlopers*, edited by Gil Ben-Herut, Jon Keune, and Anne E. Monius. New York: Routledge, 2018.

———. *Śiva's Saints: The Origins of Devotion in Kannada according to Harihara's* Ragajegalu. New York: Oxford University Press, 2018.

———. "Things Standing Shall Move: Temple Worship in Early Kannada Śivabhakti Hagiographies." *International Journal of Hindu Studies* 20, no. 2 (2016): 129–58.

Berger, John. "Mother." In John Berger, *Keeping a Rendezvous*, 43–52. New York: Vintage, 1992.

Bhagavad Gītā. Gorakhpur: Gita Press, 1998.

Bhāgavata Purāṇa. 2 vols. Gorakhpur: Gita Press, 2010.

Bhārill, Hukumcand. *Paṇḍit Ṭoḍarmal: Vyaktitva aur Kartṛtva*. Jaipur: Paṇḍit Ṭoḍarmal Smārak Ṭrasṭ, 1973.

Bhati, Jitendrasimh. *Rājasthān kī Praśāsanik Vyavasthā: Mārvāṛ ke Sandarbh Meṃ, 1300–1800 Ī.* Jodhpur: Rajasthani Granthagar, 2011.

Bhatia, Varuni. "Devotional Traditions and National Culture: Recovering Gauḍīya Vaishnavism in Colonial Bengal." Ph.D. diss., Columbia University, 2009.

Bhatti, Abdulmajid, ed. *Kāfīyān Shāh Ḥusain: Manẓūn Urdū Tarjumah*. Lahore: Panjabi Adabi Academy, 1961.

Bhūdhardās. *Pārśva Purāṇ*. Edited by Nāthūrām Premī. Bombay: Hindī Granth Karyālāy, 1918. Reprint, Mumbai: Sanmati Ṭrasṭ, 2001.

Bowker, John Westerdale. *The Oxford Dictionary of World Religions*. Oxford, New York: Oxford University Press, 1997.

Brick, David, ed. and trans. *Brahmanical Theories of the Gift: A Critical Edition and Annotated Translation of the Dānakānda of the Kṛtyakalpataru*. Cambridge: Harvard University Press, 2015.

Briggs, George Weston. *Gorakhnāth and the Kānphaṭa Yogīs*. 1938. Reprint, Delhi: Motilal Banarsidass, 1973.

Brown, Carolyn Henning. "Contested Meanings: Tantra and the Poetics of Mithila Art." *American Ethnologist* 23, no. 4 (November 1996): 717–37.

Bryant, Edwin F. *Bhakti Yoga: Tales and Teachings from the Bhāgavata Purāṇa.* San Francisco: North Point Press, 2017.

———. *Krishna: The Beautiful Legend of God. Śrīmad Bhāgavata Purāṇa, Book X, with Chapters 1, 6 and 29–31 from Book XI.* London: Penguin, 2003.

Bryant, Kenneth E. *Poems to the Child-God: Structures and Strategies in the Poetry of Sūrdās.* Berkeley: University of California Press, 1978.

Burchett, Patton. "Bitten by the Snake: Early Modern Devotional Critiques of Tantra-Mantra." *Journal of Hindu Studies* 6, no. 1 (May 2013): 1–20.

Burghart, Richard. "The Disappearance and Reappearance of Janakpur." *Kailash* 6 (1978): 257–84.

Burn, R. *Census of India 1901, Volume XVI: N.-W. Provinces and Oudh, Part I, Report.* Allahabad: Government Press, 1902.

Busch, Allison. *Poetry of Kings: The Classical Hindi Literature of Mughal India.* New York: Oxford University Press, 2011.

Callewaert, Winand, ed. *The Hindī Biography of Dādū Dayāl.* Delhi: Motilal Banarsidass, 1988.

Callewaert, Winand M., and Bart Op de Beeck, eds. *Nirguṇ-Bhakti Sāgar—Devotional Hindī Literature: A Critical Edition of the Pañc-Vāṇī or Five Works of Dādū, Kabīr, Nāmdev, Raidās, Hardās with the Hindī Songs of Gorakhnāth and Sundardās, and a Complete Word-Index.* 2 vols. New Delhi: Manohar, 1991.

Callewaert, Winand M., and Swapna Sharma, eds. *Dictionary of Bhakti.* Delhi: D. K. Printworld, 2009.

Callewaert, Winand M., and Rupert Snell, eds. *According to Tradition: Hagiographical Writing in India.* Wiesbaden: Otto Harrassowitz, 1994.

Cāṇḍiyo, Jāved, ed. *Dīvān-i Farīd.* Bahavalpur: Sirā'ikī Adabī Majlis, 1998.

Carman, John B. *The Theology of Rāmānuja: An Essay in Interreligious Understanding.* New Haven: Yale University Press, 1974.

Case, Margaret, ed., with photographs by Robyn Beeche. *Govindadeva: A Dialogue in Stone.* New Delhi: Indira Gandhi National Centre for the Arts, 1996.

Caturvedī, Paraśurām, ed. *Mīrābāī kī Padāvalī.* Allahabad: Hindi Sahitya Sammelan, 1973.

Chakrabarty, Bidyut. *Communism in India: Events, Processes and Ideologies.* New York: Oxford University Press, 2014.

Chakraborty, Ajanta. "'Backward' Tag for State Folk Artistes." *Times of India,* October 18, 2012.

Chakravarti, Ramakant. *Vaiṣṇavism in Bengal.* Calcutta: Sanskrit Pustak Bhandar, 1985.

Chakravarti, Sudhindra Chandra. *Philosophical Foundations of Bengal Vaisnavism.* Calcutta: Academic Publishers, 1969.

Champakalakshmi, Radha. "Caste and Community: Oscillating Identities in Pre-Modern South India." In *Religion, Tradition, and Ideology: Pre-Colonial South India,* edited by R. Champakalakshmi, 235–85. New Delhi: Oxford University Press, 2011.

Chandra, Satish. *Medieval India: From Sultanate to the Mughals*, vol. 2. New Delhi: Har Anand Publications, 2006.

Chandra Shobhi, Prithvi Datta. "Pre-Modern Communities and Modern Histories: Narrating Vīraśaiva and Lingayat Selves." Ph.D. diss., University of Chicago, 2005.

Chatterjee, Indrani. "Monastic 'Governmentality': Revisiting 'Community' and 'Communalism' in South Asia." *History Compass* 13, no. 10 (2015): 497–511.

Chatterjee, Kumkum. "Cultural Flows and Cosmopolitanism in Mughal India: The Bishnupur Kingdom." *Indian Economic and Social History Review* 46, no. 2 (2009): 147–82.

———. *The Cultures of History in Early Modern India: Persianization and Mughal Culture in Bengal*. New Delhi: Oxford University Press, 2009.

Chatterjee, Partha. *The Politics of the Governed: Reflections on Popular Politics in Most of the World*. New York: Columbia University Press, 2004.

Chattopadhyay, Swati. *Representing Calcutta: Modernity, Nationalism, and the Colonial Uncanny*. New York: Routledge, 2005.

Chaturvedi, Parsuram. *Uttarī Bhārat kī Sant-Paramparā*. 1951. 2nd ed. Allahabad: Bharati Bhandar, 1965.

Cherian, Divya. "Ordering Subjects: Merchants, the State, and Krishna Devotion in Eighteenth-Century Marwar." Ph.D. diss., Columbia University, 2015.

Choudhary [Chaudhuri], Radhakrishna. "Political History of North Bihar (550–1200 A.D.)." Chapter XXXV of *The Comprehensive History of Bihar*, vol. I, part II., edited by Bindeshwari Prasad Sinha, 281–330. Patna: Kashi Prasad Jayaswal Research Institute, 1974.

———. "Karnats of Mithila." *Annals of the Bhandarkar Oriental Research Institute* 35 (1954): 91–121.

Chowdhury, Rohini, trans. *Banarsidas: Ardhakathanak: A Half Story*. New Delhi: Penguin Books, 2009.

Coburn, Thomas B. "The Structural Interplay of Tantra, Vedānta, and Bhakti: Nondualist Commentary on the Goddess." In *The Roots of Tantra*, edited by Katherine Anne Harper and Robert L. Brown, 77–89. Albany: State University of New York Press, 2002.

Connolly, William E. *Why I Am Not a Secularist*. Minneapolis: University of Minnesota Press, 1999.

Cort, John E. "Bhakti in the Early Jain Tradition: Understanding Devotional Religion in South Asia." *History of Religions* 42 (2002): 59–86.

———. "The Cosmic Man and the Human Condition." In *Victorious Ones: Jain Images of Perfection*, edited by Phyllis Granoff, 34–47. New York: Rubin Museum of Art; and Ahmedabad: Mapin Publishing, 2009.

———. "Dyānatrāy: An Eighteenth Century Digambara Mystical Poet." In *Essays in Jaina Philosophy and Religion*, edited by Piotr Balcerowicz, 279–95. Delhi: Motilal Banarsidass and Warsaw Indological Studies 2, 2003.

———. "God Outside and God Inside: North Indian Digambar Jain Performance of Bhakti." In *Bhakti Beyond the Forest: Current Research on Early Modern Literatures in North India, 2003–2009*, edited by Imre Bangha, 255–86. New Delhi: Manohar, 2013.

———. "Making it Vernacular in Agra: The Practice of Translation by Seventeenth-Century Digambar Jains." In *Tellings and Texts: Music, Literature, and Performance in North India*, edited by Francesca Orsini and Katherine Butler Schofield, 61–105. Cambridge: Open Book Publishers, 2015.

———. "Singing the Glory of Asceticism: Devotion of Asceticism in Jainism." *Journal of the American Academy of Religion* 70 (2002), 719–42.

———. "Singing the Seasons: Spiritual Songs of Bhūdhardās." In *Sanmati: Essays Felicitating Professor Hampa Nagarajaiah on the Occasion of His 80th Birthday*, edited by Luitgard Soni and Jayandra Soni, 119–29. Bengalaru: Sapna Book House, 2015.

———. "A Tale of Two Cities: On the Origins of Digambara Sectarianism in North India." In *Multiple Histories: Culture and Society in the Study of Rajasthan*, edited by Lawrence A. Babb, Varsha Joshi, and Michael W. Meister, 39–83. Jaipur: Rawat, 2002.

Coward, Harold, ed. *Studies in Indian Thought: The Collected Papers of Prof. T. R. V. Murti*. Delhi: Motilal Banarasidass, 1983.

Crill, Rosemary. *The Fabric of India*. London: V and A Publishing, 2015.

———. "Vrindavani Vastra: Figured Silks from Assam." *Hali* 14, no. 2 (1992): 72–83.

Cutler, Norman. *Songs of Experience: The Poetics of Tamil Devotion*. Bloomington: Indiana University Press, 1987.

Daftary, Farhad. *A Short History of the Ismailis: Traditions of a Muslim Community*. Edinburgh: Edinburgh University Press, 1998.

Dale, Stephen F. *Indian Merchants and Eurasian Trade, 1600–1750*. Cambridge: Cambridge University Press, 1994.

Damodar. *Heer Damodar*. Edited by Muzaffar A. Ghaffaar. Lahore: Ferozsons, 2009.

Dandekar, S. V., B. M. Khuperkar, N. R. Phatak, A. K. Priyolkar, and R. N. Velingkar, eds. *Śrī Jñāneśvarī*. Mumbai: Government Central Press, 1963.

Dās, Rās Bihārī Lāl. *Tirhut in the Early Twentieth Century: Mithilā Darpan*. Edited by Hetukar Jha. Darbhanga: Maharajadhiraja Kameshwar Singh Kalyani Foundation, 2005.

Dass, Nirmal. *Songs of the Saints from the Adi Granth*. Albany: State University of New York Press, 2000.

Davis, Coralyn V. *Maithil Women's Tales: Storytelling on the Nepal-India Border*. Urbana: University of Illinois Press, 2014.

Davis, Richard H. "Bhakti Poetry: An Interview." *Journal of Vaishnava Studies* 4, no. 4 (1996): 5–16.

De, Sushil Kumar. *Early History of the Vaisnava Faith and Movement in Bengal: From Sanskrit and Bengali Sources*. Calcutta: Firma K. L. Mukhopadhyay, 1961.

Dennen, David. "The Third Stream: Oḍiśī Music, Regional Nationalism, and the Concept of 'Classical.'" *Asian Music* 41, no. 2 (2010): 149–79.

Deshpande, V. N., ed. *Smṛtisthaḷa*. Pune: Venus, 1969.

Devadevan, Manu V. *A Prehistory of Hinduism*. Warsaw, Berlin: De Gruyter, 2016.

Dhaky, M. A. "Bhūtas and Bhūtanāyakas: Elementals and Their Captains." In *Discourses on Shiva: Proceedings of a Symposium on the Nature of Religious Imagery*, edited by Michael W. Meister, 240–56. Philadelphia: University of Pennsylvania Press, 1984.

Diamond, Christopher. "City of the Turks: Urban Encounters in Vidyāpati's Kīrttilatā." M.A. thesis, University of Washington, 2015.

Digby, Simon. "The Sufi Shaykh and the Sultan: A Conflict of Claims to Authority in Medieval India." *Iran* 28 (January 1, 1990): 71–81.

———. "To Ride a Tiger or a Wall? Strategies of Prestige in Indian Sufi Legend." In *According to Tradition: Hagiographical Writing in India*, edited by Winand Callewaert and Rupert Snell, 99–130. Wiesbaden: Otto Harrassowitz, 1994.

Dimock, Edward C., Jr., and Denise Levertov. *In Praise of Krishna: Songs from the Bengali*. Garden City: Doubleday, 1967.

Dimock, Edward C., Jr., and Tony Stewart, trans. and eds. *Caitanya Caritāmṛta of Kṛṣṇadāsa Kavirāja: A Translation and Commentary*. Cambridge: Harvard University Press, 1999.

Entwistle, Alan W. *Braj: Centre of Krishna Pilgrimage*. Groningen: Egbert Forsten, 1987.

Ernst, Carl W. "The Islamization of Yoga in the 'Amrtakunda' Translations." *Journal of the Royal Asiatic Society* 13, no. 2 (2003): 199–226.

———. "Muslim Studies of Hinduism? A Reconsideration of Arabic and Persian Translations from Indian Languages." *Iranian Studies* 36, no. 2 (2003): 173–95.

———. "Situating Sufism and Yoga." *Journal of the Royal Asiatic Society* 15, no. 1 (2005): 15–43.

Fitrat, Bihārī Lāl. *Mithila in the Nineteenth-Century: The Aina-i-Tirhut of Bihari Lal "Fitrat."* Edited by Hetukar Jha. Hindi translation by Izhārūl Imām. Darbhanga: Maharajadhiraja Kameshwar Singh Kalyani Foundation, 2001.

Foucault, Michel. *The History of Sexuality*. New York: Vintage Books, 1990.

———. *Security, Territory, Population: Lectures at the Collège de France, 1977–78*. Basingstoke: Palgrave Macmillan, 2007.

Francis, Emmanuel, and Charlotte Schmid. "Introduction: Towards an Archaeology of Bhakti." In *The Archaeology of Bhakti I: Mathura and Maturai, Back and Forth*. Pondichéry: Institut Français de Pondichéry, 2014.

Gadon, Elinor. "Note on the Frontispiece." In *The Sants: Studies in a Devotional Tradition of India*, edited by Karine Schomer and W. H. McLeod, 415–21. Berkeley: Berkeley Religious Studies Series, 1987.

Geertz, Clifford. *Islam Observed: Religious Development in Morocco and Indonesia*. Chicago: University of Chicago Press, 1968.

Ghosh, Pika. *Temple to Love: Architecture and Devotion in Seventeenth-Century Bengal*. Bloomington and Indianapolis: Indiana University Press, 2005.

Glushkova, Irina. "*Dharma* and *Bhakti*: Marital Conflicts in the Vārkarī Tradition." In *In the Company of Gods: Essays in Memory of Günther-Dietz Sontheimer*, edited by Aditya Malik, Anne Feldhaus, Heidrun Brückner, and Günther-Dietz Sontheimer, 179–92. New Delhi: Indira Gandhi National Centre for the Arts in association with Manohar, 2005.

Goldman, Robert P. "Vālmīki and the Bhṛgu Connection." *Journal of the American Oriental Society* 96, no. 1 (1976): 97–101.

Gonda, Jan. *Medieval Religious Literature in Sanskrit*. Wiesbaden: Otto Harrassowitz, 1977.

Gosvāmī, Jīva. *Bhāgavata Sandarbha* (including *Tattva Sandarbha, Bhagavata Sandarbha, Paramātma Sandarbha, Śrīkṛṣṇa Sandarbha* in volume 1; *Bhakti Sandarbha* and *Prīti Sandarbha* in volume 2). Edited by Puridasa. Vrindavan: Haridasa Sarma, 1951.

Gosvāmī, Rūpa. *Kṛṣṇajanmatithividhi*. Edited by Puridasa. Puri: Shachinath Rayachaudhuri, 1948.

———. *Padyāvalī*. Edited by Puridasa. Meymensingh: Sachinath Rayachaudhuri, 1946.

Gosvāmī, Vāsudev. *Bhakta Kavi Vyāsjī*. Mathurā: Agravāl Press, 1952.

Goswami, Shrivatsa. "Gopal Bhatt: Carrier of Bhakti to the North." In *Text and Tradition in Early Modern North India*, edited by Tyler Williams, Anshu Malhotra, and John Stratton Hawley, 335–53. Delhi: Oxford University Press, 2018.

Graves, Eben. "The Marketplace of Devotional Song: Cultural Economies of Exchange in Bengali Padāvalī-Kīrtan," *Ethnomusicology* 11, no. 1 (2017): 52–86.

Greeven, Richard. *The Knights of the Broom: An Attempt to Collect and to Explain Some of the Ceremonies of the Sweepers in the Benares Division*. Benares: Medical Hall Press, 1894.

Grewal, J. S., ed. *Religious Movements and Institutions in Medieval India*. New Delhi: Oxford University Press, 2006.

Grewal, J. S., and Irfan Habib, eds. *Sikh History from Persian Sources*. Delhi: Indian History Congress, 2001.

Grierson, George A. *Bihar Peasant Life: Being a Discursive Catalogue of the Surroundings of the People of that Province*. Calcutta: Bengal Secretariat Press, 1885.

———. *An Introduction to the Maithili Language of North Bihar, Containing a Grammar, Chrestomathy, and Vocabulary*. Calcutta: *Journal of the Asiatic Society of Bengal*, 1880–81.

Grover, B. R. "An Integrated Pattern of Commercial Life in the Rural Society of North India during the Seventeenth and Eighteenth Centuries." In *Money and the Market in India, 1100–1700*, edited by Sanjay Subrahmanyam, 219–55. Delhi: Oxford University Press,1994.

Guha, Ranajit. "Dominance without Hegemony and its Historiography." In *Subaltern Studies VI: Writings on South Asian History and Society*, edited by Ranajit Guha, 210–309. Delhi: Oxford University Press, 1992.

Gupta, Charu. *The Gender of Caste: Representing Dalits in Print*. Seattle: University of Washington Press, 2016.

Gupta, I. P. *Urban Glimpses of Mughal India: Agra: The Imperial Capital (16th and 17th Centuries)*. Delhi: Discovery, 1986.

Gupta, Lina. "Tantric Incantation in the *Devī Purāṇa: Padamālā Mantra Vidyā*." In *The Roots of Tantra*, edited by Katherine Anne Harper and Robert L. Brown, 231–49. Albany: State University of New York Press, 2002.

Gupta, Nagendranath. "Vidyāpati Ṭhākur." *Journal of the Asiatic Society of Bengal* 73, no. 1 (1904): 20–24.

Guthrie, Stewart. *Faces in the Clouds: A New Theory of Religion*. New York: Oxford University Press, 1993.

Haberman, David. *Acting as a Way of Salvation: A Study of Rāgānugā Bhakti Sādhana*. New York: Oxford University Press, 1988.

———, trans. *The Bhaktirasāmṛtasindhu of Rūpa Gosvāmin*. New Delhi: Indira Gandhi National Centre for the Arts, 2003.

———. *Journey through the Twelve Forests: An Encounter with Krishna*. New York: Oxford University Press, 1994.

Habib, Irfan. "Jatts." *Brill's Encyclopedia of Sikhism*, edited by Knut A. Jacobson, Gurinder Singh Mann, Kristina Myrvold, and Eleanor Nesbitt, 263–65. Leiden: E. J. Brill, 2017.

Hallisey, Charles. *Therigatha: Poems of the First Buddhist Women*. Cambridge: Harvard University Press, 2015.

Hansen, Thomas Blom. "The Vernacularization of Hindutva: BJP and Shiv Sena in Rural Maharashtra." *Contributions to Indian Sociology* 30, no. 2 (1996): 177–214.

———. *The Saffron Wave: Democracy and Hindu Nationalism in Modern India*. Princeton: Princeton University Press, 1999.

———. *Wages of Violence: Naming and Identity in Postcolonial Bombay*. Princeton: Princeton University Press, 2001.

Hardy, Friedhelm. *Viraha-Bhakti: The Early History of Kṛṣṇa Devotion in South India*. Delhi: Oxford University Press, 1983.

Haridās Dās. *Śrī-Śrī-Gauḍīya-Vaiṣṇava-Abhidhāna*. 2 vols. Navadvīp: Haribol Kuṭir, 1957.

Harihara, Hampeya. *Nūtana Purātanara Ragaḷegaḷu*. Edited by M. S. Sunkapur. Dharwad: Kannaḍa Adhyayanapīṭha, Karnāṭaka Viśvavidyālaya, 1976.

———. *Śivabhaktimahimā Ragaḷegaḷu*. Edited by M. S. Sunkāpura. Dharwad: Kannaḍa Adhyayanapīṭha, Karnāṭaka Viśvavidyālaya, 1976.

Hariramdas. *Dayāl Jī kī Pañc Paracai*. Manuscript 24778, Rajasthan Oriental Research Institute, Jodhpur. Manuscript dated 1817 CE.

Harlan, Lindsey. *Religion and Rajput Women*. Berkeley: University of California Press, 1992.

Hastings, James Michael. "Poets, *Sants*, and Warriors: The Dadu Panth, Religious Change and Identity Formation in Jaipur State circa 1562—1860 CE." Ph.D. diss.,University of Wisconsin, Madison, 2002.

Hawley, John Stratton. "Can There Be a Vaishnava Kabir?" *Studies in History* 32, no. 2 (2016): 147–61.

———. "The Nirguṇ-Saguṇ Distinction in Early Manuscript Anthologies of Hindi Devotion." In *Bhakti Religion in North India: Community, Identity and Political Action*, edited by David N. Lorenzen, 160–80. New York: State University of New York Press, 1995.

———. "Seeing the Bhakti Movement." In *Archaeology and Text: The Temple in South Asia*, edited by Himanshu Prabha Ray, 232–67. Delhi: Oxford University Press, 2010.

———. *A Storm of Songs: India and the Idea of the Bhakti Movement*. Cambridge: Harvard University Press, 2015.

———. *Sūrdās: Poet, Singer, Saint*. 2nd rev. ed. Delhi: Primus, 2018.

———. *Three Bhakti Voices: Mirabai, Surdas, and Kabir in Their Time and Ours*. New York: Oxford University Press, 2005.

Hawley, John Stratton, and Kenneth E. Bryant. *Sur's Ocean: Poems from the Early Tradition*. Cambridge: Harvard University Press, 2015.

Hawley, John Stratton, and Mark Juergensmeyer. *Songs of the Saints of India*. New York: Oxford University Press, 1988.

Hess, Linda. *Bodies of Song: Kabir Oral Traditions and Performative Worlds in North India*. New York: Oxford University Press, 2015.

Hess, Linda, and Shukdev Singh. *The Bījak of Kabir*. San Francisco: North Point Press, 1983.

Holdrege, Barbara. *Bhakti and Embodiment: Fashioning Divine Bodies and Devotional Bodies in Kṛṣṇa Bhakti*. London: Routledge, 2015.

Hopkins, Steven P. *Singing the Body of God: The Hymns of Vedāntadeśika in their South Indian Tradition*. New York: Oxford University Press, 2002.

Horstmann, Monika. *Crossing the Ocean of Existence: Braj Bhāṣā Religious Poetry from Rajasthan: A Reader*. Wiesbaden: Otto Harrassowitz, 1983.

———. "Dādūpanthī Anthologies of the Eighteenth and Nineteenth Centuries." In *Bhakti in Current Research: Proceedings of the Ninth International Conference on Early Devotional Literature in New Indo-Aryan Languages, Heidelberg,*

23–26 July 2003, edited by Monika Horstmann, 163–77. New Delhi: Manohar, 2006.

———. *Der Zusammenhalt der Welt: Religiöse Herrschaftslegitimation und Religionspolitik Mahārājā Savāī Jaisinghs (1700–1743)*. Wiesbaden: Otto Harrassowitz, 2009.

———. *In Favour of Govinddevjī: Historical Documents Relating to a Deity of Vrindaban and Eastern Rajasthan*. New Delhi: Indira Gandhi National Centre for the Arts and Manohar, 1999.

———. *Jaipur 1778: The Making of a King*. Wiesbaden: Otto Harrassowitz, 2013.

———. "Symbiotic Antinomy: The Social Organization of a North Indian Sect." A. L. Basham Lecture. Canberra: Australian National University, 1986.

Hussain, Shah. *Kalām-i Shāh Husain*. Lahore: Paikejiz, 1979.

Hutchins, Francis G. *Young Krishna*. West Franklin, NH: Amarta Press, 1980.

Ingalls, Daniel H. H. "The Harivaṃśa as a Mahākāvya." In *Mélanges d'indianisme a la mémoire de Louis Renou*, 381–94. Paris: Éditions de Boccard, 1968.

Ishwaran, K. *Religion and Society among the Lingayats of South India*. Leiden: E. J. Brill, 1983.

———. *Speaking of Basava: Lingayat Religion and Culture in South Asia*. Boulder, CO: Westview Press, 1992.

Jain, Bhaṅvarlāl. "Jaypur ke Jain Dīvān." In *Jain Saṅskṛti aur Rājasthān*, edited by Narendra Bhānāvat, 332–39. Jaipur: Samyagjñān Pracārak Maṇḍal, 1975.

Jain, Kastūrcand Suman, and Puṣpalatā Khāg. "Prastāvnā." In *Āmer ke Digambar Jain Mandir Sāṅvlājī Neminâth ke Yantralekh*, 13–62. Śrī Mahāvīrjī: Jainvidyā Saṅsthān, 2012.

Jain, Munnī. *Hindī Gadya ke Vikās meṃ Jain Manīṣī Paṅ. Sadāsukhdās kā Yogdān*. Varanasi: Pārśvanāth Vidyāpīṭh; and Ajmer: Śrī Digambar Jain Siddhakūṭ Caityālay Ṭempal Ṭrasṭ, 2002.

Jain, Premsāgar. *Hindī Jain Bhakti Kāvya aur Kavi*. Varanasi: Bhāratīya Jñānpīṭh Prakāśan, 1964.

Jain, Ramākānt. *Hindī Bhāratī ke kuch Jain Sāhityakār*. Śrī Mahāvīrjī: Jainvidyā Saṅsthān, 1995.

Jana, Naresh Chand. *Vṛndāvaner Chaya Gosvāmī*. Kolkata: Calcutta University, 1970.

Jaoul, Nicolas. "Casting the 'Sweepers': Local Politics of Sanskritisation, Caste and Labour." In *Cultural Entrenchment of Hindutva: Local Mediations and Forms of Convergence*, edited by Daniela Berti, Nicolas Jaoul, and Pralay Kanungo, 273–306. New Delhi: Routledge, 2011.

Jha, Hetukar. "Prāchīn Mithilā meṃ Pokhar Paramparā." *Sākshya* 14 (October 2004): 325–31.

Jha, Pankaj Kumar. "Beyond the Local and the Universal: Exclusionary Strategies of Expansive Literary Cultures in Fifteenth Century Mithila." *Indian Economic and Social History Review* 51, no. 1 (2014): 1–40.

Jha, Makhan. *Civilizational Regions of Mithila and Mahakoshal*. Delhi: Capital Publishing House, 1982.
Jordens, J. T. F. *Swami Shraddhananda: His Life and Causes*. Delhi: Oxford University Press, 1981.
Kalidos, Raju. "Naṭarāja as Portrayed in the Tēvāram Hymns." *Acta Orientalia* 57 (1996): 13–56.
Kamath, Harshita Mruthinti. "Kṣētrayya: The Making of a Telugu Poet." *Indian Economic and Social History Review*, forthcoming.
Karve, I. K. "On the Road: A Maharashtrian Pilgrimage." *Journal of Asian Studies* 22, no. 1 (November 1962): 13–29.
Kāslīvāl, Kastūrcand. *Bhaṭṭārak Ratnakīrti evaṃ Kumudacandra: Vyaktitva evaṃ Kṛtitva*. Jaipur: Śrī Mahāvīr Granth Akādamī, 1981.
———. *Khaṇḍelvāl Jain Samāj kā Vṛhad Itihās*. Jaipur: Jain Itihās Prakāśan Saṅsthān, 1989.
———. *Mahākavi Daulatrām Kāslīvāl: Vyaktitva evaṃ Kṛtitva*. Jaipur: Sāhitya Śodh Vibhāg, Śrī Di. A. Kṣetra Śrī Mahāvīrjī, 1973.
———. "Prastāvnā" to Gaṅgārām Gārg, *Pārśvadās Padāvalī*, pp. *ek—āṭh*. Tonk: Digambar Jain Samāj, 1972.
Kavirāja, Kṛṣṇadāsa. *Caitanya Caritāmṛta of Kṛṣṇadāsa Kavirāja*. Edited and translated by Edward C. Dimock, Jr., and Tony K. Stewart. Cambridge: Department of Sanskrit and Indian Studies, Harvard University, 1999.
———. *Śrī-Śrī-Caitanyacaritāmṛta Ādilīlā*. Edited by Jagadīśvara Gupta. Kalikātā: Devīprasanna Rāy Caudhurī, 1889.
Keune, Jon. "Gathering the *Bhaktas* in Marathi." *Journal of Vaishnava Studies* (2007): 169–87.
———. "God Eats with Mahars: Dalits, Brahmans, and Intertextuality in the Varkari Canon." Paper presented to the conference on The Self in Bhakti, Max Weber Center for Advanced Cultural and Social Studies, University of Erfurt, June 22–24, 2016.
Khan, Dominique-Sila. *Crossing the Threshold: Understanding Religious Identities in South Asia*. London: I. B. Tauris, 2004.
Kinsley, David. *Hindu Goddesses: Visions of the Divine Feminine in the Hindu Religious Tradition*. Berkeley: University of California Press, 1986.
Knutson, Jesse Ross. *Into the Twilight of Sanskrit Poetry: The Sena Salon of Bengal and Beyond*. Berkeley: University of California Press, 2014.
Kohli, Surinder Singh, trans. *Sri Dasam Granth Sahib*. Birmingham: Sikh National Heritage Trust, 2003.
Kolff, Dirk H. A. *Naukar, Rajput and Sepoy: The Ethnohistory of the Military Labour Market in Hindustan, 1450–1850*. Cambridge: Cambridge University Press, 1990.
Kramrisch, Stella. *The Presence of Śiva*. 1981. Princeton: Princeton University Press, 1992.

Kugle, Scott Alan. *Sufis and Saints' Bodies: Mysticism, Corporeality, and Sacred Power in Islam*. Chapel Hill: University of North Carolina Press, 2007.
Lalas, Sitaram, ed. *Rājasthānī-Hindī Śabdakoś*, vol. 2. Jodhpur: Rajasthan Oriental Research Institute, 1987.
Lapierre, Dominique. *The City of Joy*. Garden City, NY: Doubleday, 1985.
Lath, Mukund, trans. *Half a Tale: A Study in the Interrelationship between Autobiography and History*. Jaipur: Rajasthan Prakrit Bharati Sansthan, 1981.
Lee, Joel. "Jagdish, Son of Ahmad: Dalit Religion and Nominative Politics in Lucknow." *South Asia Multidisciplinary Academic Journal* 11 (2015): n.p.
———. "Recognition and Its Shadows: Dalits and the Politics of Religion in India." Ph.D. diss., Columbia University, 2015.
Lele, Jayant. "The Bhakti Movement in India: A Critical Introduction." In *Tradition and Modernity in Bhakti Movements*, edited by Jayant Lele, 1–15. Leiden: Brill, 1981.
Leonard, Karen. "The 'Great Firm' Theory of the Decline of the Mughal Empire." *Comparative Studies in Society and History* 21, no. 2 (1979): 151–67.
Leslie, Julia. *Authority and Meaning in Indian Religions: Hinduism and the Case of Vālmīki*. Cornwall: Ashgate, 2003.
———. "Understanding Basava: History, Hagiography and a Modern Kannaḍa Drama." *Bulletin of the School of Oriental and African Studies* 61, no. 2 (1998): 228–61.
Little, J. H. *House of Jagatseth*. Calcutta: Calcutta Historical Society, 1967.
Lorenzen, David N. "Bhakti." In *The Hindu World*, edited by Sushil Mittal and Gene R. Thursby, 185–209. New York: Routledge, 2007.
———. *Bhakti Religion in North India: Community Identity and Political Action*. Albany: State University of New York Press, 1995.
———. "The Historical Vicissitudes of Bhakti Religion." In *Bhakti Religion in North India: Community, Identity and Political Action*, edited by David Lorenzen, 1–32. New York: State University of New York Press, 1995.
———. "Introduction." In *Religious Movements in South Asia, 600–1800*, edited by David N. Lorenzen, 1–44. Delhi: Oxford University Press, 2004.
———. *Who Invented Hinduism? Essays on Religion in History*. New Delhi: Yoda Press, 2006.
Losty, Jeremiah P. *The Art of the Book in India*. London: British Library, 1982.
———. *Krishna: A Hindu Vision of God*. London: British Library, 1980.
Lutgendorf, Philip. *The Life of a Text: Performing the Rāmcaritmānas by Tulsīdās*. Berkeley: University of California Press, 1991.
———. "Medieval Devotional Traditions: An Annotated Survey of Recent Scholarship." In *The Study of Hinduism*, edited by Arvind Sharma, 200–260. Columbia: University of South Carolina Press, 2003.
Mahāvīr Vandanā. ŚrīMahāvīrjī: Digambar Jain Atiśay Kṣetra Śrī Mahāvīrjī, 2013.
Mallison, Françoise. "The Teaching of Braj, Gujarati, and Bardic Poetry at the Court of Kutch: The Bhuj Brajbhāṣā Pāṭhśālā (1749–1948)." In *Forms of*

Knowledge in Early Modern Asia: Explorations in the Intellectual History of India and Tibet, 1500–1800, edited by Sheldon Pollock, 171–82. Durham: Duke University Press, 2011.

Mangaldas, Swami, ed. *Śrī Mahārāj Haridās Jī kī Vāṇī*. Jaipur: Nikhil Bharatiya Niranjani Mahasabha, 1962.

Mani, Braj Ranjan. *Debrahmanising History: Dominance and Resistance in Indian Society*. Delhi: Manohar, 2005.

Mann, Gurinder Singh. *The Making of Sikh Scripture*. New York: Oxford University Press, 2001.

Markovits, Claude. "Merchant Circulation in South Asia (Eighteenth to Twentieth Centuries): The Rise of Pan-Indian Merchant Networks." In *Society and Circulation: Mobile People and Itinerant Cultures in South Asia, 1750–1950*, edited by Claude Markovits, Jacques Pouchepadass, and Sanjay Subrahmanyam, 131–61. Delhi: Permanent Black, 2003.

Martin, Nancy. "Mirabai: Inscribed Text, Embodied in Life." In *Vaiṣṇavī: Women and the Worship of Krishna*, edited by Steven J. Rosen, 7–46. Delhi: Motilal Banarsidass, 1996.

McDermott, Rachel Fell. *Singing to the Goddess: Poems to Kālī and Umā from Bengal*. New York: Oxford University Press, 2001.

McGregor, R. S. *The Oxford Hindi-English Dictionary*. Oxford: Oxford University Press, 1993.

Mehta, J. L. *Philosophy and Religion: Essays in Interpretation*. New Delhi: Indian Council of Philosophical Research, 1990.

Michael, R. Blake. *The Origins of Vīraśaiva Sects: A Typological Analysis of Ritual and Associational Patterns in the Śūnyasampādane*. Delhi: Motilal Banarsidass, 1992.

———. "Women of the Śūnyasaṃpādane: Housewives and Saints in Vīraśaivism." *Journal of the American Oriental Society* 103, no. 2 (1983): 361–68.

———. "Work as Worship in Vīraśaiva Tradition." *Journal of the American Academy of Religion* 50, no. 4 (1982): 605–19.

Michelutti, Lucia. *The Vernacularisation of Democracy: Politics, Caste, and Religion in India*. New Delhi: Routledge, 2008.

———. "The Vernacularization of Democracy: Political Participation and Popular Politics in North India." *Journal of the Royal Anthropological Institute* 13 (2007): 639–56.

Miller, Barbara Stoler. *Love Song of the Dark Lord: Jayadeva's Gītagovinda*. New York: Columbia University Press, 1977.

Miller, William Ian. *The Anatomy of Disgust*. Cambridge: Harvard University Press, 1997.

Mir, Farina. *The Social Space of Language: Vernacular Culture in British Colonial Punjab*. Berkeley: University of California Press, 2010.

Mishra, Ratanalal. *Nirañjanī Sampradāy: Sādhanā evaṃ Sāhitya*. Navalagadh: Mahamaya Mandira, 1998.

Mudgal, Shubha, Aneesh Pradhan, and Kunal Ray, eds. *Shabd aur Sangeet: Unravelling Song-Texts in India*. Delhi: Three Essays Collective, 2019.

Mukhopadhyay, Harekrishna. *Bāṅglāra Kīrtana o Kīrtanīyā*. Kolkata: Sahitya Samsad, 1971.

———. "Introduction." In *Vaiṣṇava Padāvalī*, edited by Harekrishna Mukhopadhyay, 20–28. Kolkata: Sahitya Samsad, 1961.

Mullatti, Leela. *The Bhakti Movement and the Status of Women: A Case Study of Virasaivism*. New Delhi: Abhinav Publications, 1989.

Nadesan, Majia. *Governmentality, Biopower, and Everyday Life*. New York: Routledge, 2008.

Nandimath, S. C. *A Handbook of Vīraśaivism*. 1942. 2nd. rev. ed. Delhi: Motilal Banarsidass, 1979.

Narayana Rao, Velcheru, assisted by Gene H. Roghair. *Śiva's Warriors: The Basava Purāṇa of Pālkuriki Somanātha*. Princeton: Princeton University Press, 1990.

Narayana Rao, Velcheru, David Dean Shulman, and Sanjay Subrahmanyam. *Textures of Time: Writing History in South India*. New York: Other Press, 2003.

Narayandas, Swami. *Śrī Dādū Panth Paricay*, vol 1. Jaipur: Sri Dadu Dayal Mahasabha, 1978.

Nathan, Leonard, and Clinton Seely. *Grace and Mercy in Her Wild Hair: Selected Poems to the Mother Goddess*. Boulder: Great Eastern, 1982.

Neog, Maheshwar. *Early History of the Vaishnava Faith and Movement in Assam*. Gauhati: Gauhati University, 1965.

Nizami, Khaliq Ahmad. *Religion and Politics in India during the Thirteenth Century*. New Delhi: Oxford University Press, 2002.

Novetzke, Christian Lee. "Bhakti and Its Public," *International Journal of Hindu Studies* 11, no. 3 (December 2007): 255–72.

———. "The Brahmin Double: The Brahminical Construction of Anti-Brahminism and Anti-Caste Sentiment in the Religious Cultures of Precolonial Maharashtra." *South Asian History and Culture* 2, no. 2 (2011): 232–52.

———. *The Quotidian Revolution*. New York: Columbia University Press, 2016.

———. *Religion and Public Memory*. New York: Columbia University Press, 2008.

O'Connell, Joseph. "Vaiṣṇava Perceptions of Muslims." In *Caitanya Vaiṣṇavism in Bengal: Social Impact and Historical Implications*, edited by Rembert Lutjeharms, 197–217. Abingdon: Routledge, 2018.

Okita, Kiyokazu. *Hindu Theology in Early Modern South Asia: The Rise of Devotionalism and the Politics of Genealogy*. Oxford: Oxford University Press, 2014.

O'Malley, L. S. S. *Bengal District Gazetteers: Darbhanga*. Calcutta: Government Press, 1907. Reprint, New Delhi: Logos Press, 2013.

Orsini, Francesca. "Inflected *Kathas*: Sufis and Krishna *Bhaktas* in Awadh." In *Religious Interactions in Mughal India*, edited by Vasudha Dalmia and Munis Faruqui, 195–232. New Delhi: Oxford University Press, 2014.

Orwell, George. *The Road to Wigan Pier*. London: Victor Gollancz, 1937.

Otto, Rudolf. *Christianity and the Indian Religion of Grace*. Madras: Christian Literature Society for India, 1929.

Padoux, André. "What Do We Mean by Tantrism?." In *The Roots of Tantra*, edited by Katherine Anne Harper and Robert L. Brown, 17–24. Albany: State University of New York Press, 2002.

Pande, Susmita. *Medieval Bhakti Movement: Its History and Philosophy*. Meerut: Kusumanjali Prakāśan, 1989.

Patton, Laurie L. *Jewels of Authority: Women and Textual Tradition in Hindu India*. New York: Oxford University Press, 2002.

Pauwels, Heidi R. M. "Hagiography and Community Formation: The Case of a Lost Community of Sixteenth-Century Vrindavan." *Journal of Hindu Studies* 3, no. 1 (2010): 53–90.

———. "Imagining Religious Communities in the Sixteenth Century: Harirām Vyās and the Haritrayī." *International Journal of Hindu Studies* 13, no. 2 (2009): 143–61.

———. *Kṛṣṇa's Round Dance Reconsidered: Harirām Vyās's Hindi Rās-pañcādhyānī*. Richmond, Surrey: Curzon, 1996.

———. *In Praise of Holy Men: Imagining Religious Communities in Medieval India, Hagiographical Poems by and about Harirām Vyās*. Groningen: Egbert Forsten, 2002.

———. "Who Are the Enemies of the *Bhaktas*? Testimony about 'Śāktas' and 'Others' from Kabīr, the Rāmānandīs, Tulsīdās, and Harirām Vyās." *Journal of the American Oriental Society* 130, no. 4 (2010): 509–39.

Pearson, M. N. *Merchants and Rulers in Gujarat: The Response to the Portuguese in the Sixteenth Century*. London: University of California Press, 1976.

Pechilis, Karen. "To Body or Not to Body: Repulsion, Wonder, and the Tamil Saint Kāraikkāl Ammaiyār." In *Refiguring the Body: Embodiment in South Asian Religions*, edited by Barbara A. Holdrege and Karen Pechilis, 199–228. Albany: State University of New York Press, 2016.

———. "Bhakti and Tantra Intertwined: The Explorations of the Tamil Poetess Kāraikkāl Ammaiyār." *International Journal of Dharma Studies* 4, no. 2 (2016): n.p.

———. *Interpreting Devotion: The Poetry and Legacy of a Female Bhakti Saint of India*. London: Routledge, 2012.

———. "Karaikkal Ammaiyar." *Women in the World Religions and Spirituality Project*, edited by Catherine Wessinger and Rebecca Moore, 2016. www.wrldrels.org.

———. "Shiva as the Lord of Dance: What the Poetess Saw." *Journal of Hindu Studies* 6, no. 2 (2013): 131–53.

———. "The Siva Nataraja Image: Poetic Origins." *Kalakshetra Journal* 4 (February 2016): 1–16.
———. "The Story of the Classical Woman Saint, Kāraikkāl Ammaiyār: A Translation of Her Story from Cēkkiḻār's *Periya Purāṇam*." *International Journal of Hindu Studies* 10, no. 2 (2006): 171–84.
Peterson, Indira Viswanathan. *Poems to Śiva: The Hymns of the Tamil Saints.* Princeton: Princeton University Press, 1989.
Petit, Jérôme, trans. *Banārasīdās: Histoire à demi: Autobiographie d'un marchand Jaina du XVIIe siècle.* Paris: Presses Sorbonne Nouvelle, 2011.
Pinch, William R. "History, Devotion, and the Search for Nabhadas of Galta." In *Invoking the Past: The Uses of History in South Asia*, edited by Daud Ali, 367–99. Delhi: Oxford University Press, 1999.
———. *Warrior Ascetics and Indian Empires.* Cambridge: Cambridge University Press, 2006.
Pollock, Sheldon. *The Language of the Gods in the World of Men.* Berkeley: University of California Press, 2006.
Pollock, Sheldon, ed. *Literary Cultures in History: Reconstructions from South Asia.* New Delhi: Oxford University Press, 2003.
Prasad, Ayodhya (alias Bahar). *A Glimpse of Tirhut in the Second Half of the Nineteenth Century: Riaz-i-Tirhut of Ayodhya Prasad "Bahar."* Edited by Hetukar Jha. Darbhanga: Maharajadhiraja Kameshwar Singh Kalyani Foundation, 1997.
Prashad, Vijay. *Untouchable Freedom: A Social History of a Dalit Community.* Delhi: Oxford University Press, 2000.
Raghavan, V. *The Great Integrators: The Singer-Saints of India.* New Delhi: Publications Division, Ministry of Information and Broadcasting, 1966.
Raghavdas. *Bhaktamāl.* Edited by Agarchand Nahata. Jodhpur: Rajasthan Oriental Research Institute, 1965.
Ramanujan, A. K. *Hymns for the Drowning: Poems for Viṣṇu by Nammāḻvār.* Princeton: Princeton University Press, 1981. Reprint, New Delhi: Penguin Classics, 2005.
———. *Speaking of Śiva.* Harmondsworth: Penguin, 1973.
———. "On Women Saints." In *The Divine Consort: Rādhā and the Goddesses of India*, edited by John Stratton Hawley and Donna Marie Wulff, 316–24. Berkeley: Graduate Theological Union, 1982.
Ramanujan, A. K., and Norman Cutler. "From Classicism to Bhakti." In *Collected Essays of A. K. Ramanujan*, edited by Vinay Dharwadker, 232–59. Delhi: Oxford University Press, 2000.
Ramaswamy, Vijaya. *Divinity and Deviance: Women in Virasaivism.* New Delhi: Oxford University Press, 1996.
———. *Walking Naked: Women, Society, Spirituality in South India.* 2nd rev. ed. Shimla: Indian Institute of Advanced Study, 2007.

Ratte, Lou. *The Un-Colonized Heart*. Calcutta: Orient Longman, 1995.
Raychaudhuri, Tapan. "The Mughal Empire in the Bengali Literary Tradition." *Journal of Islamic Studies* 11, no. 3 (2001): 320–34.
Reddy, William M. *The Navigation of Feeling: A Framework for the History of Emotions*. Cambridge: Cambridge University Press, 2001.
Redington, James D. *Vallabhācārya on the Love Games of Kṛṣṇa*. Delhi: Motilal Banarsidass, 1983.
Reu, Vishveshvar Nath. *Marvāḍ kā Itihās*, vol. 1. 1940. Jodhpur: Maharaja Mansingh Pustak Prakash, 1999.
Richards, J. F. "Mughal State Finance and the Premodern World Economy." *Comparative Studies in Society and History* 23, no. 2 (1981): 285–308.
Rinehart, Robin. "The Portable Bullhe Shah: Biography, Categorization, and Authorship in the Study of Punjabi Sufi Poetry." *Numen* 46, no. 1 (1999): 53–87.
Rizvi, Saiyid Athar Abbas. *A History of Sufism in India, Vol. 1: Early Sufism and Its History in India to 1600 AD*. New Delhi: Munshiram Manoharlal, 1978.
Rosen, Steven. *Six Goswamis of Vrindavan*. New rev. ed. Vrindavan: Ras Bihari Lal and Sons, 2002.
Rosenstein, Ludmilla. *The Devotional Poetry of Svāmī Haridās: A Study of Early Braj Bhāṣā Verse*. Groningen: Egbert Forsten, 1997.
Rosenwein, Barbara H. *Emotional Communities in the Early Middle Ages*. Ithaca: Cornell University Press, 2006.
Rupkala, Sitaramsaran Bhagavanprasad. *Śrī Bhaktamāl with the Bhaktirasabodhinī Commentary of Priyādās*. 1910. Lucknow: Tejkumar Press, 1962.
Saha, Shandip. "Creating a Community of Grace: A History of the *Puṣṭi Mārga* in Northern and Western India (1493–1905)." Ph.D. diss., University of Ottawa, 2004.
———. "The Movement of Bhakti along a North-West Axis: Tracing the History of the Puṣṭimārg between the Sixteenth and Nineteenth Centuries." *International Journal of Hindu Studies* 1, no. 3 (2007): 299–318.
Sahai, Nandita Prasad. "Artisans, the State, and the Politics of Wajabi in Eighteenth Century Jodhpur." *Indian Economic and Social History Review* 42, no. 1 (2005): 41–68.
Sahdev, Manjula. "Adi Kavi Valmiki, or the First Classical Sanskrit Poet, Valmiki." *The Divine Life: Monthly Journal of the Divine Life Society* 48, no. 1 (1986): 12–16.
———. *Maharishi Valmiki—Vyaktitva evam Kritatva*. Patiala: Punjab University Press, 1997.
Sanderson, Alexis. "The Impact of Inscriptions on the Interpretation of Early Shaiva Literature." *Indo-Iranian Journal* 56 (2013): 211–44. www.alexissanderson.com.
———. "The Śaiva Age: The Rise and Dominance of Shaivism during the Medieval Period." In *Genesis and Development of Tantrism*, edited by Shingo

Einoo, 41–350. Tokyo: Institute of Oriental Culture, University of Tokyo, 2009. www.alexissanderson.com.
Śāstrī, Narendrakumār Jain. *Mahākavi Bhūdhardās: Ek Samālocanātmak Adhyayan*. Ajmer: Śrī Vītrāg Vijñān Svādhyāy Ṭrasṭ, 1997.
Śāstrī, Nemicandra. "Āgrā meṃ nirmit Jain Vaṅmay." In *Guru Gopāldās Varaiyā Smṛti-Granth*, edited by Kailāś Candra Jain and Gopāldās Baraiyā, 553–71. Sagar: A. Bhāratvarṣīya Di. Jain Vidvat Pariṣad, 1967.
Schelling, Andrew, ed. *The Oxford Anthology of Bhakti Literature*. New Delhi: Oxford University Press, 2011.
Schmitt, Carl. *Political Theology: Four Chapters on the Concept of Sovereignty*. Translated by G. Schwab. 1922. Chicago: University of Chicago Press, 2005.
Schouten, Jan Peter. *Revolution of the Mystics: On the Social Aspects of Vīraśaivism*. 1st Indian ed. Delhi: Motilal Banarsidass, 1995.
Schultz, Anna. *Singing a Hindu Nation: Marathi Devotional Performance and Nationalism*. New York: Oxford University Press, 2013.
Sekhon, Sant Singh, trans. *Love of Hir and Ranjha [by] Waris Shah*. Ludhiana: Punjab Agricultural University, 1978.
Seigworth, Gregory J., and Melissa Gregg. "An Inventory of Shimmers." In *The Affect Theory Reader*, edited by Gregory J. Seigworth and Melissa Gregg, 1–25. Durham: Duke University Press, 2010.
Shabadārth Srī Gurū Granth Sāhib Jī. 4 vols. Annotated by Teja Singh. Amritsar: Shiromani Gurdwara Prabandhak Committee, 1969.
Shackle, Christopher. "Between Scripture and Romance: The Yūsuf-Zulaikhā Story in Panjabi." *South Asia Research* 15, no. 2 (1995): 153–88.
———. *Bullhe Shah: Sufi Lyrics*. Cambridge: Harvard University Press, 2015.
Shackle, Christopher, and Rupert Snell, eds. *The Indian Narrative: Perspectives and Patterns*. Wiesbaden: Otto Harrassowitz, 1992.
Shah, Hussain. *Kalām-i Shāh Husain*. Lahore: Paikejiz, 1979.
Shah, Waris. *Hīr Wāris*. Edited by Shah Hasan. Ludhiana: Chetna Prakashan, 2007.
Shahab, Mas'ud Ḥasan, ed. *K͟hvājah G͟hulām Farīd*. Bahavalpur: Urdu Academy, 1963.
Sharma, Amichand. *Śrī Bālmīki Prakāś*. Delhi: Gautam Book Centre, n.d.
Sharma, G. D. "Urban Social Structure: A Case Study of the Towns of Western Rajasthan during the Seventeenth Century." In *Studies in Urban History*, edited by J. S. Grewal and Indu Banga, 70–79. Amritsar: Department of History, Guru Nanak Dev University, 1981.
Sharma, Shriram. *Patitoddhār*. Unpublished, 1919.
Sharma, Swapna. "Gadadhar Bhatt and His Family: Facilitators of the Song of Bhakti in Vrindavan." In *Text and Tradition in Early Modern North India*, edited by Tyler Williams, Anshu Malhotra, and John Stratton Hawley, 354–64. Delhi: Oxford University Press, 2018.
Sheikh, Samira. *Forging a Region: Sultans, Traders and Pilgrims in Gujarat, 1200–1500*. Delhi: Oxford University Press, 2010.

Singh, Kamalroop. *The Granth of Guru Gobind Singh: Essays, Lectures, and Translations.* Delhi: Oxford University Press, 2015.

Singh, Shyam Narayan. *History of Tirhut from the Earliest Times to the End of the Nineteenth Century.* Calcutta: Baptist Mission Press, 1922.

Singh, Simran Jeet. "The Life of the Purātan Janamsākhī: Tracing the Earliest Memories of Gurū Nānak." Ph.D. diss., Columbia University, 2016.

Snell, Rupert. *The Eighty-Four Hymns of Hita Harivaṃśa: An Edition of the Caurāsī Pada.* Delhi: Motilal Banarsidass; London: School of Oriental and African Studies, 1991.

———. *The Hindi Classical Tradition: A Braj Bhāṣā Reader.* London: School of Oriental and African Studies, University of London, 1991.

Sreenivasan, Ramya. "The Marriage of 'Hindu' and 'Turak': Medieval Rajput Histories of Jalor." *Medieval History Journal* 2, no. 1 (2004): 87–108.

Starkey, Kathryn. *Reading the Medieval Book, Word, Image, and Performance in Wolfram von Eschenbach's Willehalm.* Notre Dame, IN: Notre Dame University Press, 2004.

Stearns, Peter N., and Carol Z. Stearns. "Emotionology: Clarifying the History of Emotions and Emotional Standards." *American Historical Review* 90, no. 4 (1985): 813–30.

Stewart, Tony. "Jaban Haridās: The Sūfī Who Practiced Kṛṣṇa Jikir." Paper presented at the workshop on Bengali Vaishnavism in the Modern Period, Oxford Centre for Hindu Studies, March 28–29, 2015.

Subramaniam, Arundhati, ed. *Eating God: A Book of Bhakti Poetry.* Gurgaon: Penguin, 2014.

Subramanian, Lakshmi. *From the Tanjore Court to the Madras Music Academy: A Social History of Music in South India.* New York: Oxford University Press, 2006.

Tagore, Rabindranath. *Gitanjali.* London: Macmillan, 1913.

———. *The Lover of God.* Edited by Tony Stewart and Chase Twichell. Port Townsend, WA: Copper Canyon Press, 2003.

Talbot, Cynthia. "Becoming Turk the Rajput Way: Conversion and Identity in an Indian Warrior Narrative." *Modern Asian Studies* 43, no. 1 (2009): 211–43.

Timberg, Thomas A. *The Marwaris: From Traders to Industrialists.* New Delhi: Vikas, 1979.

Trivedi, K. K. "The Emergence of Agra as a Capital and a City: A Note on Its Spatial and Historical Background during the Sixteenth and Seventeenth Cities." *Journal of the Economic and Social History of the Orient* 37 (1994), 147–70.

Tulsīdās. *Rāmcaritmānas.* Gorakhpur: Gita Press, 2008.

Turino, Thomas. "Nationalism and Latin American Music." *Latin American Music Review* 24 (2003): 175.

Turner, Victor. "Metaphors of Anti-Structure in Religious Culture." In Victor Turner, *Dramas, Fields, and Metaphors: Symbolic Action in Human Society,* 272–99. Ithaca: Cornell University Press, 1974.

———. *The Ritual Process: Structure and Anti-Structure*. Chicago: Aldine Publishing, 1969.

Usborne, Charles Frederick, trans. *The Adventures of Hir and Ranjha [by] Waris Shah*. London: Peter Owen, 1973.

Vajpeyi, Ananya. *Righteous Republic: The Political Foundations of Modern India*. Cambridge: Harvard University Press, 2012.

Venkatesan, Archana. *The Secret Garland: Āṇṭāḷ's Tiruppāvai and Nācciyār Tirumoḻi*. New York: Oxford University Press, 2010.

Venkatkrishnan, Anand. "The *Bhāgavata Purāṇa* in History." In *The History of Vaishnavism, The Oxford History of Hinduism*, vol. 4, edited by Archana Venkatesan. Oxford: Oxford University Press, forthcoming.

———. "Ritual, Reflection, and Religion: The Devas of Banaras." *South Asian History and Culture* 6, no. 1 (2015): 147–71.

Verter, Bradford. "Spiritual Capital: Theorizing Religion with Bourdieu against Bourdieu." *Sociological Theory* 21, no. 2 (2003): 150–74.

Vidyāśaṅkara, Es. *Vīraśaiva Pāribhāṣika Padakōśa*. Bangalore: Basava Samithi, 2000.

Vrindāvandās Ṭhākura. *Śrī-Śrī-Caitanyabhāgavata Ādikhaṇḍa-mūla Śrī-Gauḍīyabhāṣya-sameta*. Kalikātā: Gauḍīya Maṭha, 1928.

———. *Śrī-Śrī-Caitanyabhāgavata Madhyakhaṇḍa-mūla Śrī-Śrī-Bhaktisiddhāntasarasvatī-Gosvāmi-ṭhākura-kṛta Śrī-Gauḍīyabhāṣya-sameta*. Kalikātā: Gauḍīya Maṭha, 1934.

Williams, Raymond Brady, and Yogi Trivedi, eds., *Swaminarayan Hinduism: Tradition, Adaptation, Identity*. Delhi: Oxford University Press, 2016.

Williams, Tyler Walker. "Sacred Sounds and Sacred Books: A History of Writing in Hindi." Ph.D. diss., Columbia University, 2014.

Yaravintelimath, C. R. *Vacanas of Women Saints*. Bangalore: Basava Samithi, 2006.

Zelliot, Eleanor. "The Medieval Bhakti Movement in History." In *Hinduism: New Essays in the History of Religions*, edited by Bardwell L. Smith, 143–68. Leiden: E. J. Brill, 1976.

Zydenbos, Robert J. "Review: Vīraśaivism, Caste, Revolution, etc." Review of *Revolution of the Mystics: On the Social Aspects of Vīraśaivism* by J. P. Schouten. *Journal of the American Oriental Society* 117, no. 3 (1997): 525–35.

CONTRIBUTORS

GIL BEN-HERUT is assistant professor in the Department of Religious Studies, University of South Florida. His research interests include premodern religious literature in Kannada, South Asian bhakti traditions, and the vernacularization of Sanskrit poetics and courtly poetry. His book *Śiva's Saints: The Origins of Devotion in Kannada according to Harihara's Ragaḷegaḷu* (2018) is the first study in English of the earliest Śaiva hagiographies in the Kannada-speaking region. It argues for a substantial rethinking of the nature and development of the devotionalism that is today typically associated with the Vīraśaivas.

DIVYA CHERIAN is assistant professor in the Department of History at Princeton University. She teaches the history of medieval and early modern South Asia. Her research is focused on the precolonial history of Rajasthan and engages with questions pertaining to law and custom, gender and sexuality, caste and state formation, and religion and politics in precolonial South Asia. She received a PhD in history from Columbia University in 2015. Her forthcoming book examines the role of newly ascendant social groups in the transformation of collective identities in the region.

JOHN E. CORT is professor of Asian and comparative religions at Denison University. He is the author of *Jains in the World: Religious Values and Ideology in India* (2001) and *Framing the Jina: Narratives of Icons and Idols in Jain History* (2010); coauthor with Lawrence A. Babb and Michael W. Meister of *Desert Temples: Sacred Centers of Rajasthan in Historical, Art-Historical and Social Contexts* (2008); and coeditor with Paul Dundas, Knut Jacobsen, and Kristi L. Wiley of *Brill's Encyclopedia of Jainism.*

RICHARD H. DAVIS is professor in the Religion and Asian Studies Programs at Bard College. His most recent publication is *The Bhagavad Gītā: A Biography* (2014). He is the author of four other books, has edited two volumes, and also wrote the text for a catalog of Indian religious prints, *Gods in Print: Masterpieces of India's Mythological Art* (2012). Currently he is continuing work on the reception history of the *Bhagavad Gītā* and on a history of religions in early South Asia.

SHRIVATSA GOSWAMI comes from a family of spiritual leaders and scholars at Sri Radharaman Mandir, Vrindavan. He often serves as a spokesman for Hinduism at interreligious forums within India and around the world and has delivered a Hibbert Lecture at Oxford. Goswami is the author, with Jack Hawley, of *At Play with Krishna* (1981), and he has been deeply involved in the publication of a number of scholarly volumes, including *Govindadeva: A Dialogue in Stone* (ed. Margaret H. Case, 1996). His regular lectures on the *Bhagavad Gītā* and the *Bhāgavata Purāṇa* have a devoted following. He is the founder and director of the Sri Caitanya Prema Samsthana, a Vrindavan-based institution that hosts scholars from around the world.

PHYLLIS GRANOFF is Lex Hixon Professor of World Religions at Yale University. She served for many years as the editor of the *Journal of Indian Philosophy*. She has written on early and medieval Indian philosophy, literature, and art and has translated modern fiction from Bangla and Odia.

EBEN GRAVES is program manager in the Yale Institute of Sacred Music. He holds a PhD in ethnomusicology from the University of Texas at Austin and was recently a Mellon postdoctoral teaching fellow and lecturer in music at Columbia University. His current book project focuses on connections between musical performance, devotional practice, and social time in contemporary West Bengal.

DAVID L. HABERMAN is professor of religious studies at Indiana University. Much of his work centers on the Krishna bhakti traditions of Braj, including *Acting as a Way of Salvation* (1988), *The Bhaktirasāmṛtasindu of Rūpa Gosvāmin* (2003), and *Journey through the Twelve Forests* (1994). His recent publications focus on Hindu attitudes toward and interaction with nonhuman entities: *River of Love in an Age of Pollution* (2006) and *People Trees* (2013). He is working on a new book about Mount Govardhan.

JOHN STRATTON HAWLEY—informally, Jack—is Claire Tow Professor of Religion at Barnard College, Columbia University. His most recently published books on India's bhakti traditions are *A Storm of Songs: India and the Idea of the Bhakti Movement* (2015), *Sur's Ocean* (with Kenneth Bryant, 2015), *Into Sur's Ocean: Poetry, Context, and Commentary* (2016), and a new art-oriented edition of *Surdas: Poet, Singer, Saint* (2018). He is coeditor, with Tyler Williams and Anshu Malhotra, of *Text and Tradition in Early Modern North India* (2018).

MANPREET KAUR is a PhD candidate in religion at Columbia University. She holds an MA in English literature and an MPhil in theater and performance studies from Jawaharlal Nehru University and has taught in both fields at Saint Stephen's College, Delhi. Her international teaching experience encompasses faculty roles in Prague, Bratislava, and Banska Bystrica, and she has participated in a binational exchange program between Saint Stephen's and Soka University in Japan. Her dissertation, currently under way, examines the performance history of the poetry of Baba Farid, both past and present.

ADITI NATASHA KINI is a writer based in New York City who works in nonfiction and screenplays. Best known for her cultural criticism, Kini has written about the South Asian diaspora, gender, and entertainment. Her chapter in this book, coauthored with William Pinch, was begun just as she was completing her MA in liberal studies at Wesleyan University.

JOEL LEE is assistant professor of anthropology at Williams College. His research and teaching interests include Dalit social history, the politics of caste and untouchability, popular religion in North India, Hindi and Urdu literature, and the social life of the senses.

CHRISTIAN LEE NOVETZKE is College of Arts and Sciences professor in Comparative Religion, South Asia Studies, and Global Studies at the University of Washington's Jackson School of International Studies. His recent books include *The Quotidian Revolution: Vernacularization, Religion, and the Premodern Public Sphere in India* (2016) and, with Andy Rotman and Will Elison, *Amar Akbar Anthony: Bollywood, Brotherhood, and the Nation* (2016).

KIYOKAZU OKITA is assistant professor in the Faculty of Liberal Arts at Sophia University, Tokyo. He is also a research fellow at the Oxford Centre for Hindu Studies. He obtained his DPhil in theology and religion from the University of Oxford in 2011; from his dissertation emerged his monograph *Hindu Theology in Early Modern South Asia* (2014). In his current project, Okita examines the complex relation between devotion (*bhakti*), aesthetic delight (*rasa*), and ethics (*dharma*) in the works of the sixteenth-century Vaiṣṇava poet-theologian Rūpa Gosvāmī.

HEIDI R. M. PAUWELS is professor in the Department of Asian Languages and Literature at the University of Washington in Seattle. Her most recent publications are two monographs—*Cultural Exchange in Eighteenth-Century India: Poetry and Paintings from Kishangarh* (2015) and *Mobilizing Krishna's World: The Writings of Prince Sāvant Singh of Kishangarh* (2017)—and a 2018 special issue of the *Journal of the Royal Asiatic Society* on vernacular views of Aurangzeb, coedited with Anne Murphy.

KAREN PECHILIS is distinguished professor of humanities at Drew University, where she teaches courses on history and comparative religion in the College of Liberal Arts History Department and in the Caspersen School of Graduate Studies as director of the Arts and Letters Program. A specialist in the history of religions, her main research interests are the history of bhakti's expression and display; intersections of gender, history, and literature; and women's contemporary experiences of tradition. Her most recent book on bhakti is *Interpreting Devotion: The Poetry and Legacy of a Female Bhakti Poet-Saint* (2012).

WILLIAM R. PINCH is professor of history and environmental studies at Wesleyan University and associate editor of the journal *History and Theory*. He is the author of *Peasants and Monks in British India* (1996) and *Warrior Ascetics and Indian Empires* (2006); editor of *Speaking of Peasants: Essays in Indian History and Politics in Honor of Walter Hauser* (2008); and coeditor of a *History and Theory* special issue titled "History and Theory in a Global Frame" (December 2015). He is currently finishing a book-length study of the rebellion of 1857, as well as a translation (with Allison Busch and Dalpat Rajurohit) of two late eighteenth-century Brajbhasha poems celebrating the Shaiva warlord Anupgiri Gosain (Himmat Bahadur).

SWAPNA SHARMA is senior Hindi lector at Yale University. She has held similar positions at the University of Chicago and the University of Leipzig. For some years she collaborated with Winand Callewaert in a number of projects undertaken at the Katholieke University, Leuven, including *The Hagiographies of Anantadās* (2000), *The Millennium Kabīr Vāṇī* (2000), and the *Dictionary of Bhakti* (2009). Her monograph *Gadādhar Bhaṭṭ Paramparā: Siddhānt aur Sāhitya* was published in 2008.

TYLER WILLIAMS is assistant professor in the Department of South Asian Languages and Civilizations at the University of Chicago. His primary research and teaching areas are Hindi language and literature, South Asian religion and aesthetics, and book history. His current research projects center on the early manuscript culture of Hindi and on merchant religious and literary culture in precolonial North India. He is the editor, with Jack Hawley and Anshu Malhotra, of *Text and Tradition in Early Modern North India* (2018).

INDEX

Page numbers in *italic* refer to illustrations.

GLOBAL
SOUTH
ASIA

Padma Kaimal
K. Sivaramakrishnan
Anand A. Yang
SERIES EDITORS

Global South Asia takes an interdisciplinary approach to the humanities and social sciences in its exploration of how South Asia, through its global influence, is and has been shaping the world.

A Place for Utopia: Urban Designs from South Asia, by Smriti Srinivas

The Afterlife of Sai Baba: Competing Visions of a Global Saint, by Karline McLain

Sensitive Space: Fragmented Territory at the India-Bangladesh Border, by Jason Cons

The Gender of Caste: Representing Dalits in Print, by Charu Gupta

Displaying Time: The Many Temporalities of the Festival of India, by Rebecca M. Brown

Banaras Reconstructed: Architecture and Sacred Space in a Hindu Holy City, by Madhuri Desai

Mobilizing Krishna's World: The Writings of Prince Sāvant Singh of Kishangarh, by Heidi R. M. Pauwels

The Rebirth of Bodh Gaya: Buddhism and the Making of a World Heritage Site, by David Geary

Making New Nepal: From Student Activism to Mainstream Politics, by Amanda Thérèse Snellinger

High-Tech Housewives: Indian IT Workers, Gendered Labor, and Transmigration, by Amy Bhatt

Privileged Minorities: Syrian Christianity, Gender, and Minority Rights in Postcolonial India, by Sonja Thomas

Mountain Temples and Temple Mountains: Architecture, Religion, and Nature in the Central Himalayas, by Nachiket Chanchani

Gandhi's Search for the Perfect Diet: Eating with the World in Mind, by Nico Slate

Marrying for a Future: Transnational Sri Lankan Tamil Marriages in the Shadow of War, by Sidharthan Maunaguru

Bhakti and Power: Debating India's Religion of the Heart, edited by John Stratton Hawley, Christian Lee Novetzke, and Swapna Sharma